The Making of Symphony Hall, Boston

Henry Lee Higginson (1834–1919), founder of the Boston Symphony Orchestra and its sponsor from 1881 to 1918. Photo by William Notman. BSO Archives.

THE MAKING OF
SYMPHONY HALL
BOSTON

A History with Documents

INCLUDING CORRESPONDENCE OF

Henry Lee Higginson
BOSTON SYMPHONY ORCHESTRA

Charles Follen McKim
McKim, Mead & White, Architects

Wallace Clement Sabine
HARVARD UNIVERSITY

BY

RICHARD POATE STEBBINS

Boston Symphony Orchestra
BOSTON, MASSACHUSETTS

Published by the Boston Symphony Orchestra, Inc.

Boston, Massachusetts 02115

© Boston Symphony Orchestra, 2000

ISBN 0-9671148-1-0
LC 00-133221

Designed by Steve Dyer

Typeset in Dante and Shelley Andante

Printed and bound by Maple-Vail Book Manufacturing,
Binghamton, New York

FIRST EDITION

Printed in the United States of America

CONTENTS

FOREWORD

IT IS THE QUINTESSENTIAL UNION OF PLACE AND INSTITUTION —
Symphony Hall and the Boston Symphony Orchestra. Established in 1881,
the BSO is the oldest permanent professional symphony orchestra in America,
and its stately home is one of the greatest performance halls in the world.

We find in this brief and eloquent study the story of this magnificent building. It was a bold move in the 1890s to propose erecting a concert hall so far from
the center of the city. It was even braver to contemplate such a project at a time
when the nation was only recently recovered from an economic depression.
Major Henry Lee Higginson, however, would not be deterred.

Once they secured the land on the corner of Huntington and Massachusetts
Avenues, Higginson and his associates turned their sights on America's most
notable architect, Charles F. McKim. Having given the people of Boston a
sparkling Renaissance-style palace for their Public Library in Copley Square,
McKim, of the New York firm of McKim, Mead & White, eagerly undertook
the task of designing Symphony Hall.

Symphony Hall stands as a monument to Higginson's foresight and
McKim's genius. Yet, as imposing and graceful as the building's exterior
appears, the true treasure lies within the walls, where the near perfection
of acoustics has given Symphony Hall a world reputation. This, of course, is
the result of the work of the early acoustical engineer, Wallace Clement
Sabine.

Construction began on June 12, 1899, and less than sixteen months later, on
October 15, 1900, the first concert was performed. This book, written to
commemorate the one-hundredth anniversary of Symphony Hall, sparkles

with the stories of those who worked to create this masterpiece. Through his own narrative voice, complemented by documents, illustrations, appendices, and a splendid essay on Sabine's work by Leo Beranek, Richard Stebbins unfolds the tale of the creation of one of America's national treasures.

WILLIAM M. FOWLER, JR., *President,*
Massachusetts Historical Society

PREFACE

T HIS BOOK MARKS THE CENTENNIAL OF BOSTON'S SYMPHONY
Hall by telling how that well-loved edifice came into being in the year
1900. The genesis of this world-famous cultural monument, the home of one of
the world's great orchestras, and the scene throughout the twentieth century
of memorable events in the life of the city and the nation, is a complex and
fascinating story, which has never before been told in full and accurate detail.

Four types of source material underpin our account of Symphony Hall's
beginnings:

- First are the contemporary published records, drawn mainly from the
  Boston newspapers of a century ago, and preserved in scrapbooks in the
  Boston Symphony Orchestra Archives and the Boston Public Library;
- Second is an abundance of visual material in the form of sketches, photo-
  graphs, and architectural plans and drawings;
- Third are the relevant personal records — most of them previously un-
  published — of those extraordinary individuals who were most closely
  involved in maintaining a framework for Boston's expanding musical life:
  Henry Lee Higginson, the founder and long-time guide of the Boston
  Symphony Orchestra; Charles Follen McKim, the leading figure in the
  stellar New York architectural firm of McKim, Mead & White; Wallace
  Clement Sabine, Harvard physicist and founder of the science of acoustics; and several of their close associates and collaborators;
- Last but not least is the hall itself, a mute but eloquent witness to the
  decisions that governed its planning and construction.

It is the personal records that give the present volume its principal claim to uniqueness. Reproduced in the following pages are some six dozen letters and documents reflecting the leadership of Henry Lee Higginson and friends in this major civic undertaking. They provide an inner history of the years-long endeavor to provide a permanent home for the Boston Symphony Orchestra and a performance space worthy of the city that nurtured it.

A significant portion of this material reposes in the BSO's own Archives. A much larger share belongs to the George F. Baker Library of the Harvard School of Business Administration, the official custodian of Higginson's papers. Other essential pieces, bearing particularly upon the role of Charles F. McKim and his firm, are preserved at the New-York Historical Society in Manhattan. Earnest thanks are due to these institutions, and to the Boston Public Library and the Harvard University Libraries and Archives, for the use of their material and for other help of many kinds. Without their cooperation, this volume could not have been successfully completed.[1]

To bring into focus a story whose elements are widely dispersed among contemporary records, an introductory narrative presents the major events in sequence and in historical context. This is followed by a selection of the documents. The volume is illustrated by the best of the sketches, photographs, and architectural plans and drawings available. Also reproduced (in Appendix A) is Professor Sabine's contemporary account of the all-important acoustical factors involved in the designing of the Symphony Hall interior. Dr. Leo L. Beranek, a Life Trustee of the BSO and the world's leading contemporary authority on concert halls and their acoustics, offers (in Appendix B) an account of certain architectural choices crucial to the design of this superb auditorium. A "Who Was Who" section (Appendix C) briefly identifies most of the persons mentioned in the text and documents.

It is a pleasure to acknowledge the counsel and unwavering support of several distinguished members of the BSO family, past and present. Leo Beranek, a longtime student of Symphony Hall's history, early threw his weight behind the project, generously shared his knowledge, and repeatedly championed the author's right of independent judgment in interpreting a sometimes ambiguous record. Bridget Carr, the BSO's gracious and accomplished Archivist, found time amid a thousand other responsibilities to exercise the diplomatic and administrative leadership essential in a cooperative project of this nature. The enthusiastic backing of Caroline Dwight Bain, Anthony Fogg, Thelma Goldberg, and Daniel R. Gustin encouraged the author to persevere despite occasional perplexities. Teresa J. Lawson effectively employed her well-honed editorial skills in shaping all parts of the volume. I also thank Helen Snively for her sharp intelligence in reading the final proofs; Steve Dyer, who successfully grappled with the multiple challenges of the book's design; and Robert Beerman of Sametz Blackstone Associates, who kindly provided the cover.

In such company and with such a theme, the author feels it a privilege as well as a duty to claim responsibility for any errors, omissions, or other shortcomings that may derogate from the volume's intended purposes.

Mihi crede, verum gaudium res severa est.
(Believe me, true joy is a serious matter.)

Lucius Annaeus Seneca
EPISTOLAE MORALES AD LUCILIUM
Letter 23

The Making of Symphony Hall, Boston

Chapter 1

THE CHANGING
SCENE

I T IS NOT AT ALL UNUSUAL FOR ONE OF BOSTON'S VENERABLE
but still vibrant institutions to have occupied the same premises for a hundred years or more. "Boston has an excellent record for keeping handsome
and worthwhile buildings in use as long as possible," observed architectural
historian Walter Muir Whitehill in 1968, "and of finding new purposes for those
that cannot be thus continued."[2]

Illustrations of this virtue are familiar: the government of the Commonwealth of Massachusetts has been at home since 1798 in Charles Bulfinch's
State House, already past its bicentennial year. Other celebrated edifices such as
the Old State House (1711–47), the Old North Church (1723), Faneuil Hall (1742),
King's Chapel (1750), Saint Paul's Cathedral (1809), Quincy Market (1826), and
the Boston Athenæum (1849) bear witness to our predecessors' care for solid
construction as well as institutional continuity.

A whole new generation of monumental buildings, predominantly of a reli-
gious character, came into existence in the later nineteenth century in response
to the gradual westward movement of population attendant on the filling in of
the Back Bay and the development of the South End. Among its more conspicuous representatives, all of them now well over a century old, are the Arlington
Street Church (1859), the New Old South Church (1875) and Trinity Church
(1877) in Copley Square; the Cathedral of the Holy Cross (1875) on Washington
Street; and the Church of the Advent (1883) between Beacon Hill and the
Charles River.

Symphony Hall (1900) belongs to a third great wave of construction that

3

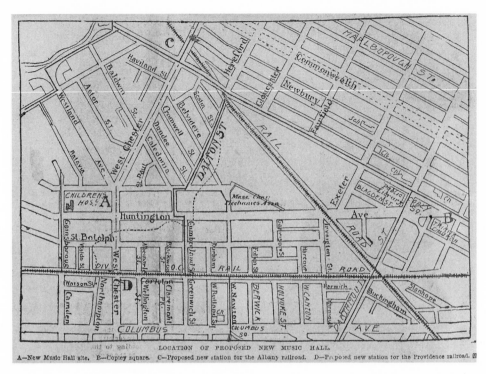

A—New Music Hall site.   B—Copley square.   C—Proposed new station for the Albany railroad.   D—Proposed new station for the Providence railroad.

Back Bay and South End: Street map indicating at "A" the location of the future Symphony Hall, from the Boston Herald, *June 15, 1893.*

took place around the end of the nineteenth century and the beginning of the twentieth. This activity endowed the growing metropolis with such landmarks as the Boston Public Library (1895), Horticultural Hall (1901), the New England Conservatory of Music (1901) and Jordan Hall (1904), as well as the Museum of Fine Arts (1909) and the Christian Science Mother Church Extension (1906). Slightly farther afield, it gave Boston the Massachusetts Historical Society (1899) and the Isabella Stewart Gardner Museum (1903) in the Fenway, the Harvard Medical School (1906) on Longwood Avenue, and, on Commonwealth Avenue, the former Temple Israel (1907), now occupied by Boston University.

Much of this third wave of construction was concentrated on or near Huntington Avenue, the thoroughfare whose name commemorates the benefactions of philanthropist Arthur Huntington to the Massachusetts Institute of Technology and other institutions. Traversing a broad extent of newly filled land redeemed from the marshy tidelands of the Back Bay, this broad and spacious avenue had seemed a natural site for the relocation of such valued cultural enterprises as the Boston Symphony Orchestra, and Symphony Hall was indeed the first such edifice to secure a position there.

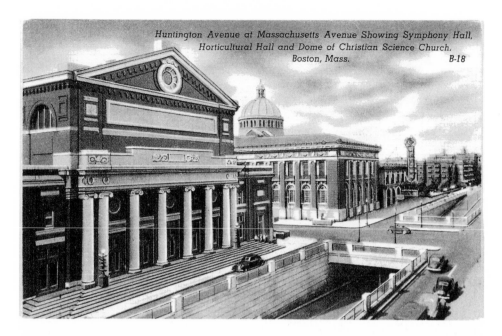

The Huntington Avenue scene, from a postcard of the 1940s showing Symphony Hall, Horticultural Hall, the Uptown Theatre (formerly Chickering Hall), and the Christian Science Mother Church Extension. BSO Archives.

Two other jewels, once included, were later torn from this glittering architectural chain. The Boston Opera House, built as recently as 1909, was demolished in 1958, its site now occupied by Northeastern University. Chickering Hall, completed in 1901 on a site just east of Horticultural Hall and subsequently known as the St. James Theatre — and later as the Uptown Theatre — was pulled down in 1968 to accommodate the enlargement of the Christian Science Center.

Also missing from our present-day perspective, though less lamented, are the Mechanics' Building, the home of the venerable Massachusetts Charitable Mechanics Association, an elongated red brick structure built in 1881 near the site of the present Prudential Center, and the former Children's Hospital, another frowning Victorian edifice dedicated in 1882 at Huntington Avenue and Gainsborough Street, just west of the present Symphony Hall.

Most of these buildings of the Huntington Avenue group exhibited a sumptuous, even palatial style of architecture that was rather new to Boston at the time of their erection. But unlike their counterparts in such foreign cities as London, Paris, or Vienna, most of them lacked the spacious environment that might have complemented the virtues of their design. (The Museum of Fine

Symphony Hall in its urban setting, from a photograph of the 1930s.
Photograph by Benjamin Morse, BSO Archives.

Arts is a significant exception.) Anchored by Trinity Church and the Public Library at one extremity and the Museum of Fine Arts at the other, the intervening structures are strung out haphazardly along a mile or so of Huntington Avenue with little reference either to one another or to any common plan.

Architectural critics have differed in their judgment of the Huntington Avenue cityscape as an architectural ensemble. Whitehill, writing in the 1960s, bitterly lamented the avenue's planlessness and its lack of any overall design that might have capitalized on the merits of the individual buildings. Even Symphony Hall, he observed, though admirably suited to its purpose, was "plumped down upon a totally undistinguished site without an inch of ground around it."

Douglass Shand-Tucci, on the other hand, writing from the perspective of the 1980s, warmly praised "the splendid new civic center — rivaling Copley Square in many ways — that emerged [early in the century] at the intersection of Huntington and Massachusetts avenues." In Huntington Avenue, with the apartment houses and street-level shops of earlier decades, Shand-Tucci saw "a distinctly cosmopolitan and even Parisian ambience" that stood in favorable contrast to "the rather staid appearance of Commonwealth Avenue."[3]

Acknowledging Huntington Avenue's unique position in the cultural life of the contemporary city, Mayor Thomas M. Menino suggested in January 1998 that the section between Massachusetts Avenue and the Museum of Fine Arts be known as the "Avenue of the Arts." This designation was later extended as far as Longwood Avenue in order to take in the Massachusetts College of Art, another venerable Bay State institution, then observing its 125th anniversary.

Mindful of the special distinction attaching to Symphony Hall as the earliest of the historic buildings that grace this thoroughfare, we may now examine the origins of a structure that has served the city well throughout the 1900s, and stands now upon the threshold of a new century and a new millennium.

2 PEMBERTON SQUARE,

BOSTON, March 11ᵗʰ 1887

My dear Eugerson

I find the land at corner of Hunt. Av. and W. Chester Park &c is like this

[sketch of the lot]

Houses built
← rear passage

H. Av. 150 ft. | 33,986 24. ft. | 152 ft. | Falmouth st.

225 ft.

W. Chester Pk.

10 feet set back on Falmouth
15 " " " Hunt. Av.
Nothing on W. Chester Park

If any public building goes on to the lot it will be for ever regretted if the whole is not taken.

I am committed to no price to you. If a part only is wanted price must depend partly on how the remainer can be used.

Geo F. D.

The future Music Hall lot, as sketched in 1887 by its owner, F. Gordon Dexter (enclosure to Document 1). Baker Library, Harvard Business School.

Chapter 2

TRIAL AND ERROR
1887–1894

IT WAS IN 1887 THAT HENRY LEE HIGGINSON, THE FOUNDER and for thirty-eight years the moral and material mainstay of the Boston Symphony Orchestra, discovered the plot of ground on Huntington Avenue on which the orchestra's permanent home would rise some thirteen years later. Its still sparsely populated neighborhood was located in an area of former tidelands and mudflats that had only recently been converted to solid ground through an engineering process begun about 1852.

Maps and photographs of the 1860s show this section of the Back Bay as submerged swampland, traversed only by a pair of railway viaducts. By the beginning of the 1880s, however, the filling process had been completed, residential blocks were being laid out, and the scene was being transformed by such new and sprawling edifices as the former Children's Hospital at Huntington Avenue and Gainsborough Street, and the Boston Storage Warehouse at West Chester Park (now Massachusetts Avenue) and Westland Avenue.

In the dynamic Boston of the 1880s, Higginson could readily be persuaded that the site to which his attention had been drawn was the city's last and "only feasible lot . . . for a Music-Hall."[4] Its owner, a "socially prominent club-man" named F. Gordon Dexter,[5] had pointed out that with the expected completion of the Harvard Bridge to Cambridge and the development of the north-south street then known as West Chester Park (later as Massachusetts Avenue), the discerning purchaser would be possessed of "a central lot on a main thoroughfare."[6]

Less advantageous, perhaps, was the locality's rather nondescript and out-of-the-way character, with no distinctive personality of its own. To the north and east it was separated from the Back Bay by the Boston and Albany Railroad, whose extensive railyards encumbered the site of the present Prudential Center; while the Providence and Boston Railroad passed within a mere two blocks on the south side, severing the district from the emerging South End.

Major Higginson, as a successful middle-aged businessman, would not have been indifferent to such mundane considerations. Born in 1834 into one of Boston's leading families — though his actual birthplace happened to be in New York City — he had attended Boston Latin School and Harvard. Forced to leave college because of poor eyesight, he had gone to study music in Germany and Austria, where he devoted four years to serious practical and theoretical study of the art, mainly in Vienna, a setting in which his steadiness of purpose was not incompatible with a mildly Bohemian life style. Though his pianistic talents did not reach a professional level, he obtained a good grounding in practical musicianship and made valuable friendships. He also conceived the somewhat extravagant idea of establishing in Boston a permanent symphony orchestra like those he had enjoyed hearing in Vienna, Leipzig, and other European centers.

Civil War duty and the need to make a fortune had deferred the realization of this visionary notion. Emerging from America's internecine conflict with a saber wound on his cheek and the military rank of Colonel, Higginson would be known throughout his life as "Major" to distinguish him from his older kinsman, Colonel Thomas Wentworth Higginson. He married a daughter of Louis Agassiz, the famous naturalist, and became the father of two children. Eventually, after one or two false starts, Higginson made a fortune in copper mining, railroads, and finance that, at length, enabled him in 1881 to realize his ambition of establishing a high-quality symphony orchestra in his own city.

The idea of a permanent, resident orchestra, made up of professional musicians performing on a regular schedule for eight months of the year, was a startling novelty in the America of 1881. Not even New York could boast of such a luxury, while Boston possessed only the occasional performances of the Harvard Musical Association to complement the offerings of touring soloists, opera companies, and local choral groups such as the already celebrated Handel and Haydn Society.

While firmly controlling the details of management, Higginson left the mu-

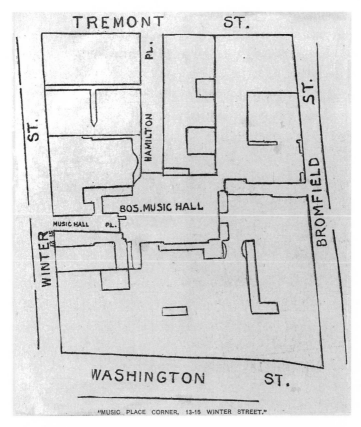

The old Boston Music Hall: Location map from the
Boston Herald, March 30, 1898.

sical leadership of the new aggregation to a succession of qualified European conductors. Over the years, he saw the orchestra progress from an unpolished assemblage of mostly local artists to a smoothly functioning professional ensemble that gained competence season by season under the musical guidance of George Henschel (1881–84), Wilhelm Gericke (1884–89), and Arthur Nikisch (1889–93). Another historic innovation, dating from 1885, was the initiation of the warm-weather Promenade concerts later known as "the Pops," designed primarily as a means of providing supplemental employment for the musicians as well as an agreeable diversion for the Boston public.

Higginson himself, meanwhile, had become a commanding presence on the Boston scene. His rugged, occasionally quirky personality, and his position in the community, were characterized with affectionate insight by his younger friend Mark A. DeWolfe Howe, the historian of the BSO and other Boston institutions:

By common consent "the Major" was the foremost citizen of Boston — the founder and sustainer of the Boston Symphony Orchestra, the princely bene-factor of Harvard College, alive to every civic responsibility, a recognized leader in the financial, artistic, philanthropic, and social life of the community. A savor of romance, heightened by the sabre-scar which the Civil war had left upon his face, was inseparable from him. There was, besides, a Yankee shrewd-ness, a bluntness of alternately severe and humorous speech, and withal a streak of sentiment which colored his telling words and generous deeds.[7]

All of these qualities would repeatedly come into play during the eight years when Symphony Hall was in the making.

The Old Music Hall

Among his numerous civic responsibilities, Higginson held a controlling inter-est in the Boston Music Hall, a center of the city's cultural life and the original home base of the Boston Symphony Orchestra. This four-story structure, built in 1852, was situated just south of Tremont Street in downtown Boston, where its shell, a survivor of many interior reconstructions, now encompasses the Orpheum Theatre. Its incommodious entrance was situated, then as now, in Hamilton Place, directly opposite the Park Street Church; the carriage traffic at the Friday afternoon Symphony "rehearsals" — which were actually full-fledged concerts — often engendered massive tie-ups in an already congested area. "The exterior," noted a contemporary handbook, "is entirely concealed by surrounding buildings, and is utterly devoid of any architectural preten-sions in its plain brick walls; but the interior is tasteful, and elegant in its pro-portions, design, and decoration."[8]

With a severely rectangular floor plan, two galleries shaped like recumbent croquet wickets, and a seating capacity of about 2600, the Music Hall had been hailed on its opening as "a grand and sumptuous affair," unrivaled in "extent, magnificence and beauty."[9] From the 1850s to the 1890s, it provided a frame-work for many stirring events, both musical and nonmusical: civic observances, prayer meetings, sermons, lectures, and debates. To an apparently increasing extent as time went on, it also accommodated what one unfriendly critic de-scribed as "prize fights, cake walks, cat and dog shows, all-night dancing parties and other uses equally objectionable and equally at odds with all ideas of pro-priety and good taste."[10]

Boston Music Hall: View of the main entrance in Hamilton Place,
from the Boston Sunday Herald, *April 24, 1892.*

Quite aside from its intrinsic merits and deficiencies, the Boston Music Hall was perennially subject to threats arising from its central position in an area of prime real estate values. For years, the musical community was intermittently alarmed by proposals "to remove the building for business improvements" and to extend Hamilton Place straight through from Tremont Street to Washington Street. It was precisely with the aim of blocking such initiatives that Higginson and his associates had purchased a controlling interest in the property in the summer of 1881 when preparations were being made for the debut of the Boston Symphony Orchestra.[11]

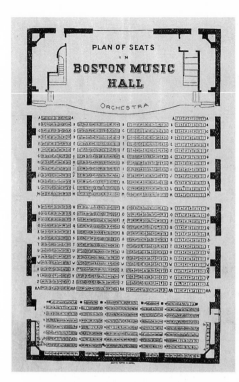
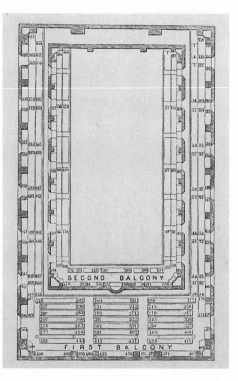

(above) *Seating plan of the Boston Music Hall, 1852–1899.* BSO Archives.

(opposite, above) *Interior of the Boston Music Hall: View toward the stage, showing the "great sounding board" installed in the mid-1880s, derisively referred to as "Mr. Higginson's woodshed roof."* BSO Archives.

(opposite, below) *View toward the rear, with the Apollo Belvedere.*
BSO Archives, from the estate of William Sturgis Bigelow.

Public enthusiasm for this once splendid edifice had waned significantly over the nineteen seasons during which it functioned as the BSO's official performance space. Typical was the judgment in 1892 of one non-Bostonian who called it an out-and-out "disgrace to the city; undesirable in every way. Badly situated, very difficult of access, dangerous of egress, and the most ill-ventilated hall that I ever saw."[12] A Brookline resident denounced it a few years later as:

> a fire trap and so wretchedly ventilated that I with several other patrons of
> the Symphony orchestra have decided this to be our last winter's experience
> of drafts and impure air. Many physicians have advised their patients to give
> up the pleasure and delight of the music, from the injury and fatigue caused
> by listening to it under such unfavorable circumstances.[13]

Major Higginson, as the Music Hall's *de facto* proprietor, could not be un-
moved by such complaints. He had long been aware that other quarters must
eventually be found if the orchestra were to continue. That was the reason for
his enduring interest in the plot of ground at Huntington Avenue and West
Chester Park, whose area (about 225 by 150 feet) was roughly half again as
large as that of the Music Hall property. Not only did Higginson keep an eye
on this choice lot of ground; he called it to the attention of various friends and
associates. In the autumn of 1892, five and one-half years after it had first come
to his notice, he took steps to bring it under his own control.

In a complicated series of transactions carried out on October 28, 1892, the
property was first sold by its owner, F. Gordon Dexter, to one John Tudor Gardiner of Brookline, acting as agent for the real purchasers.[14] Gardiner, in turn,
immediately mortgaged the property for $170,000,[15] then sold it, subject to the
mortgage,[16] to Major Higginson and three close associates: Dr. Henry F. Sears,
a pathologist and major benefactor of the Harvard Medical School; John L.
Gardner, the banker husband of the celebrated Isabella Stewart Gardner, hostess and art collector; and Charles E. Perkins of Burlington, Iowa, a Midwestern
railroad magnate and longstanding friend of Higginson.

RECRUITING THE ARCHITECT

In thus maneuvering to gain control of the land for a new music hall, Major
Higginson did not overlook the fact that he would also need an architect to determine the dimensions and design of any structure he might wish to place
upon it. Not for him was the approach adopted in the 1880s by the sponsors of
the celebrated Gewandhaus concert hall in Leipzig, Germany, a building much
discussed in American musical circles and believed by many to have served as
a model for Boston's Symphony Hall.[17]

The Gewandhaus architects were selected after a competition that at-
tracted seventy-five applicants.[18] Major Higginson, in contrast, went directly to
the man who was already at the top of his profession in America. Under date
of October 27, 1898 — the day before the land was secured — he made an in-
formal but momentous overture to the celebrated Charles Follen McKim
(1847–1909), chief luminary of the New York architectural firm of McKim,
Mead & White.

A man of Pennsylvania Quaker background and unusual personal charm,
McKim, like Higginson himself, had studied briefly at Harvard and had there-

*Charles Follen McKim (1847–1909), the architect
of Symphony Hall.* BSO Archives.

after pursued his architectural training in Paris, New York, and Boston, working with the celebrated H. H. Richardson on Trinity Church and other Boston projects. Now in his middle forties, McKim was enhancing an already brilliant reputation by his work on the new Boston Public Library — a Renaissance palace begun in 1887 and completed in 1895 — and on the resplendently classical Agriculture Building at the Chicago World's Fair, the "World's Columbian Exhibition" of 1893.

McKim's work was characterized by a sensitivity to historical styles, meticulous attention to detail, and a certain magnificence in conception and execution that featured the use of high-quality materials, lavish painted and sculptural decoration, and a well-publicized unwillingness to be defeated by inconvenient budgetary constraints. Although he and Higginson enjoyed what McKim's biographer later called "one of those friendships based on mutual admiration and confidence which were frequent in McKim's career,"[19] the Boston financier apparently felt some diffidence in approaching this princely figure with his own comparatively modest ideas.

The matter was broached in quasi-conspiratorial style in a note from Higginson, dated October 27, 1892, and written, for some unexplained reason, on the stationery of New York's Knickerbocker Club, although both Higginson and McKim would seem from the contents to have been in Boston at the time.[20] "This is a secret — please keep it absolutely," Higginson began, in his usual stubby and almost illegible handwriting.

> Two or three of us have bot [sic] the only feasible lot in Boston for a Music-Hall — [southern?] corner of West Chester Park, Huntington Avenue & a good [small?] street — 34,000 ft. in a parallelogram —
>
> No hall is intended yet, and perhaps never — but if a very good offer for the present hall comes we might have to decide in haste —
>
> I know of no one, but you, to whom I should like to entrust the work — Possibly others are as good but not for me — nor do I know if Mr. [Stanford] White [McKim's partner] is as good — nor if you or he would touch the job.
>
> Possibly you may have time to glance at the land, — then we will meet for discussion, if you choose — *I* can't give the work to any one without consultation, & I would not ask you to spend a minute on it, except just to look at the ground — which will take much more than a hall for 2500 people —
>
> If anything is done, it must be at low cost — & *perhaps* a theatre might be better.

Undismayed by this flurry of caveats, McKim responded promptly and in terms refreshingly positive — almost disconcertingly so. "We all feel that it is quite impossible to express the pleasure we have that you should wish to associate us with the development of your splendid idea for a Music Hall for the City of Boston," the architect wrote on October 29, explaining that he had received Higginson's letter at the moment of leaving and had been unable to put off his departure because of a prior commitment.[21] "[N]othing more flattering or complimentary has ever happened to our office, and . . . we shall do our best, when the time comes, to assist you to reach the result you desire." Promising an early visit in company with his other partner, William Rutherford Mead, "to look over the ground with you," McKim tactfully concluded that:

> while our ambition will be to make the building representative of the purposes for which it is intended in the best sense, we believe that this is not inconsistent with the use of simple materials and economical construction.

Oct. 27ʰ '92 —

KNICKERBOCKER CLUB
319 FIFTH AVENUE.

Dear McKim,

This is a secret — please keep it absolutely —

Two or three of us have hit the only feasible lot in Boston for a Music-Hall — southern corner of West Chester Park, Huntington Avenue & a good small street. 34.000 ft. in a parallelogram —

No Hall is intended yet, & perhaps never — but if a very good offer for the present hall comes

Opening of a dialogue: Part of a letter from Major Higginson to McKim,
October 27, 1892, broaching the subject of a new Music Hall for Boston
(Document 2). New-York Historical Society.

With the ice thus broken, matters moved rapidly forward in spite of McKim's involvement in current projects in Chicago as well as Boston, where he was hard at work on the new Public Library building. Arranging to have the exact dimensions of the proposed music hall property telegraphed to him in Chicago, he also made plans for more intensive study during a forthcoming European trip. "There isn't a day that I don't dream about that Music Hall," he wrote Higginson on November 10, 1892.[22] "I am most anxious to see the lot and have your views, and a large part of the pleasure of my vacation on the other side will be studying a practical application of them from the best existing examples."

McKim even asked to take with him to Europe a survey of the Huntington Avenue plot with the adjoining streets and points of the compass.[23] In complying, Major Higginson furnished him with a detailed syllabus of the features he considered appropriate for a music hall to house the Boston Symphony Orchestra. Writing in pencil and in haste on the eve of the architecture's departure, he laid down a detailed statement of requirements as seen from his experienced perspective.[24]

The Major did not intend that the new building should hold more people than the old, despite the burgeoning growth of the city's population, which more than quadrupled during the second half of the nineteenth century.[25] The concert-going public, though large and enthusiastic, did not increase in anything like the same proportion, and it was Higginson's judgment that there was no need to exceed, or even necessarily to equal, the 2600-seat capacity of the current Music Hall. "The [new] hall should hold about 2200 to 2500 people — not more," the Major wrote, without explaining his reasons. Even 2200 would be a more than generous allotment by the standards of European concert halls. Leipzig's New Gewandhaus, for example, had a seating capacity of only 1560.

As for the proposed structure's other characteristics, Higginson's ideas seemed consciously aimed at correcting some of the deficiencies of the existing building. The proposed hall, he said, should have:

> an ample stage for an orchestra of 90 men and for a chorus of 300 singers if
> need be; two or three adjoining small rooms for tuning the instruments, for
> overcoats, hats, etc. and for the singers; have a good space for an organ which
> can be set into the wall. The hall must have ample exits — on several sides if
> may be — and ample corridors and staircases. It should be on the street level

I think and have perhaps two galleries of small dimensions. I think that it should be lighted from the top only, i.e. from windows in the top or in the highest part of the side walls. I say all this on account of quiet — to keep out sounds from the world.[26]

Not less decisive than these physical attributes was the need for economy, Higginson emphasized. "As I must bear the burden of the new hall, perhaps quite alone, and as I keep my purse fairly depleted all the time, I must not — cannot — spend too much money for a new hall," Higginson insisted. He also asserted that he had "no notion of the cost of a new hall," although he suggested that the land alone would probably be worth $200,000 by the time a hall could be built. The existing Music Hall, he said, had originally cost less than $200,000, although it had required much upkeep and modernization and had paid him no return since its purchase in 1881.

Scattered among these major points were other suggestions for McKim's consideration: the possibility of "a sounding board of some kind or a stage shut in by an alcove, rounded or angular"; the possibility of including an additional small hall seating 700 or 800 for chamber music, lectures, etc.; the merits, known or reputed, of various concert halls in Vienna, Leipzig, Paris, and elsewhere; the names of knowledgeable and distinguished acquaintances whom McKim might consult in the Austro-Hungarian capital; and Higginson's own liking for "round-arched Norman or Lombard architecture" and for "brick and brick ornament."

"I always like the severe in architecture, music, men and women, books, &c. &c.," he added. In his use of the word "severe," Major Higginson may have been influenced by recollections of the Latin motto prominently displayed on the portal of Leipzig's New Gewandhaus: *Res severa verum gaudium*, a quotation from Seneca that can be translated as "True joy is a serious matter."[27] That, at any rate, was the spirit in which Higginson habitually exercised his self-imposed responsibility for maintaining the Boston Symphony Orchestra and ensuring it a proper performance space.

"I've no present purpose of building," the prospective client reminded McKim, adding, however, that a good offer to purchase the existing Music Hall "might precipitate matters." "As I understand it," he said, "we could not well have a hall before the fall of '95, eh? or still later? *Can you guess at the cost?*"

"All of which is respectfully submitted," Higginson concluded. "I'd have this typewritten but then might miss you. If you care for it you'll have it typewrit-

Portal of Leipzig's New Gewandhaus (1884–1944), with Latin inscription.
Stadtgeschichtliches Museum Leipzig.

ten." McKim did indeed have the letter typewritten, and evidently paid close and continuing attention to its contents. Nor did he lose sight of the music hall project during his months in Europe, although there is no basis for the later assumption that his principal business abroad had been to inspect the leading concert halls in quest of a model for Boston. Years later, he reminded Higginson that he had not only studied the plan of Leipzig's New Gewandhaus but had conferred, at the Major's behest, with conductors Charles Lamoureux in Paris and Wilhelm Gericke and Hans Richter in Vienna.[28]

More concretely, in Paris McKim enlisted the help of a young American named John Galen Howard, who had been studying architecture at the Ecole des Beaux-Arts and negotiating with the artist Puvis de Chavannes about the murals that the latter would execute for the Boston Public Library. In consultation with Professor Victor Laloux of the Beaux-Arts, Howard is said to have worked out three different sets of studies or sketches for a music hall such as was proposed for Boston. The first, according to McKim's biographer,

> was worked up according to McKim's own preferences — a semicircular plan. The second, elliptical in form, was believed by M. Laloux to promise the best acoustical properties. The third, rectangular in shape, represented the views of M. Lamoureux, director of the concerts of the Cirque d'Été and of the Grand Opera.[29]

Months would pass before Howard's sketches could be forwarded to McKim from Paris, and only then, apparently, would it be possible for the architect to answer Higginson's urgent inquiries about cost. An interim response was, however, offered on April 28, 1893, by McKim's partner, William R. Mead, at a moment when McKim himself was in Chicago. From the estimates they had obtained, Mead wrote, he believed the proposed music hall, "can be built in the very simplest manner for three hundred thousand dollars ($300,000)." But, he added,

> to do it in a creditable manner would I think require more money. This estimate contemplates a building devoted entirely to Music Hall purposes and from which no rent from shops would be received. It would contain the necessary vestibules and stairs, a large and small Music Hall, and certain rooms for instruction and administration.[30]

These figures, McKim explained to Higginson a few days later, had been the outcome of "a number of schemes" worked up in the past three months in Paris and New York — "of which the last has seemed to both Mr. Mead and myself the most practical, economical and desirable." The nature of this preferred scheme he did not specify, although it is clear from later developments that he strongly inclined to a semicircular or amphitheatric design. "Before proceeding further," McKim added, "I should like to have the opportunity of going over the several schemes with you with a view to determining the policy which you intend to pursue. We can meet here or in Boston as you prefer."[31]

THE MUSIC HALL CRISIS

As we shall see, McKim's ideas would soon begin to take shape, and a plaster model of a preliminary design would be unveiled in January 1894. However, Boston's musical public had thus far received no hint of this activity. Throughout the Symphony season of 1892–93 — the BSO's twelfth — its patrons made their customary way to the Music Hall in Hamilton Place. They may have grumbled at the shortcomings of the building, but they cheered the orchestra's performances under the brilliant if mercurial Arthur Nikisch, then in the third and, as it turned out, final year of his Boston engagement.

There had been a moment of alarm in March 1893 when it was rumored that the Music Hall in Hamilton Place was about to be sold and the orchestra left homeless. But Higginson himself had promptly allayed these anxieties, assuring the press that the concerts would go on and that he had not talked to the Music Hall's directors about any sale, although he did not doubt that "a fair offer," if made, would be accepted. Somewhat disingenuously, Mr. Higginson added that with regard to the perplexing problem of a site for a possible new hall, he was "no nearer a solution of the problem today than he was when it was first propounded."[32]

This air of innocence could not, however, be long maintained in face of the much graver threat to the Music Hall — and the BSO — that developed from an unexpected direction at the beginning of June. This was "An Act to Provide for Rapid Transit in Boston and Vicinity," passed by the State Legislature and approved by the Governor on June 10, 1893.[33] Designed with a view to relieving the chronic congestion prevalent in downtown Boston, it mandated the construction of a north-south elevated railroad line that would run from Causeway Street to Franklin Park and would pass straight through the premises of the Boston Music Hall.

Details of this remarkable legislation provided — subject to approval by a majority of Boston's then all-male electorate — for the creation of a Metropolitan Transit Commission charged with taking possession, "by purchase or otherwise," of a strip of land for the right of way of the proposed rapid transit line. This done, the commission was to initiate prompt measures for the construction of the elevated railroad, and it was also to determine whether or not "any subway for street railway tracks and cars" should be built, either on the strip itself or in any part of Tremont or Boylston streets. Through downtown Boston, the "strip" was specifically required to run "between Tremont and

Washington streets" and to have a width between twenty-five and thirty-five feet: wide enough to doom the Music Hall and anything else that lay in its path.[34]

A conversation with Mayor Nathan Matthews persuaded Major Higginson that this so-called "Back Alley Plan" would almost surely be ratified by the voters at a special election to be held in September. (The vote was later put off until the state election in November.) If it was indeed approved, the Boston Symphony could find itself without a home as early as the beginning of the 1894–95 season, then only fifteen months away. The moment could scarcely have been more inconvenient, for Higginson already faced the urgent necessity of engaging a new conductor to replace the departing Nikisch, and of renegotiating the contracts of the individual members of the orchestra.

The Major was not inclined, in the uneasy economic climate prevailing in June 1893, to try to meet the emergency by personally mobilizing the sums required to procure an alternative performance space. "It seems to me that the concerts are my share, after all," he told the *Boston Herald*:

> It has been a great risk and a great responsibility, as everybody knows. I think there is risk about it. I don't want to carry the load. I have all I can do anyway. There are enough other gentlemen interested in the plan to carry it along.[35]

This did not mean, of course, that Higginson was washing his hands of the problem. On the contrary, he was already in touch with some of these "other gentlemen," and was engaged with them in working out a comprehensive strategy to deal with the situation. Its basic ingredient would be a high-pressure fund-raising campaign directed toward construction of a suitable building on the plot of ground at Huntington Avenue and West Chester Park, a plot whose existence was now for the first time made known to the public.

An opening call to action was sounded in a public statement, attributed to "several prominent gentlemen," that appeared in most of the city's half-dozen daily newspapers on June 14, 1893. In it, these unnamed gentlemen revealed that "an option" on a possible site for a music hall — i.e., the property at Huntington Avenue and West Chester Park — had already been taken, "at a fair price." However, these gentlemen warned, unless the sum of $400,000 to build a new hall could be raised within the next ten days, the concerts of the Boston Symphony Orchestra "must be abandoned indefinitely" (one paper said "definitively").[36] According to unofficial statements attributed to Higginson and others, about one-fourth of the amount sought would be for the land (which had been mortgaged for $170,000 the year before) and the remainder for the proposed building.

A second statement, dated June 17 and published on the 19th, outlined a more sedate and regular process whereby the proposed hall would be built under a formal act of incorporation, shares being issued to subscribers in the amount of $100 each.[37] Urgent action was needed, the statement reiterated, in order that the new hall might be finished by October 1, 1894, a date less than fifteen months away.

Named as the source of this second statement were three prominent citizens who, it was asserted, had been "asked to act as a committee for the building of a new hall for music in Boston." One of the three was Higginson himself; the other two were his friends Edward W. Hooper, the treasurer of Harvard College, and the same Dr. Henry F. Sears who had joined in purchasing the Huntington Avenue property the year before. These three, whom we may designate informally as the "Committee of Three," would form the active nucleus of the music hall enterprise over the next several years.

Edward W. Hooper (1839–1901) was to play a role second only to Higginson's own in the transactions leading up to the building of Symphony Hall. The son of a scholarly physician and a Transcendental poetess, Hooper was widely connected among Boston's elite. Notable among his kinfolk were the late Colonel Robert Gould Shaw, the Civil War hero and commander of the all-Negro 54th Massachusetts Regiment; William Sturgis Bigelow, the Orientalist and art collector, who would become Hooper's fellow director in the New Boston Music Hall corporation; and Mrs. Caroline Sturgis Tappan of "Tanglewood" in the Berkshires, the future summer home of the Boston Symphony Orchestra.

Hooper's sister was the tragic Clover Adams, wife of historian Henry Adams; this extraordinarily gifted woman had inexplicably committed suicide in Washington in 1885. Hooper's mother, Ellen Sturgis Hooper, had also attempted to take her own life. His wife, a musician and the mother of their five girls, had died of natural causes in 1881, but Hooper's own death in 1901, after a fall from the window of his Beacon Street home, would not escape the suspicion of suicidal intent. Yet in spite of these personal griefs, and occasional minor eccentricities, Hooper was credited with highly effective management of Harvard's finances over a long period. Known also as a discriminating patron of the arts, he was described by his friend Higginson in laudatory terms:

*Edward William Hooper (1839–1901), treasurer of Harvard College and
a key figure in the creation of Symphony Hall.*
Photograph by William Notman, courtesy of Harvard University Archives.

He was as near golden as any man ever was: a high-minded gentleman, keen
as a briar. Hooper knew how to look into things with excellent judgment and
with forethought. He was the best kind of a man, and yet so appreciative of
other people.[38]

Hooper was a conspicuous participant in the campaign for a new music hall
initiated by the statements of June 14 and June 17, 1893. But Higginson himself
did not shun personal association with the project. On June 20, he released a
statement in his own name in the form of identical letters to the editors of the
principal Boston newspapers. In a frank description of the problems he faced
as sponsor of the BSO, the Major made it clear that he was appealing not to the
cupidity but to the conscience of his fellow citizens. The marketing of shares
in the new music hall was no money-making scheme, he emphasized, but de-
served the support of the public as a matter of civic responsibility. Again he

warned that unless a new hall could be assured promptly, "I must disband the orchestra, and finally abandon the Symphony concerts."[39]

All through that midsummer week, subscriptions trickled in from wealthy business and community leaders, Higginson relatives, and ordinary music lovers. By Friday, June 23, $268,000 of the needed $400,000 had been sub-scribed. Saturday, which was understood to be the final deadline, brought a flood of pledges that carried the ultimate total to $407,000.[40]

In announcing the success of the subscription drive, the committee fol-lowed Higginson's example in distancing itself from any notion that the stock was likely to be profitable. The new hall, the committee indicated, would be built "to serve the purposes of music in the best way possible," and the stock was "not expected to be a regular dividend paying security."[41] A realization that the venture was in no sense a means of self-enrichment was reflected also in the list of subscribers, which, as one journalist commented, "reads like what a severely critical social mentor would put forth as the 'best set' in the city. Very many of them are women prominent in social ways, a fact which, perhaps as much as anything else, takes it out of the ordinary run of business."[42] We do not know how much of the needed sum was subscribed by Major Higginson personally. A quarter of a century later, he acknowledged ownership of 140 shares of music hall stock with a face value of $14,000.[43]

As they awaited the results of Higginson's appeal, Bostonians excitedly can-vassed every aspect of the situation, most especially the site proposed for a new music hall. To many, the Huntington Avenue location seemed excessively remote and unappealing for a number of reasons, notably the proximity of two railroad lines with their noise, smoke and soot. At the same time, it was recognized that more desirable locations, such as the former Public Library building on Boylston Street or a site near the new Public Library in Copley Square, would in all probability be prohibitively expensive.

The Panic of '93

There was wonderment in Boston that so large a sum of money — nearly half a million dollars — could be raised in a mere ten days' time, especially consid-ering "the very disturbed state of financial matters throughout the United States this summer."[44] Indeed, the Music Hall crisis was hardly more than a ripple compared to the tidal wave that threatened to engulf the nation as a whole in these same midsummer weeks.

*Emil Paur (1855–1932), conductor of the Boston
Symphony Orchestra, 1893–1898.*
BSO Archives.

Indicative of the suddenness of this threatening situation was the experience of historian Henry Adams, Edward Hooper's brother-in-law (who, as a younger contemporary of Henry Higginson at Boston Latin School, remembered the leadership of "Bully Hig" in stone-throwing battles on Boston Common). Arriving in Lucerne, Switzerland, on July 22, 1893, the historian "found letters from his brothers requesting his immediate return to Boston because the community was bankrupt and he was probably a beggar." Adams later wrote: "Blindly some very powerful energy was at work. . . . Men died like flies under the strain, and Boston grew suddenly old, haggard, and thin."[45]

Among those hard hit by the threatened collapse — touched off by the failure of a London banking house and aggravated by an alarming outflow of gold from the United States — was the founder of the Boston Symphony. "I've not been away from the office for even part of a day, during this summer, unless when in New York on duty — and I shall not go away," Higginson admitted in mid-August. Indeed, the Major looked "as if he had grown five years older," novelist Henry James reported to his brother William. "I got an idea the first time I saw him of what the strain must have been."[46]

Although it would be years before the nation fully regained its equilibrium, by autumn the sense of acute panic had largely subsided. Returning to Washington in mid-September, Henry Adams found that the storm had "partly blown over, [and] life had taken on a new face."[47] In Boston, the BSO began its thirteenth season at the Music Hall on schedule under the leadership of Austrian-born Emil Paur, whom an eleventh-hour recruiting effort had brought from Leipzig under a five-year contract. A welcome development was the rejection of the dreaded Rapid Transit scheme at the state election on November 7, 1893. The closeness of the tally — 27,109 to 23,980 — made it clear that the threat had been real.

With the plan for a north-south elevated line defeated, the focus of Boston's transit problems would shift to the building of elevated rail lines outside the city center, and the construction of a subway for electric streetcars along Tremont and connecting streets. The first segment of the Tremont Street subway — actually the first such line in the nation — would run from Park Street to an exit in the Public Garden not far from the present Arlington Street stop. Opened September 1, 1897, it would carry a part of the distinguished audience that assembled for the opening of the new Symphony Hall on October 15, 1900.

FOUNDING THE "NEW BOSTON MUSIC HALL"

Although the immediate threat to the Boston Symphony had passed, Major Higginson and his associates remained convinced that a new music hall would be needed eventually, even though not immediately. Weeks before the vote on the Rapid Transit plan, the "Committee of Three" had issued a circular letter, dated October 30, 1893, in which the 400-odd subscribers to the music hall scheme were invited to remit one-half the amount of their subscriptions by November 15, 1893, and the balance by May 15, 1894. As soon as paid-in pledges reached $200,000, the letter stated, a corporation would be organized with authority to issue capital stock to a maximum of $500,000, and the shareholders would be consulted about the purchase of the needed land and the plans for the building.[48]

Subscriber response to this summons was so prompt and positive, despite the nation's shaky economic condition, that the corporation — to be known

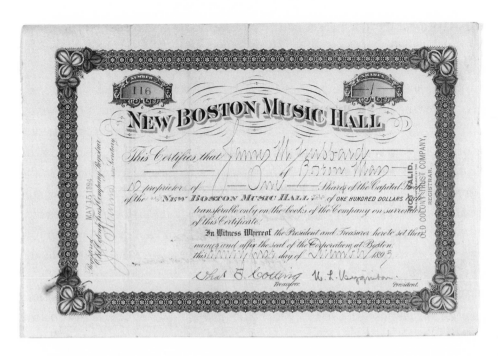

Share of capital stock of the New Boston Music Hall, issued December 21, 1893.
BSO Archives.

throughout its forty-year existence as the "New Boston Music Hall" — could be organized under Massachusetts law as early as December 30, 1893, and the interested stockholders could assemble for an organizational meeting on January 6, 1894.[49]

Named as directors of the infant corporation were Henry L. Higginson, with the title of President; Edward W. Hooper and Henry F. Sears, Higginson's associates on the "Committee of Three"; William Sturgis Bigelow; and Charles Edward Cotting, a younger man with a head for details who was already clerk of the old Music Hall corporation and now became Clerk and Treasurer of the new association as well. Mr. Cotting, like his colleagues, came of an old Boston family identified with the city's urban development. "In his business career," said his 1920 obituary, "he was connected as a director or trustee with many financial institutions, including numerous Boston trust companies and various real estate trusts."[50]

The principal business of the January 6 meeting, aside from ratifying the choice of directors, was to approve the corporation's purchase of the Huntington Avenue property — which, it was now explained, had already been secured on behalf of the stockholders at a cost of $170,000, the amount of the mortgage taken out in 1892. In accordance with authority voted at the meeting, the lot was formally conveyed to the New Boston Music Hall by its four interim purchasers on January 10, 1894.[51]

Acquisition of a building lot, the stockholders were cautioned, did not necessarily mean "that the work of preparing plans for a building was to be commenced right away or even in the near future." In fact, they were informed, it was "impossible to tell when any move toward that end will be made." In the meantime, it was stated, no plans for such a building had been "solicited by the Directors." What was, however, now revealed officially for the first time was that the New York firm of McKim, Mead & White had been looking at Boston's music hall problem and had offered a "suggestion" for the interior of a music hall, one "entirely different from anything in New England." This "suggestion," it was explained, had been embodied in a plaster model that would shortly be placed on exhibition in the new Boston Public Library building, where it was hoped that the public would "see it and criticise it fully."

Essay in Plaster

Like some previous public utterances by Major Higginson and members of his group, these first disclosures to the stockholders of the New Boston Music Hall offered less than a complete account of the relevant facts. It was, no doubt, technically accurate to say that no plans for a new music hall had been "solicited by the Directors," but it was also true that some of these gentlemen had remained in direct contact with the McKim firm and, as far as we know, had done little if anything to discourage that firm's interest in moving ahead on the music hall project.

McKim himself had continued to be actively concerned with this undertaking throughout the months of uncertainty over the Rapid Transit plan. He had apparently forwarded to Higginson in early July of 1893 a set of preliminary "plans, sections and interior perspective at quarter scale" for a new music hall, followed a few days later by an "elevation and exterior perspective" of such a building.[52] Later in the summer, McKim had written to Edward Hooper about his desire to illustrate his architectural concept with a three-dimensional wood and plaster model, and Hooper, after consultation with Sears and Higginson, had authorized McKim to spend up to $1200 for such a purpose.[53]

The gratified architect, interpreting the Bostonians' unexpectedly liberal gesture as a "vote of confidence in the plan as it stands," had promptly engaged a man named Hall to carry out the work with the help of five assistants, and had expansively stated that his firm would even bear half the cost.[54] By December 21, 1893, he was able to inform Hooper that the model was practically ready for inspection by the Committee, and that it would, if agreeable, be placed in one of the rooms of the still unfinished Boston Public Library building.[55]

Such was the background of the "suggestion" that had been brought to the notice of the New Music Hall stockholders at their meeting on January 6, 1894. Two days later, the model was placed on public display in what was then called the "Catalogue Room" of the Public Library building (presumably the "Catalogue and Shelf Department," just left of the main entrance, as seen on early plans of the building).

Quite apart from the architectural concept it was supposed to illustrate, the mere existence and physical characteristics of this unusual contraption sufficed to create a minor sensation in the press and public. A box-like structure twelve feet square and seven feet high, it was raised five feet above the floor and offered prospective viewers a choice of approaches. They could, from below, pass their heads through a kind of trap door and survey the interior from approximately stage level, or they could mount a special set of external stairs and peep through one of the tiny windows. What lay within was, as the Music Hall stockholders had been told, something "entirely different from anything in New England." It was, perhaps regrettably, a concept that would never be realized, despite its manifold attractions.

THE GREEK THEATRE PLAN

McKim's idea, as here presented to interested Bostonians, was a realization in gleaming imitation marble of the architect's early "semicircular" plan for a music hall. In its essential characteristics, it recalled the ancient Greek amphitheatres seen and admired by well-traveled Bostonians at Delphi, Taormina, and other ancient Hellenic sites. Having made his bow to the Renaissance in designing the Boston Public Library, McKim had been irresistibly impelled to revisit the classical forms of Greece and Rome that he had used so effectively at the Chicago World's Fair.

Unlike its Greek and Roman antecedents, a Greek theatre for New England would need, of course, to be roofed over and protected against the elements,

The Greek Theatre Plan: Model displayed in the Boston Public Library,
January 1894. View toward the stage.
Photographs by Joseph Livermore Stebbins, Boston Public Library, Print Department.

but its external form was not apparent from the model, and seems not to have been determined at this stage.[56] Inside, the design was unmistakably based on familiar classical elements: seats rising in tiers, following the curves of the amphitheatre; a level space — the "orchestra" or "pit" — that could accommodate additional seats; and a proscenium or stage for the musicians, also rising in tiers and surmounted by what one newspaper described as a "double sounding-board . . . forming a sort of vast, imperceptible funnel." (Others likened it to the mouth of a trumpet.) Conspicuous, too, was a "wide and commodious lobby, from which two doors enter directly into the amphitheatre, while from either hand a wide ambulatory leads entirely around the theatre to the stage."

Also included in the design was a characteristic McKim touch, "an appropriate statue, allegorical in nature, in the rear of the stage, and a line of statues in niches around the hall."[57] The statuary, an essential ingredient in

The Greek Theatre Plan: View toward the rear. JLS photo, BPL Print Department.

the architect's design, had been a subject of more than casual consultation between McKim and the sculptor Daniel Chester French, the creator of Concord's "Minuteman," Cambridge's "John Harvard," and, later, the seated President in the Lincoln Memorial at Washington. Already meditating on a plan for the bronze doors of the Boston Public Library, French had also experimented, at McKim's invitation, with a design for a sculptured frieze for the music hall.

As a part of this exercise, French had overseen the preparation of the diminutive sculptured figures that graced the model, and had even gone so far as to submit to McKim an estimate of the cost of providing the proposed hall with all needed statuary, including twelve or fourteen casts from the antique. This could be done, French had intimated, for the rather modest total of $28,500.[58] The sculptor himself, however, had not been well satisfied with the results of his own experiments, and his name was not included in the official publicity when the model was exhibited in Boston.[59]

Statuary aside, the proposed music hall could not fail to engage the rapt at-

The Greek Theatre Plan: Side view, stage left. JLS photo, BPL Print Department.

tention of the Boston press, ably briefed by G. E. Wolters, the Boston representative of the McKim firm. Practically every newspaper published sketches of the wonders on display at the Public Library. Abundant statistics cataloged the interior dimensions of the proposed hall (150 by 143 feet), its seating capacity (2500), its stage capacity (120 musicians and 350 choristers), its corridor width (18 feet), and its visibility, fireproofing, acoustical arrangements, cloakroom accommodations, and so forth.[60] It was noted that the proposed building would be set back some distance from the street, perhaps leaving room for shops on the Huntington Avenue side. The principal entrance would be located on Falmouth (now St. Stephen) Street, rather than on either of the two avenues.

"It is beyond the possibility of a doubt," the *Boston Transcript* exulted,

> that if this project is accepted Boston will shortly possess one of the most beautiful structures devoted to music in the world. Every line, every proportion, and every detail . . . attests the creation of a masterpiece of architecture worthy to be the shrine of the best music.

The Greek Theatre Plan: Side view, stage right. JLS photo, BPL Print Department.

Other papers seemed happy to agree. The *Boston Journal*, for example, hailed what it called "a most beautiful structure, a delight to the eye of the architect and equally a wonder and pleasure to the sight of the layman."[61]

Yet the enthusiasm was less universal than some later accounts suggest.[62] Various difficulties of a practical nature were cited, and there were some complaints about the remoteness and inconvenience of the site, the questionable propriety of employing out-of-town architects, and the lack of provision for grand opera, a genre normally produced in the forty-year-old Boston Theatre on Washington Street. A lady in Jamaica Plain registered dismay at the "immense" size of the cloakrooms and the apparent expectation that Symphony patrons would henceforth appear in evening dress, to the discomfiture of more modest music lovers.[63]

Of more decisive weight were the reservations felt by the directors of the New Boston Music Hall. These men were not without taste, nor could they deny that McKim had devised an appealing plan, one that satisfied many of the desiderata Higginson had outlined at the beginning. Yet there seemed room for doubt on various points, especially about the acoustical implications of this untried scheme. McKim himself had been highly optimistic in this regard:

> The plan seems to us to sustain itself in its structural and architectural possibilities, and as regards acoustics, we believe that the wedge-form stage walls and the succession of rising concentric arches immediately behind and above the orchestra offers a series of sounding boards of the best.[64]

But Edward Hooper later spoke of "objections" voiced by "some of the subscribers, notably Mr. Higginson," on the score of "acoustic defects." Higginson himself told a stockholders' meeting that the plan had "included some innovations, and the directors were afraid to adopt it."[65] Higginson and his associates knew little of acoustics, which at that time were a mystery even to specialists. But they were keenly aware of their responsibilities within the corporate framework, and unwilling to make a costly mistake that would involve other people's money as well as their own.

Such doubts were reinforced, moreover, by misgivings of a more general character. The country as a whole remained in the grip of severe economic depression. The year 1893 had seen the failure of 15,000 business enterprises and 158 national banks. By mid-1894, the number of unemployed would reach four million. "For business reasons we must now go slowly," Edward Hooper warned McKim on February 14, 1894. "We wish to have your plans perfected and safe estimates of cost obtained (at our expense) before we adopt any plan."[66] In April came word that the Boston Symphony was omitting its customary spring tour in the South and Midwest, supposedly because of a shortfall in concert-hall receipts.[67]

With Hooper temporarily out of the country, Major Higginson personally intervened on April 23, 1894, to impose an indefinite moratorium on the music hall project. In a brief and otherwise casual note to McKim, he pronounced what would amount to a death sentence on the Greek theatre scheme:

> [I]t has seemed to me best to wait awhile before building — No one cares to put out fresh money, no one knows about the plans of transit — or can guess at the future — therefore we should wait — Edward H[ooper] & I agreed as to this point before his sailing.[68]

McKim's response was prompt and tactful, though understandably lacking in enthusiasm:

I have received your letter in regard to the Music Hall, and while I regret that it is not likely to be pushed through to completion this summer, as we had hoped, I recognize that once built it must stand for success or failure, and am therefore quite willing to regard the necessity as fortunate which forbids its immediate construction.[69]

Writing to Hooper that summer, the architect revealed a little more of his personal disappointment and his reluctance to let the project drop:

I daresay you have returned [from abroad] with models in your mind's eye newer and fresher, but until I know positively from you that the form of the Greek theatre must go, I propose to cherish my faith in it.[70]

It was later said that McKim had found an alternative use for the Greek theatre design in his plan for an Academic Theatre at Columbia University, but that plan, too, remained unrealized.[71] Not until after World War II would modern concert-hall architecture begin to free itself from the traditional rectangular model and to experiment successfully with such innovations as polygonal ground plans and amphitheatric seating.

In the meantime, the authorities of the Boston Public Library were pressing to have the plaster model removed from the library premises, and McKim suggested to Hooper that his clients either let his firm take care of the matter or "entrust the work to someone familiar with plaster construction."[72] From the surviving evidence, it would appear that the corporation elected to have the model removed and stored for a time at its own expense.

Almost five years later, in April 1899, Major Higginson was reminded by Mr. Cotting that he had intended to offer the model back to McKim and, if the architect declined, to have it "broken up."[73] All trace of this curious construction has since vanished, and there remains only a set of contemporary photographs in the Print Department of the Boston Public Library to commemorate what may have been an unrealized masterpiece.

INTERVAL, 1894–97

There now began an interval that would end only with the sale of the old Music Hall in Hamilton Place after a delay of nearly four years. Boston, during these years, continued to feel the severe effects of the economic depression which had begun in 1893. As Henry Adams described it:

The convulsion of 1893 left its victims in dead-water. . . . While the country braced itself up to an effort such as no one had thought within its powers, the individual crawled as best he could, through the wreck, and found many values of life upset. . . . Much that had made life pleasant between 1870 and 1890 perished in the ruins.[74]

Boston, the first American city to acquire a permanent professional symphony orchestra, was rapidly falling behind in the creation of modern concert facilities. New York's Carnegie Hall had opened in 1891, and Baltimore's fine new Music Hall, subsequently renamed the Lyric Theatre, began operation in 1894. Like the future Symphony Hall, the Baltimore edifice was reputed to be patterned after Leipzig's New Gewandhaus, a favorite supposition of American music lovers in the 1890s.

In Boston, there was "nothing new" on the concert hall front, Mr. Higginson told an inquiring reporter in November 1894:

I thought that it was generally understood that so long as the old Music Hall remained there would not be a new one. If the present hall were sold tomorrow, then a new hall would of course have to be provided at once. But so long as the old hall stands without danger of alteration or removal on account of rapid transit schemes or any other causes, the plan for a new hall is not likely to be pushed. Then, too, this is not a time to ask people for money for any such project. The model of the New Music Hall, that was shown in the new Public Library building, is still in possession of the committee and is stored in this city.[75]

A formal statement along similar lines was addressed to the stockholders of the New Boston Music Hall by its directors on November 17, 1894:

After careful inquiry, your directors are satisfied that so long as the old Music Hall is used as a public hall the income from the new Music Hall would not be sufficient to pay even its current expenses for taxes and administration. They therefore have been unwilling to advise you to build until the fate of the old Music Hall shall be settled.[76]

The shareholders were assured, however, that their subscriptions had already "done much good" by forestalling the threatened breakup of the orchestra and securing the lot on which "a new and better Music Hall will soon have to be built in the interest of music in Boston."

The 363 paid-up stockholders had an opportunity to comment on this reasoning at the annual meeting of the New Boston Music Hall, held on February 20, 1895, in the premises of the old Music Hall. But "the rows of empty chairs," according to the *Boston Transcript*, "seemed to indicate that the interest with which the project was inaugurated had largely died away."[77] Among the scraps of information revealed at this meeting was the fact that $2,000 had been paid as a commission to McKim, Mead & White, and $2,600 to T. Dennie Boardman, a prominent realtor who had been in charge of collecting subscriptions.

Three possible lines of action for the future were now available, Edward Hooper told the meeting: building a new hall, liquidating the corporation, or leaving matters as they stood. Major Higginson, as president of the corporation, spoke for the third alternative. The Huntington Avenue site was an "excellent" one, he asserted; the value of the property was increasing, and would doubtless yield a fair return if it ever became necessary to sell. With no apparent dissent, the officers of the corporation were reelected and the future of Boston's musical infrastructure was left in abeyance.

Three more years would pass before an improving economy brought with it an acceptable bid to purchase the old Music Hall, thus removing the principal obstacle to its replacement. Though lacking any current mandate from the corporation, McKim remained a vital presence on the Boston scene, not least because of the controversy over his would-be gift to the Public Library of Frederic MacMonnies's bronze sculpture of a nude "Bacchante and Child." The new library building, constructed at a cost of over two and one-half million dollars exclusive of land, was formally opened on March 11, 1895, and Major Higginson was among the speakers at a gala reception given by the architects to celebrate the event.[78]

Edward Hooper, whose position as treasurer of Harvard College gave him important responsibilities in connection with the University's building program, remained in contact with McKim about a possible master plan for the area of Cambridge between the Harvard Yard and the Charles River. In addition, he and Higginson undoubtedly had McKim in mind as architect of choice for another of the Major's contemplated benefactions. This was the proposed Harvard Union, a students' clubhouse made possible by a Higginson gift of $150,000 in 1899. (It is now a part of the Barker Center for the Humanities.) But a formal invitation to undertake this project would not be tendered until after McKim's return to duty as architect of the New Music Hall.[79]

Chapter 3

STEPS TOWARD
PARNASSUS
1898–1899

GRADUS AD PARNASSUM — "STEPS TO PARNASSUS," THE mountain sacred to Apollo and the Muses — is the title of a celebrated eighteenth-century treatise on counterpoint, and of a well-known nineteenth-century book of exercises for the pianoforte.[80] The words well characterize the sequence of events that, in 1900, culminated in the creation of Symphony Hall, an enduring American memento of the transition between the nineteenth and twentieth centuries.

By the latter part of 1897, the United States had at length begun to experience a vigorous recoil from the economic disaster that had loomed so threateningly back in 1893. One indicator among many was an increase in the prices offered at the annual auction of subscription tickets for the Boston Symphony's 1897–98 season, its seventeenth. A more decisive harbinger was the news, early in 1898, that the old Boston Music Hall had at last found a purchaser: a Boston real estate group reputed to be acting on behalf of anonymous New York interests.

Terms of the sale, said to be set at about $450,000, were fixed at a special meeting of the old Music Hall's directors on March 10, 1898. Under the agreed arrangement, the property was to be leased back to Major Higginson, the former owner, for the next two years so that the Symphony concerts could continue without interruption.[81] This provision would give the sponsors of the new music hall a reasonable interval in which to provide an alternative auditorium.

*Wilhelm Gericke (1845–1925), conductor of the Boston
Symphony Orchestra, 1884–1889 and 1898–1906.*
BSO Archives.

Through much of the ensuing year, such questions were overshadowed by
more immediate national concerns, especially the war with Spain that followed
the destruction of the battleship *Maine* in Havana harbor on February 15, 1898.
Major Higginson himself became much involved in actions to promote the
welfare of the American fighting forces, especially the mission to Cuba of the
hospital ship *Bay State*, for which he personally contributed a check for $10,000
when the Legislature was slow to appropriate the needed funds.[82]

Another claim on Higginson's time was the pleasant task of arranging the return of Wilhelm Gericke to conduct the BSO as successor to Emil Paur, whose
five-year contract was allowed to expire at the end of the 1897–98 season. A letter Higginson wrote to Gericke on April 11, 1898, shows that the music hall
question was much on his mind, and that he was determined to review all possibilities before making any new commitment:

I forgot to tell you last week that the Music Hall has been sold, but that I have control of it for two years. During that time we will build a new hall. The ground for it has been bought and the plan has been made, but I think we shall need a new plan or some alterations. I shall be very glad to see some good [plans?] and shall be much pleased if you can bring me the measures and the plan of the Vienna hall, the Leipsic [sic] hall and any other which may occur to you. I do not care about the ornaments in the room but about the way it is shaped, its galleries, etc., etc. We shall have a new hall built here certainly and would like to get as much wisdom about it beforehand as possible.[83]

McKim Redux

Fighting with Spain had come to an end and Gericke was back on the BSO's podium before any definite initiative was taken in the music hall matter. Mr. Hooper reviewed the status of the question in a note to Higginson dated October 22, 1898, in which he suggested that McKim be asked to carry on the project, but on a drastically reduced scale. "Since our last Music Hall meeting," Hooper wrote,

> I have given much thought to the question of an architect, and I am decidedly of the opinion that it is unwise as well as unfair to employ anyone except McKim, if he consents to abandon his old [Greek theatre] scheme, & take up cheerfully our new plan, at a cost not to exceed two hundred thousand dollars (exclusive of furniture). This would mean either more subscriptions or a small mortgage debt.[84]

Hooper's reasoning was quite in line with Higginson's own views, as embodied in a cautious and deferential letter the Major wrote to the distinguished architect on October 27, 1898:

> We, the directors, have been discussing the matter for some time among ourselves and, considering that the money subscribed belongs to so many people, we feel afraid to try any experiments. While we hanker for the Greek theatre plan, we think the risk too great as regards results, so we have definitely abandoned that idea. We shall therefore turn to the general plan of our Music Hall and of the halls in Vienna and Leipsic [sic], the latter being the best of all, and Mr. Cotting will ask for a plan on those lines.[85]

"We have 18 months in which to complete our work," Higginson continued,

> and we have, at the outside, $200,000 (probably somewhat less) to spend. With the slender income which this new hall will give us, we must keep within that sum so as to incur no debt. We therefore hesitate as to whether this scheme, devoid of poetry and charm, will have enough interest to bring you in person over here and give your own thoughts and time to the completion of the work. Will you kindly tell us your wishes in the matter? We are all greatly obliged to you for the beautiful plan, which we should much like to use if we dared to run the risk. All this must seem very stupid to you, but we cannot help it.

Replying with his usual promptitude and tact, McKim wrote next day from New York that he was willing either to withdraw from the project or to bow to the directors' wishes:

> Let me say that if you feel it will be to your interest, and that of the Directors . . . please eliminate us from further connection with the problem. On the other hand, having, as you will recollect, studied the Leipsic plan, and having met Lamoureux, in Paris, and Richter and Gericke, in Vienna, at your instance, I naturally feel great interest in the final development of the scheme, whatever form may be adopted, or however inexpensive or simple its character.[86]

The architect therefore proposed that G. E. Wolters, who had previously served as Boston representative on the Public Library project and the Greek theatre plan, should revisit Boston to gather data for a preliminary sketch embodying the sponsors' latest views.

With every evidence of relief, Higginson wrote again on October 31, 1898, after consultation with the other directors, to suggest an early visit by Mr. Wolters and to reemphasize some of the points already made, especially on the score of economy. "Will you allow me to say," he concluded, "that it gives us very great pleasure to go on with you. Our doubt has been to ascertain whether you cared to do the work or not, and your reply made it very clear."[87]

Mutual understanding being thus reestablished, it was time to determine what the architects could devise within the stringent limitations Higginson had laid down. With the data gathered by Wolters in Boston, McKim found it possible to outline a number of alternatives. His own favorite, described as echoing the proportions of the Leipzig concert hall (the so-called New Gewandhaus), was felt by both the architect and his colleagues to stand out by virtue of its "compactness, simplicity and economy." The architectural firm's preferred design was also approved by Mr. Hooper on a stopover in New York, and its practicability was further certified by McKim's favorite building contractor, O. W. Norcross of Worcester, Massachusetts.[88]

Such, then, was the plan McKim commended to the directors of the New Boston Music Hall when he met with them in Boston on December 1, 1898. In a discussion lasting more than three hours, the various possibilities were again reviewed, and the architect was asked to work out "a relatively elaborate and careful plan for submission . . . when the time [came] for final decision on building the structure."[89] The general idea of the preferred plan, it was stated, was "founded on the best German music halls," among which the most suitable for orchestral concerts had been found to be those whose length was about twice their width. (This description exactly fit the main hall of the Leipzig Gewandhaus, which measured 124 feet in length by 62 feet in breadth.)

The Boston plan would differ from the usual German pattern, the *Herald* explained, since it would include two galleries rather than a single one, and would dispense with the lower hall "for lounging and ante-room purposes" that was usual in German concert halls.[90] The building would necessarily be a modest one, the *Herald* added, since it must be fireproof and its cost must be limited to about $300,000, or $10 a square foot. (This figure, it may be noted, was already half as large again as the maximum that had recently been mentioned by Hooper to Higginson and by Higginson to McKim.)

A modest, fireproof building with a hall about half as wide as it was long, two galleries, and a stage at the end, and costing not more than $300,000: such was the modest concept out of which Symphony Hall was to emerge, like a musical creation evolving from a single thematic nucleus. Many minds and diverse talents would be drawn upon in the process of refinement and realization, as the nineteenth century moved toward its close and "Boston's new temple of music," as the *Herald* later called it, was readied for its inauguration on October 15, 1900. Their contributions would add up to a striking memorial of human efforts linked in the pursuit of an artistic and, at the same time, severely practical ideal.

THE SABINE FACTOR

We come now to the third and, in some ways, the most attractive among the gifted individuals who helped to shape the Symphony Hall we know today. A bronze plaque unveiled in the building in 1946 has commemorated Wallace C. Sabine's achievement for generations of Symphony Hall patrons:

WALLACE CLEMENT SABINE

1868–1919

PIONEER IN ARCHITECTURAL ACOUSTICS

SYMPHONY HALL

THE FIRST AUDITORIUM IN THE WORLD

TO BE BUILT IN KNOWN CONFORMITY

WITH ACOUSTICAL LAWS

WAS DESIGNED IN ACCORDANCE

WITH HIS SPECIFICATIONS

AND MATHEMATICAL FORMULAE

THE FRUIT OF LONG AND ARDUOUS RESEARCH

THROUGH SELF-EFFACING DEVOTION TO SCIENCE

HE NOBLY SERVED THE CAUSE OF MUSIC

HERE STANDS HIS MONUMENT

This is a fitting tribute to the scientific achievement and the personal qualities of the young man from Ohio who, "in less than twenty years brought architectural acoustics from the empirical state, in which success with any new structure was a happy accident . . . to the status of a reasoned science and a precise art."[91]

The steps by which Professor Sabine arrived at this result are detailed in his *Collected Papers*, published three years after his untimely death in 1919 at the age of fifty.[92] Boston music lovers may take pride in knowing that the sudden illumination that rewarded his years of patient experiment, providing a sound theoretical basis for the new science, came to him as he was preparing for a role in the New Boston Music Hall project.

As a junior member of Harvard's physics department since 1889, Sabine had begun to ponder the scientific basis of acoustics when he was asked, in 1895, to see what could be done about the acoustical shortcomings of the auditorium

*Wallace Clement Sabine (1868–1919), acoustical advisor
on the design and construction of Symphony Hall.*
From a 1906 photograph, *Harvard Graduates Magazine*, 1919.

of the recently opened Fogg Art Museum, a now demolished building situated in Harvard Yard. In countless experiments carried out over the next three years, mainly at night, with quantities of equipment, hundreds of seat cushions, and other sound-absorbing materials, the young unmarried professor had acquired a more precise idea of "the relation . . . between the volume, the shape of the room, and the location of its absorbing components, and the resulting acoustical quality."[93]

Sabine's work had been sufficiently promising to gain the attention of Harvard's President, Charles W. Eliot, who was a friend of Major Higginson, a warm supporter of the Boston Symphony, and one of the earliest subscribers to the New Boston Music Hall.[94] In the autumn of 1898, President Eliot learned from Higginson of the latter's hopes for an early start on the new hall, and of his uneasiness about the structure's acoustical quality, which no architect seemed able to guarantee. It was but natural that Eliot should mention Sabine's investigations as a possible key to solving Higginson's problem.

Sabine hesitated on learning of this initiative, and apparently asked for time to pull together his experimental data. According to his biographer, the young professor devoted himself "for a fortnight . . . to a feverish perusal of his notes, representing the labors of the preceding three years. Then, suddenly, at a moment when his mother was watching him anxiously, he turned to her, his face lighted with gratified satisfaction, and announced quietly, 'I have found it at last!'"[95]

Sabine's mother recounted her son's discovery to an older daughter, apparently no stranger to abstruse mathematical concepts:

> He took the set of experiments he made two or three years ago, when he covered the seats, floor, and walls with cushions, taking successive observations, and plotted them. By letting the abscissas equal the amount of the cushions, and the ordinates be the duration of sound, he gets a perfect hyperbolic curve, $xy = a$ constant $= k$. This makes everything definite. His whole face smiles, though he is very tired.[96]

Sabine lost no time in sharing his insight with President Eliot, to whom he wrote on Sunday, October 30, 1898:

> When you spoke to me on Friday in regard to a Music Hall I met the suggestion with a hesitancy the impression of which I now desire to correct. At the time, I was floundering in a confusion of observations and results which last night resolved themselves in the clearest manner.
>
> You may be interested to know that the curve, in which the duration of the residual sound is plotted against the absorbing material, is a rectangular hyperbola with displaced origin; that the displacement of the origin is the absorbing power of the walls of the room; and that the parameter of the hyperbola is very nearly a linear function of the volume of the room.[97]

"This [discovery] opens up a wide field," Sabine assured his patron. One need only collect further data on the "absorbing power" of the building material, he claimed, in order "to predict the character of any room that may be planned, at least as respects reverberation." The principle thus enunciated has been reformulated in layman's terms by Dr. Leo L. Beranek:

The Sabine reverberation formula says that the reverberation time [what Sabine called "the duration of the residual sound"] is directly proportional to the cubic volume of the hall — the bigger the volume, the longer the reverberation time — and inversely proportional to the number of seat cushions present.[98]

Once in possession of this new formula, Sabine's confidence in its validity and universal applicability seems never to have wavered. Some eyebrows would be raised, during the months of Symphony Hall's construction, by the pertinacity of this otherwise modest and reticent young professor in insisting "that the application of the scientific principles resulting from his experiments would guarantee successful results."[99] Sabine's temerity was emphasized by musicologist H. E. Krehbiel in an article in the *New York Tribune* of October 16, 1900, the day after the formal dedication of Symphony Hall:

> Ever since Mr. Sabine laid his formula of proportions and materials before the architects of the hall . . . , he has maintained that there was as little question about the desired outcome as there was in the minds of the architects about the appearance of the structure. In view of certain memorable failures, . . . this attitude seemed very daring. . . . [E]xamples of mystery surrounding the laws of sound made Mr. Sabine's claim that his determinations concerning architectural acoustics left remaining no element of doubt touching the excellence of the music hall yet to be built seem very venturesome, to say the least.[100]

Krehbiel would conclude, however, that Sabine's confidence had been "justified and rewarded."

President Eliot responded to word of his protégé's discovery by alerting Major Higginson, who had by then obtained McKim's consent to resume responsibility for the Music Hall project. We do not know just when the Major first talked to Professor Sabine, but apparently the acquaintance got off to an excellent start. Sabine's biographer reports that:

> At the first conference between the two men, Major Higginson was deeply impressed by the young scientist's replies to his searching questions. Sabine's exposition of any subject always possessed unusual clarity, and his quiet conviction imparted to his hearer his own calm confidence. Higginson was a man of equally strong individuality, slow to entrust his affairs to others; but,

when once satisfied as to the ability of his agent, he backed him with all the force of his dynamic temperament. Before Symphony Hall was finally completed, this characteristic was to stand young Sabine in good stead![101]

Higginson also wrote warmly of the relationship so happily begun, though he is vague about the timing of discussions with his new acquaintance:

> We went over many points, and Sabine gave me his ideas. I remember his saying that angles were necessary; that clear sound did not come well from curves, and, therefore, in making the stage we must remember that fact; also that the room of the stage should not be too high nor the stage too deep. He not only gave the advice, but examined the plans with care and settled the points of doubt. He explained to me why the sound was better when the raised floor was taken out. At the same time, it was necessary for the great concerts of the season that the floor should rise from front to back, and he marked out how that should be done.[102]

GEWANDHAUS OR MUSIC HALL?

Professor Sabine's introduction into the music hall project occurred at a moment when the planning process was already gaining momentum. Major Higginson, it will be recalled, had written McKim on October 27, 1898, that the directors of the New Boston Music Hall had definitely abandoned the Greek theatre idea and were turning instead to "the general plan of our Music Hall and of the halls in Vienna and Leipsic, the latter being the best of all." Consistent with the directors' intention to ask for a plan along those lines, McKim, at the meeting of December 1, 1898, had undertaken to prepare "a relatively elaborate and careful plan . . . founded on the best German music halls" (described as being "about twice as long as they are wide"), with provision for two galleries and a stage at one end.

A plan — or set of plans — in implementation of this program appears to have been drawn up with minimal delay, for we possess a detailed critique from an administrative perspective by BSO manager Charles A. Ellis, who submitted his comments on January 6, 1899, with an apology for delay.[103] Presumably these were the same plans that Professor Sabine was able to study "for some days" prior to an important meeting with Higginson and Hooper that took place on January 25, 1899.

(above) *The Leipzig Gewandhaus, exterior view, with the Albertina Library at the right.*

(opposite) *The Leipzig Gewandhaus, general floor plan, showing orchestra level at right, balcony level at left.*

All Gewandhaus views in this volume are of the so-called Second Gewandhaus (previously called New Gewandhaus), which was built in 1884, was largely destroyed by Allied bombing in 1944, and, since its replacement by an ultra-modern "New Gewandhaus" after World War II, has been referred to retrospectively as the Neues Konzerthaus, or New Concert House. Stadtgeschichtliches Museum Leipzig.

Some indication of the nature of these first tentative plans since the abandoned Greek theatre project may be gleaned from a highly technical treatise on "Architectural Acoustics: Reverberation," published by Professor Sabine during the spring of 1900 while Symphony Hall was under construction. Its final installment, published June 16, 1900, under the title, "Calculation in Advance of Construction," deals specifically with acoustical matters pertaining to Boston's new music hall, and is reproduced as an Appendix to this volume.[104] Although it leaves a number of questions unanswered, Sabine's analysis of the acoustical considerations involved in planning the new hall provides by far the clearest and most convincing information on the subject that we possess.

Following the abandonment of the Greek theatre plan, Sabine recalls by way of introduction, the sponsors of Boston's new music hall had reverted to "the conventional rectangular form" as the basis of further planning. It had, he

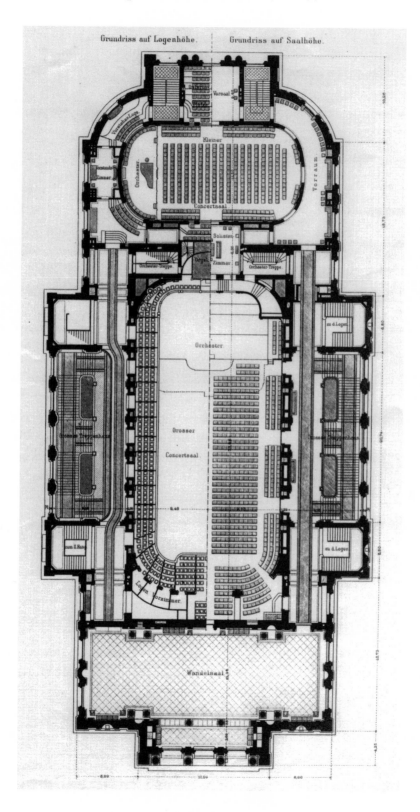

said, been the intention of the new music hall's "building committee" — a rather shadowy, seldom mentioned body, presumably some kind of subcommittee of the directors —

> to follow the general proportions and arrangement of the Leipzig Gewand-
> haus, so enlarged as to increase its seating capacity about seventy per cent;
> thus making it a little more than equal to the old hall. At this stage calculation
> was first applied.

The object of this design, as Sabine describes it and as it has been interpreted by Leo L. Beranek, would have been to increase the seating capacity of the proposed hall by about 70 per cent — from the Gewandhaus's maximum of 1560 to a target figure of 2600 — by simply increasing all of the Gewandhaus's linear dimensions by a factor of 1.3, or 30 per cent — a procedure which would have had the incidental effect of doubling the volume of the proposed hall.[105] Sabine's statement that "At this stage calculation was first applied" is taken by Beranek to mean that Sabine on entering the project made calculations which exposed the impracticability of the whole idea and led directly to its abandonment.[106]

It is important to note that Sabine attributes this plan neither to McKim, the architect, nor to any other individual, but only to the "building committee" of the New Boston Music Hall. Irrespective of its authorship, it was Sabine's contention that implementation of such a plan would have resulted in nothing less than an acoustical disaster. Its fatal consequences, he wrote, would have arisen not only from the differing dimensions and volumes involved but also from other weighty technical factors, notably the nature of modern building materials and their sound-absorbing characteristics:

> Had the new Music Hall been enlarged from the Leipzig Gewandhaus to
> increase the seating capacity seventy per cent, which, proportions being pre-
> served, would have doubled the volume, and then built, as it is being built, ac-
> cording to the most modern methods of fireproof construction, the result,
> unfortunately, would have been to confirm the belief [that the whole subject
> of acoustical design is beyond control].

In terms of his own reverberation formula, Sabine explained, such a procedure would have resulted in an unacceptably lengthy reverberation time of 3.02 seconds, compared to the actual reverberation times, as he calculated them, of 2.30 seconds for the Gewandhaus, 2.44 seconds for the old Boston Music Hall, and an anticipated 2.31 seconds for the new hall then under construction.[107]

There can, then, be little doubt of our good fortune that the plan as Sabine describes it was never implemented, and that instead of an acoustical monstrosity the new music hall turned out to be among the finest in the world. What remains for us to consider is what model or models were followed, if the Gewandhaus model was rejected as Sabine describes. What Sabine has to tell us on this subject is, briefly, that there was no single model. His statement on this point is unequivocal:

> While several plans . . . were thus cursorily examined [in the preliminary discussion of plans for the new hall], the real discussion was based on only two buildings — the present Boston Music Hall and the Leipzig Gewandhaus; one was familiar to all and immediately accessible, the other familiar to a number of those in consultation [and fully documented in the literature available to them].[108]

Sabine himself appeared, at one point in the winter of 1899, to be recommending the Boston Music Hall as an alternative model to the Gewandhaus. "The seating capacity of your hall," he wrote to Higginson on February 14, 1899,

> is so different from that of the Leipzig Music Hall that it cannot be a copy, and a comparison would be misleading — as misleading as any attempt at either linear or proportioned imitation. The old hall approaches more nearly the new in seating capacity, and, moreover, it is a more familiar standard.[109]

In his June 1900 article, however, Sabine expressly rejected the assumption that the new Boston Music Hall (Symphony Hall) was copied from either the Gewandhaus or the old Music Hall:

> It should, perhaps, be immediately added that neither hall served as a model architecturally, but that both were used rather as definitions and starting points on the acoustical side of the discussion. The old Music Hall was not a desirable model in every respect, even acoustically, and the Leipzig Gewandhaus, having a seating capacity about that of [Harvard's] Sanders Theatre,

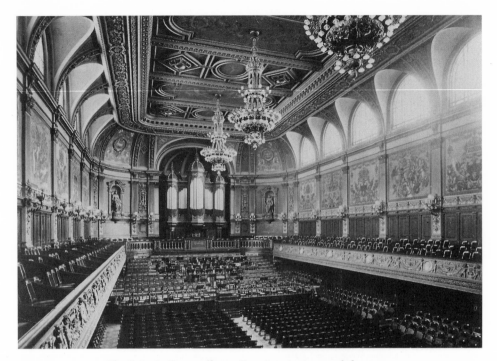

The Leipzig Gewandhaus: Interior view toward the stage.
Stadtgeschichtliches Museum Leipzig.

1500, was so small as to be debarred from serving directly, for this if for no other reason. . . . The new Boston Music Hall is, therefore, not a copy of the Gewandhaus, but the desired results [i.e., the increased seating capacity] have been attained in a very different way.[110]

This statement does not, of course, negate the many obvious resemblances between the old Boston Music Hall and Symphony Hall in regard to interior decoration, seating arrangements, and the like, but it does expressly rebut the notion that Symphony Hall was designed as a deliberate copy of the older building.

It is curious that virtually none of this argument over models and proto-types is reflected in the contemporary documentation that has come down to us, mainly in the letters exchanged by Higginson, McKim, and some of their associates. Although full of absorbing detail, this correspondence scarcely touches on the subject of derivation, imitation, or the ways in which the new building evolved as an organic whole.

One revealing comment is found, however, in a letter written by Sabine to McKim on May 1, 1901, half a year after Symphony Hall was opened:

The Leipzig Gewandhaus: Interior view toward the rear.

You remember how the hall was shortened from the idea of an enlarged Gewandhaus, the ceiling lowered, the stage recessed, and the second gallery inserted to maintain the seating capacity to the required amount, — not to enter more intricate considerations.[111]

From these and other scattered comments, it is clear that the hall McKim initially proposed was felt to be excessively long from front to back, and was materially shortened in the final plan; that the desired increase in seating capacity had consequently to be sought by other means; and that these means appear to have included a redesign of the stage so as to permit more seating in the front of the hall, an extension of the second balcony along the sides as well as the rear of the hall, and possibly a reduction in the space between rows of seats.

To follow this complex process in detailed, orderly sequence is simply not possible with the limited information at our disposal. What can, however, be done is to examine the pertinent records of conferences, epistolary exchanges, and ad hoc decisions. Knowing the end result, we can better appreciate the way in which it grew out of the specialized discussions that took place during the crucial first six months of 1899.

ADJUSTING THE PLANS

Unlike his ill-fated Greek theatre scheme, McKim's "rectangular" plan of December 1898–January 1899 was never rejected out of hand by Major Higginson and his associates. So far as we can judge from the available records, it was subjected to important modifications but remained the basic design for the future Symphony Hall. Our first specific intimation of the way this transformation occurred is found in Higginson's letter to McKim of January 26, 1899, in which he summarized a discussion held the previous day with Professor Sabine and Edward Hooper, his trusted associate in music hall matters.[112]

As treasurer of Harvard, Hooper had been aware of Sabine's work; indeed, there are indications that he may have been involved with President Eliot in recommending Sabine for the Fogg Museum assignment.[113] But although the young professor's association with the music hall project had been agreed upon as far back as October 1898, it would appear that McKim, the architect, had yet to be informed of it. In his letter of January 26, therefore, Higginson devoted a good many words to explaining who Sabine was and what he had thought of McKim's plans. "We here have considerable opinion of Professor Sabine," Higginson wrote.

To judge from Higginson's account of the January 25 meeting, the conferees were not much concerned about the relative merits of the Gewandhaus or the Music Hall, but focused their entire attention on plans for the new hall that was now to be built. Professor Sabine, Higginson reported, had liked McKim's plans "very much in some respects," particularly the low ceiling and rising floor. But, Higginson warned, there were also serious reservations — not only on Sabine's part, but on his own and Gericke's as well — with regard to the proposed length of the hall:

> Professor Sabine thinks the hall altogether too long. How long it should be he does not venture to say, considering that partly a matter of experiment and partly a matter of calculation, [a stage] which he has not yet reached, but he is very much afraid of the long tunnel which we have laid out. In this I entirely agree with him and so does Mr. Gericke.

Returning to this issue at the end of his letter, Higginson reiterated his vigorous opposition to the 160-foot overall length of the hall, as contemplated in McKim's plan:

The new plans make the distance on the floor, from the front of the stage to
the back wall, 121 ft. 8 in. The additional space of almost 40 ft. is above in the
galleries. That is, from the front of the stage to the back wall of the galleries
is 160 ft. I believe that size altogether too much. Perhaps we can venture with
a hall of 120 feet, but I should think that was the extreme.

What the architect had envisaged was undoubtedly a lengthy hall: the proposed floor length "from the front of the stage to the back wall" was approximately 1.3 times that of the Gewandhaus or the old Music Hall, and the overall length of 160 feet, including the extraordinarily deep galleries, would have
greatly exceeded that of either of those halls. Figures for the breadth and
height of the hall McKim proposed are not available, although Beranek has
suggested a width of 75 feet — the actual width of Symphony Hall — and a
height of 62 feet.[114] But the length — the feature so sharply criticized by Higginson and his associates in January — stood out as the principal issue, and was
to be greatly modified in the revised and "final" plans submitted by the McKim
firm in early March of 1899.

Other areas in which Sabine's influence was particularly felt will be considered shortly. In the meantime, the professor had a belated first meeting with
McKim at the architect's New York offices on Saturday, February 25, 1899.
McKim, according to his letter to Higginson next day, was as much impressed
"by the force and reasonableness of [Sabine's] arguments, as by the modest
manner in which they were presented." The pair spent two hours together,
McKim reported, "in going over the plans, and in a thorough consideration of
the unsettled points." Implying that the "points in doubt" had been "removed
to [Sabine's] satisfaction," McKim suggested that the plans could — and indeed
must — be finalized without further delay.[115]

Sabine, too, reported that the meeting had been "both pleasant and satisfactory." McKim, he said, had promised "not to lengthen the hall beyond the
dimensions shown on the plan already submitted to you." In addition, the
architect had accepted, and even appeared to welcome, a proposal to extend
the second balcony along the sides of the hall. But he had steadfastly resisted
the Major's idea of squeezing an additional row of seats into each of the side
balconies.[116]

On this last point, Higginson capitulated handsomely in a note to McKim of
early March:

> I've been filled with admiration at your self-abnegation even more than your
> knowledge & ingenuity & skill. . . . I accept your decision as to the galleries &
> am sorry to have interfered at all with your ideals.[117]

At the same time, the Major pointed out, it should be remembered that each
seat lost or gained would have an immediate effect on the financial results.

Sabine's biographer was not a little impressed by the tractability of the
McKim firm at this crucial juncture. "It is greatly to the credit of such distinguished architects as McKim, Mead & White," he wrote,

> that they should have been willing to accede to Major Higginson's insistence
> to accept the coöperation of a young and little known physicist in preparing
> their plans for the new building, yet by so doing they became the first of their
> profession to make use of the new science. Sabine tested the plans from the
> standpoints of loudness, of interference, of resonance, and of reverberation,
> and the architects made such alterations as were necessary to conform to the
> epoch-making ideas on which rested his guarantee of the acoustical perfec-
> tion of the new auditorium.[118]

Neither then nor later did Major Higginson and his associates allude to any
radical change of direction, such as an abandonment of the Gewandhaus concept in favor of some other plan. The Major, at a meeting of New Music Hall
stockholders on February 15, 1899, seemed even to minimize the difference between the Gewandhaus and Boston's old Music Hall. The new hall, he stated,
while "fashioned on the lines of the 'Leipsic plan,' . . . would [at the same time]
be very much like the present hall."[119] Although the *Boston Transcript*, *Globe*,
and *Post* all quoted Higginson as indicating that the new hall would be "after
that of Leipsic," the *Evening Record* credited him with the statement that of the
half-dozen plans that had been worked over, "the idea most approved was to
have something similar to the old hall."[120]

That there was and remains confusion in the public mind about the architectural antecedents of Symphony Hall is not surprising in view of the contra-
dictory information provided by the best-informed contemporaries. Even after
the building was completed, the *Boston Herald* of September 20, 1900, declared
it to be "practically a reproduction of the famous music hall at Leipsic," while
the *Transcript*, four days later, expatiated with equal authority on the likeness
of the new edifice to the old Boston Music Hall.[121]

The rest of us can only fall back upon Professor Sabine's assurance that

neither the Gewandhaus nor the Boston Music Hall "served as a model architecturally," though "both were used . . . as definitions and starting points on the
acoustical side of the discussion."[122] Such a statement, in its sobriety and pre-
cision, reflects the qualities that made of Sabine not only an outstanding scientist but an outstanding human being. Although our knowledge of some phases
of the Symphony Hall story is inevitably incomplete, we do possess abundant
evidence of Sabine's constructive influence — and of the good sense and good
will of his collaborators.

SABINE'S CONTINUING ROLE

Great as was his reliance on Sabine's advice, Major Higginson was not the man
to deny himself the benefit of wider consultation. He was already acquainted
with Professor Charles R. Cross of the Massachusetts Institute of Technology,
a more senior physicist who had some background in acoustics and had
worked with Alexander Graham Bell on the development of the telephone. In
a lengthy conversation with Higginson on March 23, 1899, Professor Cross
went over the Music Hall plans with a good deal of care and found himself in
almost entire agreement with his Harvard colleague. He did, however, offer a
number of practical suggestions, focusing particularly on the types of material
to be used in the walls of the auditorium.[123]

Professor Sabine, meanwhile, continued to make himself available, quietly
and tactfully, throughout the planning and construction of the new hall — at
the same time enriching his own knowledge and understanding in acoustical
and other matters. As he later wrote to President Eliot: "This work has brought
me in contact with a nonacademic world that has been delightful, and if through
it I have been of public service I am very glad."[124] Some idea of the character
of Sabine's continuing role can be gleaned from one of his own reminiscences
from this period:

> Mr. Higginson, Mr. Gericke, the conductor of the orchestra, and others con-
> nected with the Building Committee expressed opinions in regard to a num-
> ber of auditoriums. These buildings included the old Boston Music Hall, at
> that time the home of the orchestra, and the places visited by the orchestra
> in its winter trips, Sanders Theatre in Cambridge, Carnegie Hall in New York,
> the Academy of Music in Philadelphia, and the Music Hall in Baltimore, and
> in addition to these the Leipzig Gewandhaus. By invitation of Mr. Higginson,

the writer accompanied the orchestra on one of its trips, made measurements of all the halls, and calculated their reverberation.[125] The dimensions and the material of the Gewandhaus had been published, and from these data its reverberation also was calculated. The results of these measurements and calculations showed that the opinions expressed in regard to the several halls were entirely consistent with the physical facts. That is to say, the reverberation in those halls in which it was declared too great was in point of physical measurement greater than in halls in which it was pronounced too small.[126]

One of many subjects on which Professor Sabine made an important contribution had to do with the heating and ventilation of Boston's New Music Hall, a matter only tangentially related to his acoustical researches but central to the development of the hall's unique heating and cooling system. In his letter of January 26, 1899, Higginson reported that:

> under the floor of the hall, [Sabine] would like to have two or three chambers, in which should be exhaust fans. . . . Heat the air above and draw it down through [the] floor, thus carrying off all dust from the hall and making the temperature even, as far as it may be so. So far as the effect on the music goes, he thinks this will be good; a strong upward current or draught carries the music away from the audience; if it is a downward draught, whatever there is in the theory, it will bring the music to the audience.[127]

Professor Sabine's resourcefulness, tact, and diplomatic skill bore good fruit in various other instances. Most important, no doubt, was his design for the stage, later hailed by his biographer as his "crowning triumph in readjusting the Symphony Hall plans."[128] Sabine himself explained the way in which his concept differed from that of the Gewandhaus and the old Music Hall:

> The three halls are of nearly the same length on the floor; but in the old hall and in the Gewandhaus the platform for the orchestra is out in the hall, and the galleries extend along both sides of it; while in the new hall the orchestra is not out in the main body of the room, and for that reason is slightly farther from the rear of the hall; but this is more than compensated for in respect to loudness by the orchestra being in a somewhat contracted stage recess, from the side walls of which the reflection is better because they are nearer and not occupied by an audience. Also it may be noted that the new hall is not so high as the old and is not so broad.[129]

The actual stage, as Sabine's biographer describes it, is "practically a square wooden sounding box, which throws the music directly forward to the audience."

> The delicate perforated design above the cornice of the organ, the sloping up of the floor, and the inward slope of each side, forms the unusual construction. [Sabine] indicated that the orchestra must sit behind the line of the proscenium arch, and warned that if rows of seats were removed to enlarge the stage for choruses, the acoustics would have to be sacrificed.[130]

This last point highlights what has been perhaps the most significant weakness of the finished design, the comparatively small size of the stage — what he called the "somewhat contracted stage recess." Although the recessed stage was originally designed with the aim of gaining additional floor space to meet Higginson's target of 2600 seats, this gain, unfortunately, had to be achieved at the expense of the onstage area allotted to the musical performers. It thus proved necessary, on the very first occasion when music was performed in the new Symphony Hall, to violate Sabine's injunction in order to accommodate the large chorus on hand for a performance of Beethoven's *Missa Solemnis*.

The inconvenience of the constricted stage area would often be felt in the years ahead, although the twentieth century would be less inclined than the nineteenth to mobilize huge choral forces. In defense of the Sabine concept, it may be remarked that the BSO of his day was smaller than in ours. From a personnel of 72 in its first season in 1881–82, it had increased only to a total of 83 (including a librarian) in 1898–99, and it seldom attained a strength of even 100 before the Koussevitzky era that began in the 1920s.[131] Paradoxically, the larger orchestra of today is claimed to be more effective acoustically, even though less well adapted to its architectural frame.[132]

A STATELY PLEASURE-DOME

Such issues lay far in the future in March of 1899, when the staff of McKim, Mead & White was preparing definitive plans for submission to Major Higginson and his fellow directors. The presentation of this material was choreographed with a minuteness that showed how seriously it was regarded by the architects as well as their clients.

McKim arranged ahead of time for the plans and drawings to be brought from New York by George B. de Gersdorff, a young Harvard graduate who was

*A New Boston Music Hall: Architect's rendering, March 1899, attributed to
Theodore O. Langerfeldt.* BSO Archives.

then working in the McKim firm and who would later oversee the construction
of the Harvard Stadium. To ensure their delivery to Mr. Higginson on Sunday
morning, March 12, 1899, Mr. de Gersdorff was instructed to take the midnight
train from New York on Saturday, deliver the drawings at the Higginson resi-
dence early Sunday morning, return later in the morning to go over them with
the client, and remain in Boston until Monday, if needed, to answer questions
and give any required explanations.[133]

The eagerly awaited material did arrive on Sunday morning as planned, and,
more remarkably, the Boston press was able to celebrate the event the very
next day with well-composed, well-written feature articles describing every detail of the splendid edifice Major Higginson had commissioned.[134] Enhancing
the presentations were drawings based on the architects' official rendering, a
roseate watercolor presentation attributed to a Boston artist, the German-
born Theodore O. Langerfeldt. Slightly romanticized in its details, it still bears
an uncanny resemblance to the Symphony Hall of one hundred years later.

This was the first time the exterior of the proposed edifice had been submitted to public scrutiny, and it must be said that it bore few visible marks of
the stringent economy on which the corporation's directors had insisted. If its

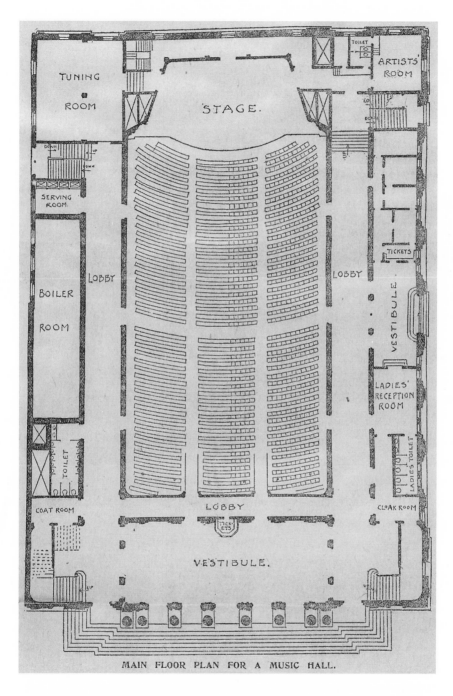

MAIN FLOOR PLAN FOR A MUSIC HALL.

Symphony Hall: The original main floor plan as published in the Boston Globe, *March 14, 1899. Selected architectural drawings by McKim, Mead & White are reproduced below at pp. 145–150.*

Symphony Hall from the southeast, from an early photograph. The turret at the rear of the hall marks the intersection of St. Stephen Street and Westland Avenue, on the site of the present bank building. BSO Archives.

outlines betrayed a certain austerity, and if the head-on view of the Huntington Avenue facade appeared a trifle stark and angular, the diagonal perspective across the intersection of Huntington and Massachusetts Avenues offered an especially harmonious and satisfying composition.

Described in the press as everything from neoclassical or Greek Revival to North Italian Renaissance, the structure would be likened at different times to an "armory," a "great brick barn," and a "vast warehouse or train station."[135] To more sympathetic observers, its classic portico, gabled front, and well-proportioned lateral members might equally well have suggested the lofty nave and broad side aisles of one of Rome's basilican churches.

Certainly the new "Boston Music Hall" (as it was conspicuously identified in the drawing, by handsome lettering across its front), had little in common with the marbled opulence of the Leipzig Gewandhaus, and only a faint generic kinship to Vienna's Musikverein (Music Society), another model Higginson had commended to the architect's attention. But the founder of the BSO might well have felt that his personal taste for "the severe in architecture," for

Symphony Hall: The Massachusetts Avenue façade, showing the extended marquee which replaced the shorter "marquise" in the 1920s. Photograph by Lincoln Russell, 1983. BSO Archives.

rounded arches and modestly decorative brick work, had been respected in a manner that contributed materially to the overall effect.

The proposed interior, too, already bore a marked resemblance to the Symphony Hall we know today. A ground-floor plan published in the *Boston Globe* of March 13, 1899, shows the hall, the stage, the corridors, and the anterooms in substantially the form and proportions that we find them a century later. The principal differences are the layout of the aisles and the location of some of the coatrooms, retiring rooms, and offices.

The dimensions of the auditorium, the subject of such vigorous discussion a few weeks earlier, were now specified as 140 feet in length, 75 feet in width, and 61 feet in height. The stated length still exceeded Major Higginson's suggested maximum of 120 feet, and it differs also from the authoritative measurements given by Sabine in his June 1900 article, which cited a length of 130 feet, a width of 75 feet, and a height of 59 feet.[136] These discrepancies, however, apparently arise from architectural variations such as the sloping floor, curved stage front, and recessed balconies, not from any significant modification of the final overall dimensions proposed by the architects.

The enthusiasm of the Boston press corps fell short only of its reception of the Greek theatre plan some five years earlier. "Taken all in all," the *Transcript* declared, "the plans include many improvements over the old hall's arrangement, and promise to yield a structure which will be desirable both as a whole and in detail."[137] The *Herald* hailed the building as "one of the finest and handsomest yet designed for this city."[138]

Major Higginson's personal reaction is not on record, but it appears that he immediately wrote McKim proposing certain specific changes, at the same time promising that no others would be demanded. Still worried about the length of the hall, he appears to have chosen this moment to revive a suggestion put forward in his original directive to the architect back in 1892.[139] This was the idea of including under the same roof with the main hall a second, smaller hall for chamber music, lectures, and the like. Such a feature was commonplace in European concert halls such as the Gewandhaus and the Vienna Musikverein, and was found as well in New York's Carnegie Hall and even Boston's old Music Hall.

Noting that McKim had provided for a spacious "foyer," measuring 75 by 28 feet, at the rear of the second balcony, Higginson apparently suggested that the space in question be enlarged — and the auditorium correspondingly shortened — in such a way as to create a separate chamber-music hall seating 450 to 500 people. This could be done, McKim responded promptly, provided that the reduction of the main hall did not exceed seven feet. If such a change were to be made at all, the architect added, he would recommend that the foyer be brought down from the second to the more accessible first balcony level.[140]

The latter suggestion was in fact incorporated in the finished building, although no chamber music hall was created and the dimensions of the various rooms were not substantially altered. The amenities of Symphony Hall were thus enriched by the creation of two separate locales for promenading and social intercourse: the Hatch Room, originally known as the "Vestibule," at orchestra level; and the Cabot-Cahners Room, replacing McKim's intended "Foyer," at first balcony level. But no provision was expressly made for chamber music. Its twentieth-century devotees would have to rely mainly upon nearby Chickering and Jordan Halls, both of which opened soon after the turn of the century, the latter continuing in full vigor at the century's end.

Inevitably there were other details requiring modification for reasons of economy, legality, or practicality. A legal analysis found that the proposed porch or portico on Huntington Avenue needed to be scaled back to comply with a city ordinance requiring a fifteen-foot setback from the Avenue, and that the steps on the Massachusetts Avenue side would probably require a special dispensation from the municipal authorities.[141]

More serious from an artistic point of view were the cost-saving modifications of the exterior that were demanded by the directors and reluctantly accepted by the architect, who found himself obliged to acquiesce in the sacrifice of many of his most characteristic inspirations. The external statuary McKim had planned would never materialize, and the proposed slate roof was downgraded to ordinary copper — a metal which, appropriately enough, had been the foundation of Higginson's fortune. Also discarded with little ceremony were such details of exterior decoration as the harp-like finial that would have crowned the pediment, and the decorative eaves or chénaux resembling those of the Boston Public Library.

"I have again talked to the Directors," Cotting advised McKim, in exercise of his watchdog function, "and they will not consider the chenaux for one moment."[142] Cotting's letters abundantly document his zeal for trimming what to him were useless excrescences. "As you will notice," he wrote the architects on May 8, 1899, "I am trying to save every dollar possible but of course I do not wish to cut anything out which from a practical point of view you consider necessary for the good of the structure."[143]

Opinions may differ as to the seriousness of these departures from McKim's concept. Architecture critic Robert Campbell has suggested that the elaborate exterior decoration McKim had planned would have projected "a sense of festivity, as if the hall were dressed for a special occasion." Writing in 1981 at the time of the BSO's centennial, Campbell lamented that, "with its frosting, the exterior of Symphony Hall [would have had] a pleasant, if boxy, elegance. As built, stripped of its trim, it is clumsy and dull."[144] Most Bostonians of McKim's and Higginson's own generation were more admiring.

COUNTING THE COST

The pecuniary considerations that forced the curtailment of McKim's decorative scheme were much on the minds of the New Music Hall directors throughout the months that preceded the beginning of construction. Their basic problem, familiar in that day as in ours, was a lack of adequate funds for what they wanted to accomplish. Of the $402,500 that had been pledged by approximately 400 subscribers in 1893, some $208,750 had thus far been collected from those 364 individuals who had redeemed their pledges and could now be counted as paid-up stockholders. Most of the amount paid in thus far appears to have gone for the purchase of the land ($170,000) and for taxes and other expenses.[145]

In November 1898, the "Committee of Three" (Hooper, Sears, and Higginson) had renewed their request for payment of the remaining subscriptions, so that new stock could be issued before the building contracts were signed. In addition, they had urged the subscription of a further $98,500 to bring the corporation's capital stock up to the legal limit of $500,000.[146] These proposals had been approved at a special meeting of stockholders on January 11, 1899, at which time it was indicated that the new building would cost in the neighborhood of $250,000, a considerable increase over the outside figure of $200,000 that had recently been given the architect.[147]

Noting that construction must be completed by April 1, 1900, when his lease on the old Music Hall would expire, Higginson also revealed on this occasion that three of the directors, acting as private individuals, had purchased some land immediately west of the proposed hall (i.e., on the site of the present Cohen Wing) in order to ensure that it would remain in friendly hands and could be secured at cost if it were ever needed.[148]

Another review of current plans took place at the regular annual meeting of the New Boston Music Hall corporation, held on February 15, 1899, and attended by some twenty-five stockholders, among whom, a reporter noted, were six ladies. After outlining preparations for the building, Mr. Higginson quelled without difficulty an attempted insurrection by Fred P. Bacon, a former music editor of the *Boston Herald*, who had been noisily campaigning against the whole idea of constructing a music hall in preference to an opera house or dual-purpose building. Bacon's effort foundered, at least for the time, when it was revealed that the proxies he held represented only nine shares of stock.[149]

As the time for decision drew nearer, the directors' insistence on a strict "pay-as-you-go" policy appears to have weakened. At another special meeting on March 28, 1899, with only about a dozen stockholders present but with plenty of others represented by proxy, it was formally voted to build the New Music Hall substantially in accordance with the plans submitted by McKim, Mead & White, which were displayed on the walls of the committee room.

Symphony Hall: The Stage Door and St. Stephen Street.
Photograph by Lincoln Russell, 1983. BSO Archives.

Mr. Hooper, in urging prompt payment of the unpaid 10 per cent of the original subscriptions, admitted for the first time that even this would not be enough. "We shall need more money," he warned.

> We will be glad if the stockholders will increase their subscriptions. Of course we shall go on and build the hall, even if we have to take a small mortgage on the structure. We shall not abandon the enterprise. We need about $500,000. There has been paid in now about $360,000, and about $260,000 of this has been expended.[150]

In further elaboration, the "Committee of Three" advised subscribers on April 17, 1899, that although stock paid for and issued had by then reached a total of $361,200, the committee still awaited payment not only of the remainder of the amount subscribed (which by then had increased slightly to $407,000), but of a suitable additional sum within the authorized limit of $500,000:

> It is to be hoped that, with the improved conditions of business since 1893, some additional subscriptions, either from the old subscribers or others, may bring the capital stock up to the maximum amount, so as to provide for the best possible building on the large and valuable lot already paid for.[151]

This appeal was echoed by Higginson himself in an open letter addressed "to the public of Boston" and published in the *Transcript* of June 5, 1899. The directors had been fortunate, Higginson wrote, in having obtained a building site which was already worth $120,000 more than they had paid for it. But the cost of the hall itself, estimated at $500,000, had still to be financed, and the funds immediately available needed to be increased from their present level of $166,000 to at least $300,000 before the contracts were signed. Even then, said the Major, in order to meet the full cost of the hall, including the organ and seats, it would be necessary to obtain a mortgage in the amount of $200,000.[152]

The results of these appeals were less than impressive. According to Higginson's later figures, the subscribed capital of the corporation grew by only $3,700 (to a total of $410,700), prior to the inauguration of the new hall in October 1900.[153] With building costs now certain to exceed the available resources by a wide margin, it was obvious that the only possible course was to borrow the difference — a difference which, moreover, seemed to increase almost from day to day.

A special meeting of stockholders took the bull by the horns on June 12, 1899. According to the *Transcript*, only four individuals were present, but they represented an adequate 1,400 shares of stock. With Mr. Hooper in the chair, the meeting voted to authorize the borrowing of not more than $325,000 — rather than the $200,00 mentioned by Higginson a week earlier — at 3½ percent interest for a term of not more than ten years. The only dissenter was Fred P. Bacon, again as proxy and this time holding a mere five shares.[154] Details of a mortgage loan for the full amount of $325,000 were concluded the next day with Boston's Provident Institution for Savings.[155]

In an important corollary arrangement completed on July 6, 1899, the New Boston Music Hall corporation leased its entire Huntington Avenue property to Major Higginson personally for a period of ten years commencing on completion of the building.[156] Under this plan, the Major explained, it would fall to him "to pay the taxes, the cost of administration and the interest on the mortgage — probably $40,000 in all yearly — and to pay to the stockholders of the hall any earnings beyond these above expenses." In this way, Higginson pointed out, "the stockholders are for ten years at least free from possibility of loss, except that of interest on their investment, and they may enjoy an increase of value."[157]

Such at least were the expectations of 1899. In point of fact, however, the new hall would from the first operate at a loss. No dividends would be paid to the stockholders, and funds to meet the annual deficit would come straight out of Higginson's own pocket. The result, as he lugubriously pointed out a few years later, was an annual drain of upwards of $13,000, over and above the orchestra's annual deficit of $20,000.[158]

That the founder and benefactor of the BSO was not altogether surprised by this development is suggested by the ruminations in his open letter of June 5, 1899:

> I venture to lay these facts before a public which has been for eighteen years invariably kind and generous to me, and to add that my share of the musical enterprise during all this period has been heavy and can never be light. The invariable experience of the world has been that artistic or educational undertakings of a high order cannot succeed without subsidy. Of that I was sure eighteen years ago, and am quite content with the results gained. The old hall is entirely unfit for its uses, and a new hall must be built at once or music be without a home in Boston.[159]

And built it soon would be: ground was broken a week later.

Chapter 4

THE HALL IS BUILT
1899–1900

W HETHER BY ACCIDENT OR DESIGN, EXCAVATION AT THE
site of the new hall began on the very day — June 12, 1899 —
when the stockholders' representatives were approving the necessary financial arrangements. There was little time to lose, for the expiration of
Mr. Higginson's lease on the old Music Hall was less than ten months away.
(He was, however, able to extend the lease to the end of April, 1900, so that the
orchestra's nineteenth season could be brought to a decorous close before the
new owners took over.)

The commencement of building operations brought into increased promi-
nence the person of the chief builder, Orlando W. Norcross (1839–1920),
known as O. W. Norcross. As a young Civil War veteran, O. W. had joined
his brother James A. Norcross in founding what had become the nationally
known firm of "Norcross Brothers, General Contractors" or "Contractors and
Builders." Based in Worcester, Massachusetts, where O. W. Norcross resided,
the firm had its own quarries and had carried on extensive building operations
both in Boston and elsewhere in the country. Among its later projects would be
the New York Public Library and the buildings still occupied by the Harvard
Medical School.[160]

In support of its Boston operations, the Norcross firm maintained both a
local office and a yard on Huntington Avenue. Its practice of assuming responsibility for all phases of building operations, from start to finish, had especially recommended it to McKim and his colleagues. Major Higginson, too, appeared to welcome the close rapport between architect and builder. Discussing

O. W. Norcross (1839–1920), the builder of Symphony Hall.
Richard Herndon, *Boston of Today* (1892).

McKim's qualifications for further work at Harvard, the Major wrote with dry humor to President Eliot that McKim had:

> a great faculty for using spaces well . . . a great eye for proportions, and, if . . . looked after, will restrain his desire for ornament. . . . He can also work economically if he wishes. Mr. Norcross's criticism of Mr. McKim's Music Hall plan was this: that it was a very economical building and that he, after several days [presumably in reviewing the plans], could only cut off $300 in the expenses, and that only in the foundations. I think this speaks pretty well for Mr. McKim.[161]

Of the commencement of excavation work at Huntington and Massachusetts Avenues, the *Boston Transcript* reported that "there were no impressive ceremonies. No high official raised the first lump of earth in a brand new shovel, and there were no speeches. A gang of men with heavy carts was let loose in the big lot, under the sharp orders of the boss, and now the formerly quiet corner is full of bustle and business." Fifty men and twelve two-horse carts, according to the *Transcript*, were engaged upon the first phase of the project, which was "to excavate deep enough for the piles to be driven for the foundation."[162]

This preliminary operation had been expected to take about a week; but in even less time than that, work was brought to a standstill by an unexpected difficulty. It had been realized from the first that the new music hall, like other buildings in the locality, would be built on the mixed terrain left over from the last glacial period and overlaid by the land-filling operations of recent decades. Major Higginson had acknowledged that "the basement of the hall will be very low, as we can go down but a little distance on account of tide water, therefore the space under the floor will be small. This is said in relation to a place where we may put the benches etc. from the stage."[163]

Test borings at twelve locations on the building site in April 1899 had revealed that while there was a firm substratum of clay some twenty-eight feet below the surface, to reach it would necessitate passing through successive layers of sand, soft peat mud, and coarse sand and gravel containing some water.[164] It had been the intention of the contractors to drive wooden piles into this mixture to a depth of twenty-six to twenty-eight feet, rather than taking the easier course of trusting to concrete alone to support the heavy machinery that would be installed in the building.

But when the time came to put this plan into execution, it was found that the spruce piles "broomed up" at a depth of about nine feet and simply could not be driven down through the stratum of sand and gravel. In one group of twelve piles, the contractors were able "to get [only one] pile down through the gravel into the clay; in at least four cases . . . the piles broke completely off just above the level of the gravel, and in several other cases they broke above the surface of the ground."[165]

Fortunately, an engineering opinion from a now unidentifiable source pointed a way out:

> Gravel appears to be very compact and of such quality as to make a very satisfactory hard pan upon which to rest foundations, and in my opinion it would be entirely superfluous, even if it would be possible, to drive piling through it. If concrete footings are placed low enough to be well bedded in the gravel, and the tops carried to grade 5, you could set foundations which would undoubtedly be capable of carrying the building without settlement. Allowing that the load you have figured does not exceed 12 tons per pile, it would, in my opinion, be perfectly safe to allow the concrete footings of the same size now shown in the drawings. In case the load should exceed 12 tons

per pile, it would perhaps be advisable to increase proportionally the area of the footings over those now shown.[166]

The builders were instructed to proceed in accordance with this advice, and no further problems are reported in relation to the building's substructure, which has endured with exemplary solidity throughout the past hundred years.

Gaps in the available documentation make it difficult to establish the precise sequence of events at the music hall construction site, but the *Boston Transcript* of October 20, 1899, reported that the warm-weather months had been well utilized and "work . . . is progressing rapidly":

> The stone foundation is finished and the walls on the two sides of the big building back from the street and that on the Massachusetts avenue side are already up to the first gallery. The structural steel is being set and the floors, posts and other interior construction are in hand. Over all stand the staging and the skeleton framework complete.[167]

The *Transcript* described in detail the laying of the stone foundations, which had required "excavation nineteen feet below the level of the sidewalk."

> When the old bed was finally reached, solid concrete five feet in depth was laid and on this was built five more solid feet of granite. To overcome the tidewater while the excavating was in progress, steam pumps were kept constantly at work and these were in use until the concrete flooring was laid. The walls of the cellar are now finished. They were built of pressed brick and on their outer side two heavy coats of pitch were laid to prevent moisture from entering.

Work above ground, on the walls and on the steel structure, had been slowed, the *Transcript* noted, by a heavy boom-time demand for structural steel:

> Every rolling-mill in the country is going full blast with all the force it can handle and yet the demand from all the large cities is so great that few if any contracts made by the steel producers are being filled on time. . . . The contractors fear that despite their best efforts, they will be held back on account of [this] in the near future.

Noting that the contractors were employing some eighty-five men — "carpenters, brick-masons, laborers, stone-masons, etc." — the *Transcript* drew attention to one recent manifestation of "the desire of the Music Hall corporation to make the new site perfect in every respect":

> An electric trolley pole stands directly in front of what will be the Massachusetts avenue entrance to the building. H.L. Higginson, the corporation's president, had his attention called to this fact and, acting immediately on the suggestion offered him, he petitioned the Elevated Railway Company to have it removed. The petition was rushed through the hands of the various officials until it came to the division chief, who at once issued orders to have the objectionable pole removed.

Bostonians of a century later may well admire the flexibility and responsiveness of this nineteenth-century transit corporation.

Positioning the Organ

Both Higginson and McKim had been much involved that autumn in plans for the erection of a second building, the Harvard Union in Cambridge, the contract for which was formally approved by the University at the beginning of November.[168] Eager to make a start on this new project, the architect responded with irritation to a difficulty that arose just at this time with reference to the placement of the magnificent, ultramodern organ being built for the new music hall by George S. Hutchings, head of the highly regarded Boston-based organ firm of that name. (This was the predecessor of the present Aeolian-Skinner organ, installed in Symphony Hall in 1949.)

In haste to complete the design of the wooden paneling around the stage of the new hall, McKim had found himself at a standstill because there had as yet been no decision about how the organ would be fitted into the labyrinth of passageways and spaces behind the stage at first and second balcony levels. Mr. Hutchings, in hopes of gaining more space for his organ, had gone to Major Higginson with a request that the height of the ceiling above the stage be increased from 36 to 44 feet. McKim, he claimed, had already agreed to such an increase. However, this the architect vehemently denied when the matter was brought to his attention, pointing out that he had no authority to make such decisions but that the need for a solution was urgent.[169]

Thus under pressure from two directions, Higginson turned to Professor Sabine to clarify the acoustical implications of the Hutchings proposal. "Will this affect us at all in the matter of the sound?" he asked. "Mr. Hutchings wishes his space for his pipes, but of course I am unwilling to grant it to the injury of the Orchestra."[170]

The further progress of the dispute is narrated by Sabine's biographer:

> Sabine immediately investigated the problem, and reported to Major Higginson that if Mr. Hutchings would change the arrangement of two pipes, his organ would not only fit the space allotted, but, in Sabine's opinion, would be greatly improved in tone. This was heresy! "That young man is very courteous," Hutchings sputtered when Major Higginson gave him instructions to follow Sabine's suggestion; "but I was making organs before he was born!" Higginson stubbornly declined to yield, and the arrangement of the pipes was changed.[171]

Sabine himself has left a record of a Saturday afternoon discussion with Hutchings in which he endeavored to persuade the older man that the best solution would be to install an open grille, such as now runs along the sloping ceiling in front of the organ.[172] This typically creative intervention led in due course to the most happy results, according to Sabine's biographer:

> During the intermission at the opening concert [October 15, 1900], attention was attracted by a tall, elderly gentleman, with streaming white locks, pushing his way through the crowd toward Sabine, who was promenading in the foyer with his wife [whom he had married two months earlier]. Reaching his arm over the shoulders of those standing between, Hutchings grasped Sabine's hand, exclaiming, "Young man, that is the best organ I ever built. I take back everything I said!"[173]

The final arrangement of the organ space was vividly described by a reporter from the *Boston Globe*, two days before the formal opening of the hall:

> Entrance through a door at the side, on a level with the first balcony, revealed a sort of an alleyway, extending 50 feet or so, right through the organ to the opposite side of the stage, and 60 or 70 feet upward to the ceiling of the hall.
>
> Climbing ladders and straddling across chasms, which to have missed one's footing would probably have meant a broken neck, the investigators found themselves in the very middle of the vast complexity of pipes of every conceivable size.

JEFFERSON PHYSICAL LABORATORY,
HARVARD UNIVERSITY,
CAMBRIDGE, MASS.,

Nov 12 1899

Dear Mr. McKim,

I spent Saturday afternoon with Mr Hutchings. I think he is persuaded, although no final decision has been reached, that the best result, best even from the standpoint of his organ, would be an open grill, similar to that which you are placing in several sections of the ceiling, forming a strip along the sloping ceiling in front of the organ and reaching across the whole stage. I should like to inquire whether this will be architecturally possible. I feel very sure that it will furnish more of an outlet for his swell and pedal organs than would the display pipes even if the ceiling were raised, as he wishes it, eight feet. I feel very sure, also, that Mr Hutchings will agree with this after he has thought it over, but whether it is architecturally possible or artistically desirable is another matter, and I do not want to urge it except with your entire agreement. If you would like to have me, I shall be very glad to come down to New York to talk it over any other points that may have come up.

When you have the details of the hall finished I should be very glad if I could get at them

The Symphony Hall Organ: Excerpt from a letter of Professor Sabine, November 12, 1899, suggesting a grille for the organ housing (Document 42).
New-York Historical Society.

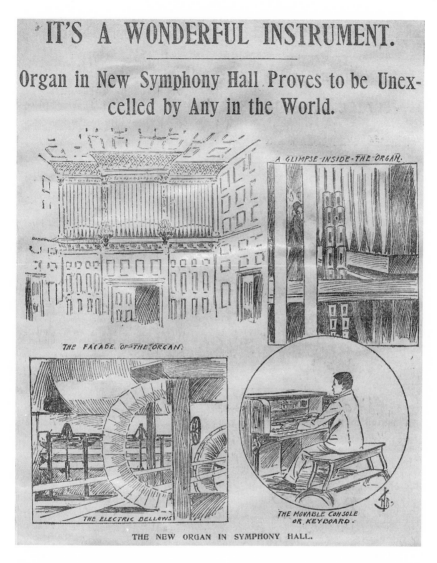

IT'S A WONDERFUL INSTRUMENT.

Organ in New Symphony Hall Proves to be Unexcelled by Any in the World.

THE NEW ORGAN IN SYMPHONY HALL.

The Symphony Hall Organ: Drawings from the Boston Globe, *October 13, 1900.*

Against the back wall were the great 16 to 32 footers, and immediately around the visitors, and stretching away in every direction, was what looked like a most wonderful bric-a-brac display, the thousands of metallic reeds, resembling an endless collection of those attenuated vases in which a cluster of three or four long-stemmed roses are usually displayed.

When the organist turned on the music, letting loose the full power of all the "wind-jammers" and the half-ton pipes, the sensation experienced of being in the midst of it all was calculated to give one an idea of what it was like to be on the bridge of the Olympia with Dewey at the battle of Manila. [174]

A Search for Words

Another source of growing anxiety for the architect was Major Higginson's dilatoriness in supplying inscriptions to fill the spaces provided for that purpose on the Huntington Avenue facade. A liberal use of inscriptions was an essential feature of McKim's architectural style and, as he had written to Higginson in November:

> We feel that nothing imparts such dignity and scholarly character, as the wise use of inscriptions, and are depending largely, in the case of your Music Hall, upon their use. They may be either commemorative, or express the value of Music in some great sentence — which, however . . . must fall within the number of letters specified [to fit the space and be legible].[175]

Never averse to delegating responsibility to those whom he trusted, Higginson promptly turned the matter over to two friends and fellow directors, Edward Hooper and William S. Bigelow. They in turn consulted with others, particularly with one E.H.B. — probably Dr. Edward H. Bradford, a faculty member and later dean of the Harvard Medical School. Bigelow and Bradford promptly unearthed two rather obscure quotations from Shakespeare: "Here will we sit and let the sounds of music creep in our ears," from *The Merchant of Venice* (V, i); and "Let rich music's tongue unfold the imagined happiness," from *Romeo and Juliet* (II, vi). Hooper, for his part, suggested for a side panel on Massachusetts Avenue a long form of the date 1899 in Roman numerals: MDCCCLXXXXVIIII.[176]

Apparently unenthusiastic about this submission, McKim again addressed himself directly to Higginson on December 1, 1899, enclosing photographs of buildings exemplifying the kind of inscribed panels he had in mind. "Since writing you the other day," he explained,

> I feel that the most dignified thing to do, in view of its size, would be to make the inscription rather a page out of the history of the Institution, as at Columbia [University], and referring, or not, as may be thought best, to the public spirit and munificence of the promotors, rather than any sentence or quotation taken from however great a source. [177]

The inspiration leading to the foundation of a permanent orchestra for the advancement of music, McKim suggested with a touch of flattery, "seems

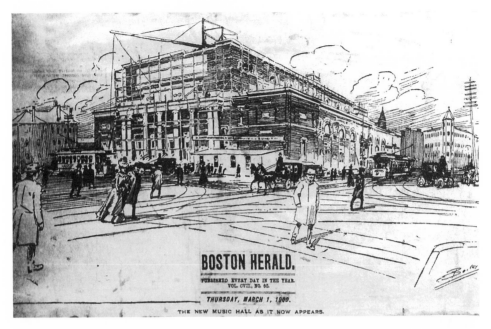

Symphony Hall under construction: Drawing from the Boston Herald, *March 1, 1900. The turreted building on the right is a storage warehouse on the site of the present Church Park apartments.*

text enough for an inscription that would justify three times the space at our command."

But Edward Hooper, as Higginson's close associate, considered that this was quite the wrong approach. He had "given much thought to the matter," he wrote McKim on December 19, 1899, "and . . . consulted many judicious persons about it, with little result." The new hall, Hooper emphasized, was not a work of philanthropy, as McKim appeared to think, but the creation of a joint-stock company, one whose very name was subject to possible change in the future. It was Hooper's judgment, therefore, that the panels had best be left blank until the stones were in place, at which time tentative lettering could be drawn in chalk and its effect discussed while the possibility of changes remained open.[178]

Such caution was visibly exasperating to the architect, who began to fear that his clients' irresolution would cause delays all along the line. The most he could obtain from Higginson, in a meeting during Christmas week of 1899, was an intimation that the latter might seek an opinion from Harvard's President Eliot, whose authority in such matters was widely recognized.[179] Further delay, McKim warned on December 29, would slow the entire con-

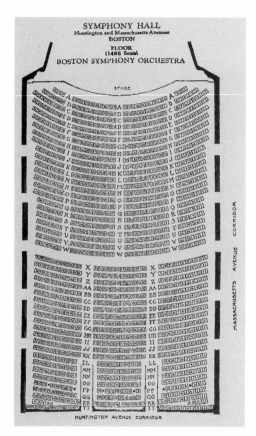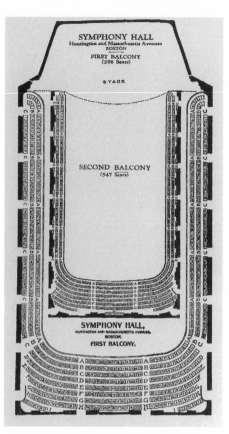

Symphony Hall's Interior: (left) *Plan of seats on the main floor, 1900,*
showing a redesign of the aisles as recommended by Major Higginson.
(right) *Plan of the seats in the first and second balconies, 1900.*
Boston Public Library, Music Department.

struction process and delay the removal of scaffolding from the front of the
building.[180]

Yet the scaffolding was still in place in mid-March of 1900, when two Boston
newspapers printed what was probably the first published photograph of the
rising edifice.[181] Other factors than Higginson's procrastination bore much of
the responsibility, however, for the threatened steel shortage had by this time
become a reality and the expected completion date of the hall, originally set
for April 1, 1900, had in January been put forward to "some time in the summer."[182] By March, however, the builders were more optimistically predicting
that the 200 men then engaged upon the enterprise — and soon to be aug-
mented by an "army" of plasterers — would finish their job around the first of
June.

"The walls are practically closed in," the *Transcript* reported on March 1, 1900:

> the roof is built, except that part over the Huntington avenue end, and the façade on Huntington avenue is practically completed. Enough of the two balconies has been built to give one an idea of their great strength. The framework is of different sizes of girders and stringers, while supporting the entire framework are posts set far in so as not to obstruct the view of persons in the rear seats.[183]

Matters relating to the hall's internal equipment and adornment were by this time claiming urgent attention. McKim and his team had much ado to deal with Major Higginson's anxious inquiries and to convince him that matters — aside from the inscriptions — were under control.[184] One fruitful suggestion from the Major's side was his plea for the addition of a center aisle to facilitate access to the seats at orchestra level, "at least as far back as the first cross aisle."[185] After an initial objection by de Gersdorff of McKim's office, the Higginson proposal was adopted, to the lasting benefit of patrons in the higher-priced seats; for structural reasons, a similar realignment for the back part of the hall was deemed impracticable. [186]

Immersed in the details of decorative plaster work and of watercolor versus oil paint, McKim continued to plead for a decision on the inscriptions so that the lettering could be carved and the scaffolding removed.[187] His wonted tact was beginning to wear thin at times. "We are all disappointed about the inscription on the Huntington Avenue front," he wrote to Higginson on April 24, 1900:

> The panel designed to carry it, and supported in arrangement by the columns below, forms an important part of the whole composition of the front (already sufficiently denuded by Mr. Cotting's ruthless economies), and if the inscription is now also taken away from us, in addition to the loss of the Cotting details above alluded to, I fear the building will look, when it is finished, more like a deaf, dumb and blind institution, than a Music Hall.

"But I am not so unreasonable as this sounds," McKim added.

> I recognize the difficulty of getting what you want, so I suppose we must be content to wait until you can agree as to what is best to put there; but I urge you solemnly not to abandon the inscription, without which the panel intended for it will be meaningless, and the facade on Huntington Avenue unintelligible.[188]

Goodbye Music Hall

More was involved in the inscription difficulty than the choice of some sententious utterance to impress the casual passerby. The very name of the future hall had yet to be determined, and its selection would continue to hang fire for several months longer. Up to this time, it had been generally assumed that the new hall would inherit the name as well as the functions of the old Boston Music Hall. Indeed, the incised words, "The Boston Music Hall," had been prominently displayed in the architectural drawings submitted by the McKim firm back in March 1899. On the same assumption, the letters "BMH" had been incorporated into a monogram, still visible today, in the cast-iron railings of the marble stairways leading to the balconies.[189]

But these expectations had been thwarted by developments at the old Music Hall. That historic if shopworn property, it now appeared, would not after all be torn down and replaced. Instead, it was being reconstructed in anticipation of an early reopening. After many rumors and more than one false start, the property had lately come under the control of theatrical interests whose spokesman and manager, Boston realtor Henry W. Savage, had announced the intention of refurbishing it from top to bottom and creating a wholly new theatre for concert, opera, or dramatic presentations.[190]

This development, the very thing the Higginson group had so feared in 1893, seemed less alarming in 1900, although it undeniably would complicate the naming of the New Music Hall. It also heightened popular interest in the final BSO performances in the older edifice, where the orchestra's nineteenth season reached a festive conclusion under Gericke's leadership on Saturday, April 28, 1900.

"Music Hall ended its tonal career . . . in a blaze of glory, in which floral decorations, frenzied huzzahs, speech-making, and other unusual excitement blended," reported the Boston *Daily Advertiser*. The musicians' stands and the "conductor's rack" were decorated with flowers. Beethoven's Ninth Symphony dominated the program; Gericke was repeatedly recalled, and both he and Higginson made impromptu speeches.[191]

The Higginson address, according to *Advertiser* critic Louis C. Elson,

> was . . . informal, but contained some most welcome statements, among
> which one may mention the allusion to the fire-proof character of the new
> hall and the mention of Mr. Gericke's indefinite retention as conductor. He

[Higginson] thanked the public, the musicians, the conductor, everybody except the critics, whose task is well-known to be a thankless one.[192]

Scarcely had the strains of the Ninth Symphony died away, another paper reported, "when a gang of workmen began the task of tearing out the interior and making preparations for the new theatre, concert hall and what-not which is to occupy the place of the famous old structure next season."[193] Major Higginson, it was reported, had given orders for careful removal of the clock and all of the statuary, which included a copy of the Apollo Belvedere as well as Thomas Crawford's statue of Beethoven, now in the New England Conservatory. But he may not have anticipated the depredations of a crowd of souvenir hunters, including one or two of his own senior aides, who in the following days secured numbered seat plates and other, more valuable trophies.[194]

Thus untidily ended the forty-eight-year history of the original Boston Music Hall. No one could then have foreseen the series of reconstructions and reincarnations that would carry the building and its memories down into our own time. But even before Symphony Hall was opened in October 1900, a rebuilt "Boston Music Hall" was back in business in Hamilton Place, offering "Continuous Refined Vaudeville" with tickets priced at 25 cents and 50 cents. In 1905, the remodeled and renamed "Empire" theatre reopened on the same site, this time with an entrance directly from Washington Street. In 1906 it became the "Orpheum," the name it still holds. As such, it served for decades as a glamorous motion picture palace of the Loew chain and, more recently, as a less than first-class venue for concert and dance events.[195]

With the old Music Hall no longer available and the new one not yet ready, the BSO had needed a temporary site for its warm-weather Promenade Concerts, or "Pops" as they were being officially called for the first time in this, their fifteenth season. A stopgap solution was at hand in the spacious if unattractive Mechanics' Building on Huntington Avenue, beyond the railroad yards and a half-mile short of the new music hall now under construction.

Here the Pops of 1900 entertained their loyal audience through May and June, led as was customary by Max Zach and then by Gustave Strube, both from the BSO string section. Judging by press comment, most patrons found Mechanics' Building an improvement over the Music Hall in terms of space, ventilation, and overall comfort, although some reservations were voiced about its acoustical properties.[196] An innovation of permanent interest was the installation of a ticket office telephone with the number, "1492, Back Bay."[197]

Later in the year, the number was transferred to the new Symphony Hall, where its four digits, familiar to every schoolchild in America, would remain constant through all the technological changes of the next hundred years.

What's In a Name?

Work on the BSO's future home went steadily forward while the Pops were running their carefree course. What remained to be done at the new hall lay principally in the field of interior decoration. With Major Higginson's agreement, the McKim firm had engaged a certain H.M. Lawrence to superintend the painting of the entire interior for a fee of $500, plus $100 for traveling and living expenses. Edward F. Caldwell of New York was focusing on electrical and lighting arrangements.[198] Alfred R. Wolff, also from New York, was responsible for installing the heating and ventilating apparatus. Louis H. Mudgett, who had been manager of the old Music Hall, was preparing to serve in a similar capacity in the new Huntington Avenue building.

On hurried visits to Boston, McKim examined the effect of his color choices under both natural and electric light, finding to his own relief that he would not be afraid "to go into court on the result."[199] Major Higginson, meanwhile, did his best to speed things along where there was evidence of delay, at the same time causing some delays of his own by a lack of timely decision on such pending questions as those relating to stage lighting and the tuning of the organ.[200]

In August 1900, the Major retreated to his summer home in Manchester-by-the-Sea, leaving it to BSO Manager Ellis — the "best manager in the country," Higginson once called him — to keep him informed on a twice-weekly basis.[201] By August 13, Ellis could report that the iron work on both balconies was being completed, except for "attaching eight cupids" whose arrival had been delayed. On August 15, all the staging was down; twenty-two men were installing the seats; and the electrical fixtures, though delayed by a strike, were being manufactured as fast as possible. "Nobody is being hindered and there are no complaints," Ellis wrote.[202]

The painting in the auditorium and lobbies was practically complete by August 18; eleven men were gilding the balcony fronts, and a larger force was to be "put on next week." Most of the seats were in place, and were being numbered and lettered; the pipes for the front of the organ were being gilded; and the platforms for the orchestra were ready for painting. "A performance

Charles A. Ellis (1855–1934), manager of the Boston
Symphony Orchestra, 1885–1918.
New York Tribune Illustrated Supplement, 1898–99.

could be given tonight, if it were necessary, without the organ," Ellis reported on August 21.[203]

On August 24, Ellis could write that "work at the hall is going on without any hitches, and the building seems to be very near completion":

> What it lacks most is a proper title. "New Music Hall" is rather common and would convey the impression to strangers that it was a variety theatre. Mr. Savage continues to use the title "Boston Music Hall" for the old building, and it would ["would" is crossed out] will lead to confusion. Can we not call the new building "Higginson Hall"?[204]

The available record shows no response by Higginson to this reasonable inquiry, but the blankness of the appointed space above the portals of Symphony Hall, still noticeable a century later, is proof enough that Ellis's suggestion failed to commend itself to the person most immediately concerned.

After viewing the hall in its nearly completed state, Major Higginson alluded tersely to the matter of nomenclature in a letter addressed to "Messrs. McKim, Mead & White" on August 28, 1900. "We are without a name for the hall and you may be able to suggest something," he wrote. "Will you kindly think of it and write me? We should advertize [sic] the tickets very soon and . . . from some particular place."[205]

Just who suggested the name "Symphony Hall," which entered into circulation without recorded public discussion, is unlikely to be determined so long after the event. Most Bostonians appeared to like the name, though some predictably objected that in featuring the symphony it seemed to ignore the claims of other kinds of music.

"I wish to say that it all seems to me very handsome," Mr. Higginson observed on completing his own inspection.[206] Praising the color effect, the rise from front to back, the appearance of the stage and the sound of the organ, he did complain about "two or three small matters . . . objectionable points." The second row of the second balcony had been pushed too far forward by pilasters and radiators, and some forty seats would probably have to come out, with a loss in revenue of perhaps $1,000 a season. The steps on the Massachusetts Avenue side, he said, protruded "into the street," in spite of earlier warnings, and the resultant legal problems with the city might, he worried, cost him another thousand or two, "and a great deal of dirty work."

Nevertheless, Higginson wrote, "I wish to thank you for your trouble and for your energy in pushing up the completion of the hall, but I hope this energy will last a little longer until the hall is in concert order." More gracious acknowledgments were reserved for the "report" the Major intended to deliver at the inaugural ceremonies.

THE VIEW FROM WITHIN

Monday, October 15, 1900, was the date set for the formal opening, but Bostonians did not have to wait so long for a glimpse of their city's new "Temple of Music," as the *Herald* called it on September 20, 1900. The new auditorium was opened during the week beginning Monday, September 24, for the customary auction of season tickets for the coming twentieth season of the orchestra. Priced nominally at $7.50 and $12.00 for a season of twenty-four concerts, the tickets were subject to a premium or surcharge based on the desirability of particular seats, determined by a bidding process conducted by a professional auctioneer. Thus, for the 1900–01 season, the recently widowed Isabella Stewart

AUCTION SALE OF SEATS AT SYMPHONY HALL.

Auction Sale of Seats at Symphony Hall, September 1900.
Boston Public Library, Music Department.

Gardner paid a previously unheard-of premium of $560 each for two $12.00 seats (First Balcony Right, A15 and A16) for the twenty-four concerts of the Saturday evening series.[207]

Bostonians who came to the hall that week were almost uniformly delighted by the freshness and sparkle of its pristine interior. "To those who expected magnificence or flowery adornment the hall will be something of a disappointment," the *Herald* of September 20 conceded,

> but it is safe to say that no similar structure in this or any other city has been treated, from the viewpoint of decoration, in a manner so satisfying. The interior of the hall is elegant in the extreme, but it is the elegance of simplicity. The color scheme, if such it can be called, is in cream and gold, and these colors are applied in the simplest way, and in the best of taste. The effect is artistic and aesthetic. There is nothing obtrusive anywhere; nothing to draw one's attention away from the music.

"In shape and construction," the *Herald* approvingly if inaccurately continued,

> the hall is practically a reproduction of the famous music hall at Leipsic. The modifications of this plan adopted are so technical that the average person, who had seen the hall at Leipsic, would probably fail to note that there had been any modifications at all.

Boston Symphony Orchestra: Season ticket for the 1900–01 season. Fixed-price tickets were sold at auction subject to a supplementary charge.

Boston Public Library, Music Department.

More noticeable to the average visitor was the new hall's resemblance in size, shape, and arrangement to the old Boston Music Hall. The new edifice "had a dearly familiar look," the *Transcript* commented. "Indeed, it seemed just like the old stand freshened up to the dazzling point." Some patrons were actually seen wandering the aisles in search of their habitual seats.[208]

Early visitors to the hall were much impressed by the care taken to ensure the comfort and convenience of future audiences. "The arrangement of the new hall is so admirable in every way that there are no poor seats anywhere," the *Boston Evening Record* asserted.[209] Praised, too, was Major Higginson's munificence in reserving the entire second balcony, with a capacity of 505 seats, for Friday afternoon "rush" patrons at 25 cents per seat. Contemporary (1900) sources give the total seating capacity of the hall as 2,569 (floor, 1,466; first balcony, 598; second balcony, 505). The Symphony Hall box office currently lists a total of 2,625 seats (floor, 1, 486; first balcony, 598; second balcony, 541).

Some key features of the new hall, including its ventilation and the all-important matter of its acoustics, remained untested for the moment, but the *Boston Sunday Herald* undoubtedly summed up the general feeling when it declared that the BSO would "at last occupy a home worthy of its reputation."[210] Even more positive would be the judgment voiced by H.E. Krehbiel of the *New York Daily Tribune*, after attending the opening night observances: "It can safely be said that for its purposes Boston has the most beautiful, appropriate and admirable hall in the United States."[211]

The record would be incomplete, however, without an unattributed opinion expressed in New York's prestigious *Musical Courier*, whose Boston informant often took a jaundiced view of Major Higginson's endeavors:

> The building has been described, but it must be visited to learn of its cheerlessness and to feel the stern effect of architectural angularity. It has all the aspect and atmosphere of a religious establishment, and no matter if Beethoven's name is carved on the proscenium arch and a copy of the Apollo Belvedere is fixed in one of the cold niches at the end of the hall, it still feels like an armory or a prayer house, where ritual is considered paganism.[212]

This, however, was decidedly a minority view.

"CASTS OF CHARACTER"

One noteworthy imperfection in the hall as seen in September 1900 was the emptiness of all but one of the sixteen generously proportioned niches that lined the side and rear walls of the auditorium above the second balcony. As in his unrealized design for the Greek theatre, McKim had planned for the new music hall a row of antique statues overlooking the audience, six on each side and four more at the back. The concept was more than a mere decorative scheme, for, as Professor Sabine later recalled, the statues "were a part of the original plan not only artistically . . . but acoustically."[213]

Plaster casts from the antique were obtainable with little difficulty from the Roxbury atelier of the Brothers Caproni, the leading Boston firm involved in the importing and casting of reproductions of antique and modern statuary. But no funds had been provided for what the New Music Hall directors apparently regarded as merely one of the frills and furbelows of the architect's scheme. Defeated on so many other points, McKim apparently had thought it useless to wage a battle over this one.

Thus only one of the available niches was occupied as the hall began its public career. As in the old Music Hall, an oversized reproduction of the Vatican's Apollo Belvedere was so placed as to overlook the auditorium from one of the four rear niches, a little to the left of center as one faced the stage. Apollo's presence in the hall was a comforting link with tradition, although the nude deity's unwonted whiteness prompted speculation as to whether he had

Symphony Hall: Interior view toward the rear, ca. 1900, with the Apollo Belvedere.
BSO Archives.

been given a bath or, as seems more likely, replaced by a fresh cast.[214] In any event, his lonely appearance and somewhat asymmetrical position emphasized the incompleteness of the design as a whole.

Two additional statues, one representing the Greek dramatist Euripides and the other a second Apollo — this one clothed, and with a lyre — would be installed on opposite sides of the auditorium during the winter of 1900–01, halfway through Symphony Hall's inaugural season. (Both were later moved to other positions.) But the preparation and installation of these colossal effigies, averaging some seven and one-half feet in height, was an undertaking of no small magnitude. Not only were no further funds believed available for such a purpose, but there apparently were no long-range plans for making good the deficiency.[215]

Surprisingly, however, these difficulties were to be overcome within the space of a few months by the vigorous yet wholly unostentatious initiative of Mary Lee (Mrs. John W.) Elliot, an artistic Higginson cousin from Beacon Street in the Back Bay. Distressed by the hall's unfinished appearance, Mrs. Elliot apparently

Symphony Hall: Interior view toward the stage, ca. 1901, showing "two colossal statues, that of Apollo, with his lyre, and of Euripides [which] stand as sentinels over the vast space" (Boston Transcript, February 16, 1901). Both statues were later repositioned. BSO Archives.

contacted the architect and inspired him to reexamine the matter, not with Major Higginson but with Professor Sabine and Daniel Chester French, McKim's sculptural consultant on the Greek theatre scheme. By May 1, 1901, Sabine was responding to McKim's inquiries by reminding him of the importance of the statuary in the original conception and assuring him that the statues "will not in the least affect the reverberation in the hall."[216]

Mrs. Elliot wrote again to McKim on February 19, 1902:

> If you would still like to have me try to get the money for the statues, it seemed to me that this would be a good time, and that we need say nothing to Mr. Higginson, but have them put in quietly during the summer. It would be a pleasure to me to do it, for the sight of those empty niches always makes me sad.[217]

Endowed with executive as well as artistic talent, Mrs. Elliot and one other woman are said to have organized two hundred "friends of the Symphony" to

Symphony Hall: Statuary along the east wall. Shown, left to right, are the Apollo Citharoedus, Mnemosyne (also called Girl of Herculaneum), Dancing Faun, Demosthenes, and Seated Anacreon. BSO Archives.

scrape together the necessary funds. The donors' names remained secret, but the *Boston Herald* reported that the funds were solicited by two ladies, one of whom, a resident of Beacon Street, had also been "superintending the placing of [the] treasures in their little shrines." Some of the statues were obtained from the Caproni galleries, and others were imported by the Capronis from the European museums where the originals were located. In choosing the subjects, it was reported, the ladies had been advised by McKim himself.[218]

As the result of this burst of activity, by October of 1902 all but two of the empty niches had been filled — or were about to be filled — by plaster casts of antique statues, the majority of them in the locations they occupy today. Only two niches remained empty for some years longer, to be filled eventually by the "Satyr with Infant Bacchus" from the Naples Museum and the "Standing Anacreon" from Copenhagen.[219]

Only a few of these looming figures were directly related to the art of music. As sculptor French pointed out to McKim, "I put a lot of study and investigation into this thing [at the time of the Greek theatre project], and the conclusion that I arrived at was that it is not possible to find sixteen antique statues of musical proclivities appropriate to a Music Hall."[220] But all of the figures were at least antique, though some had been pieced together from scattered elements. A few were already familiar to Bostonians from casts in the Boston Athenæum or the Museum of Fine Arts. Others were quite new to "the Athens of America," and were expected to provide an educational as well as an artistic stimulus to future concertgoers.[221]

THE SOUNDS OF MUSIC

An imposing array of ticket holders and invited guests made solemn entry into the new Symphony Hall on the inaugural evening of Monday, October 15, 1900. Among the guests were over 400 stockholders of the New Boston Music Hall, awarded free tickets by Major Higginson in spite of Mr. Ellis's advice to the contrary.[222] The event provided a glamorous distraction from an ongoing presidential campaign, in which Republican President William McKinley soon afterward scored a second electoral victory over Democratic candidate William Jennings Bryan.

"No more brilliant or important event has ever figured in the musical history of Boston," the *Herald* gloated, enumerating the splendors of Symphony Hall's inaugural evening: Mr. Gericke and his musicians; a chorus of over 250, mainly from Boston's Cecilia Society; eminent soloists; a splendid organ; and "an audience which represented the best brains and culture of the commonwealth." It was indeed "a most brilliant audience for Boston," the *New York Daily Tribune* concurred.[223]

According to Philip Hale of the *Boston Journal*, the audience was "entirely in evening dress," although the *Herald* noted that only one "society woman" appeared with bare shoulders and décolleté. Such caution was undoubtedly well-advised, for many in the audience would shiver through the evening in what one journalist described as "chilling draughts" from a "$75,000 ventilation [system] blowing the very hair off one's head."[224] However, such torments, familiar enough in the old Music Hall, would be mitigated if not eliminated by the time the regular Symphony season opened later that week.

A Bach chorale ("Grant us to do with zeal / Our portion whatsoever") and Beethoven's *Missa Solemnis* in D — in what was said to be its first complete American performance[225] — made up the musical part of the inaugural pro-

SYMPHONY HALL
HUNTINGTON AND MASSACHUSETTS AVENUES

Inaugural Concert

MONDAY EVENING, OCTOBER FIFTEENTH
NINETEEN HUNDRED, AT EIGHT O'CLOCK

L. van Beethoven

Missa Solennis

in D, for Chorus, Solo Quartet, Orchestra, and Organ

PERFORMED BY

THE BOSTON SYMPHONY ORCHESTRA

ASSISTED BY

THE CECILIA SOCIETY AND OTHER
SINGERS

AND THE FOLLOWING SOLOISTS:

MME. CLEMENTINE DE VERE
MISS GERTRUDE MAY STEIN
MR. EVAN WILLIAMS
MR. JOSEPH S. BAERNSTEIN

Conductor, WILHELM GERICKE
Solo Violin, MR. FRANZ KNEISEL
Organ, MR. J. WALLACE GOODRICH

Program for the Inauguration of Symphony Hall,
October 15, 1900. BSO Archives.

gram. These highly praised but rather atypical works could not in themselves be rated an adequate test of Professor Sabine's acoustics, but the initial public response to the sound of the hall was in the main extremely favorable, and this reaction would be confirmed and strengthened as time passed. H.E. Krehbiel of the *New York Tribune* would declare that Sabine's confidence in the hall's acoustical excellence, which had earlier seemed "very venturesome, to say the least," had been "justified and rewarded."[226] The *New York Evening Post* suggested that "it would not be surprising . . . if mellowing time made [Symphony Hall] a Stradivarius among halls."[227]

William Foster Apthorp of the *Boston Transcript*, who was also the BSO's official program annotator, praised the new organ, played by J. Wallace Goodrich of the New England Conservatory, as "about as perfect as an instrument of its sort can be." He was, however, decidedly critical of the dimensions of the stage, which he described as "just large enough to contain the Symphony Orchestra, with hardly a square foot of space wasted."

To make room for the chorus, Apthorp explained, the first five rows of seats in the auditorium had been removed and a part of the orchestra brought forward, so that "nearly all the strings and wood-winds [were] out in the hall, not on the stage proper."[228] Apthorp therefore withheld detailed comment on the acoustics of the new hall until the following Saturday, when the orchestra would return to its normal position for the opening concert of the Symphony season.

Apthorp's judgment, when that time came, was less than favorable. Reporting dubiously on the "disorienting" novelty of the sound, he conceded its astonishing clarity and smoothness, but complained that it lacked "body" and "fulness," and had a "thin and ineffectual" quality:

> The hall itself seems perfectly dead to [the music]. It does not awake to the orchestra's call and vibrate with it. Things that should sound heroic and awakening, seem merely polite and irreproachable.[229]

Two years later, after he had been succeeded by Philip Hale as BSO program annotator, Apthorp permitted himself a still harsher judgment. "We have not yet met the musician," he wrote, "who did not call Symphony Hall a bad hall for music. Expert condemnations of the hall differ, as far as we have been able to discover, only in degrees of violence."[230]

Leo Beranek finds this condemnation "surprising in the light of Symphony Hall's subsequent widespread acceptance by musicians and critics."[231] He has suggested that any adverse acoustical judgments of this period probably originated with visiting European conductors and soloists. Accustomed to performing in smaller halls, such artists might well have found that music played in Symphony Hall, especially with the smaller-sized, ninety-piece orchestras of the period, "sounded weaker or thinner than what they were accustomed to hearing."[232]

OPENING OF BOSTON'S BEAUTIFUL SYMPHONY HALL.

Exceedingly Large and Refined Audience Enjoys the Initial Performance Under the Direction of Wilhelm Gericke.

OPENING NIGHT OF THE SYMPHONY CONCERTS IN THE NEW MUSIC HALL.

Opening Night of the Symphony Concerts in the New Music Hall.
Sketch from the Boston Globe, *October 16, 1900.*

Beranek's own judgment, almost a century later, rates Symphony Hall among the top three halls in the world in overall quality, on a par with Amsterdam's Concertgebouw and the Grosser Saal or Great Hall of Vienna's Musikverein.[233] This is an opinion with which few Bostonians are likely to differ.

Professor Sabine himself wrote in May 1901 that he had heard no negative comment on Symphony Hall's acoustics during its first several months of operation.[234] But Sabine was not a highly communicative man, and the extent of his personal satisfaction — or, possibly, discontent — with the final result of

"POP" CONCERT SEASON OPENS WITH A BIG CROWD AND ENCORES AND DOUBLE ENCORES.

OPENING NIGHT OF THE "POPS" AT SYMPHONY HALL.

Opening Night of the "Pops" in Symphony Hall's second season, May 5, 1902.
Sketch from the Boston Herald, *May 6, 1902.*

his labors is unknown to us.[235] What is clear, however, is that Sabine's association with Symphony Hall brought him instant celebrity and powerfully advanced his career. Ahead of him lay honorary degrees, a full professorship, the deanship of Harvard's Graduate Schools of Applied Science, consultancies on numerous architectural projects, and valiant civilian service to the Allied cause in Europe and America, mainly in the field of aeronautics, in the First World War. Sabine died within weeks of the conclusion of that conflict, and could not know of the bronze plaque commemorating his work on the hall he had helped to design. But one hopes that he was pleased by Major Higginson's note of appreciation, a week after the opening ceremonies in 1900:

> Just a word to thank you for your pains and success in the Hall. Of both no doubt exists. I have never heard the music as now. You have proved here that the Science of Acoustics exists in a definite form. You have done a great part of the hall, and every one thanks you.[236]

A point too seldom noted is that Sabine received no material reward for his work on Symphony Hall. "Sabine never asks anything for his advice or assistance," Major Higginson wrote to another correspondent. "He made the acoustics in Symphony Hall what they are, and I could never persuade him to take one penny."[237]

PARTING WORDS

Between the Bach and Beethoven choral masterpieces at Symphony Hall's inaugural ceremony were two spoken numbers: a long-awaited "report" by Major Higginson, and a poem written and delivered by Owen Wister, a Higginson friend from Philadelphia who is now remembered chiefly for his 1902 novel *The Virginian*. Wister's "Ode to Instrumental Music," formally entitled "The Bird of Passage," proved to be the low point of the evening, distinguished by neither poetic merit nor effective delivery. Conceding that it contained "excellent thoughts, excellently expressed," H.E. Krehbiel found it "too long," and said it "occupied so much time as to try the patience of the audience."[238] "One could not help sympathizing with Mr. Higginson, who stood courteously near the poet until he had ended," the *Boston Courier* reported.[239]

Major Higginson's own contribution, delivered just before Wister's poem, touched the higher end of the scale. "After the splendid Bach chorale was rendered," the *Herald* reported,

> Mr. H.L. Higginson stepped upon the stage and rendered what he was pleased to term a "report." He was given an inspiring greeting, the entire audience rising to do honor to the man who has done so much to make Symphony Hall possible. A well meant but poorly planned attempt to cheer him in no way detracted from the sincerity and meaning of the tribute which was paid.[240]

Most striking, in this first coherent account of how Symphony Hall came into being, are the personal modesty of the man who had refused to give his name to the building, and his generous acknowledgments of those who had lent their talents to the enterprise. "If it is a success," he said, "the credit and your thanks are due to four men — Mr. McKim, Mr. Norcross, Professor Sabine, of Harvard University, and last, but not least, Mr. C.E. Cotting, who, with his wide experience, guarded our slender purse."[241] One can only speculate why the Major omitted mention of his friend "Ned" Hooper, who was present in the hall but who would die just a few months later. If Hooper was not publicly praised on this occasion, it was probably by his own wish.

Of special interest to many in the audience were Higginson's disclosures about the cost and financing of the new hall, subjects which had been obscured rather than clarified by piecemeal announcements in the preceding years. "Our capital is $500,000," Higginson now confirmed, "of which $410,700 has been subscribed, and, as this sum was far too small, the directors have borrowed the remaining cost, which is about $350,000, making the total cost rising $750,000. They mortgaged the hall with reluctance, but had no other course, as the money was essential."

Later and more precise figures would place the adjusted cost of the land for Symphony Hall at about $188,000, construction of the building at about $583,000, and the two together at about $771,000.[242] While this total was nearly double the original estimate of 1893, it was still comparatively modest by the standards of the time: construction and decoration of the Boston Public Library had cost over $2.5 million.[243]

Higginson's concluding sentences were pitched in a more elevated key, and may possess even greater relevance for a time like ours in which the function and value of symphonic music are perhaps less widely understood than a century ago. Extolling the philanthropic outlook of "certain citizens of Boston" who had built the hall "without regard to return in money," the BSO's founder articulated what would now be thought a classical, even archaic view of the responsibilities of the private sector. By their action, Higginson declared, the creators of the hall had shown their care:

> . . . for the happiness, the convenience, the education of the inhabitants for twenty miles around this spot; and it is fitting in a republic that the citizens and not the government in any form should do such work and bear such burdens. To the more fortunate people of our land belongs the privilege of providing the higher branches of education and of art.

Few today would maintain with Higginson that "the privilege of providing the higher branches of education and of art" should be left entirely to "the more fortunate people of our land." But even fewer would challenge his lavish praise of the orchestra he had himself created, or deny the recognition to which he was entitled as its founder and longtime guarantor. Nor could there be reasonable dissent from his assertion that the BSO and its leaders, over the preceding two decades, had "done our city and our country signal and intelligent service, such as ennobles and educates a nation." Such words, though absent from the facade of Symphony Hall, may still have a place in the hearts and minds of those who love the building and its now century-old tradition.

A silent presence at the opening ceremonies was that of Charles Follen McKim, the architect of Symphony Hall. To him the Major paid tribute not for his artistic genius, but for the "absolute cheerfulness" with which he had abandoned his "pet idea" — the Greek theatre — and, in executing a plan that was "not entirely to his liking," had "given up many hopes, wishes, and fancies because the directors had no more money."

McKim, like Sabine, appears to have left no significant comment on a building which, though hardly one of his capital achievements, can certainly not be ignored in any summary of his contributions. Architectural critic Robert Campbell has attributed McKim's persistent silence in the matter to lingering pique over the rejection of his Greek theatre scheme and the dismissal of so many of his subsequent suggestions. The architect ought, however, in Campbell's opinion, to have taken pride in what turned out to be a "very Bostonian building":

> It has the qualities that the more traditional kinds of Bostonians like to think they possess. It's defiantly unfashionable, free of all ostentation, frugal, and durable. It's a building that could look a little better but couldn't work any better. McKim should have been pleased.[244]

With the dawning of the new century, the architect could look forward to further years of high creativity, in his chosen profession and in the organization and leadership of the American Academy in Rome. But deteriorating health would take its toll, and he would often bemoan the growing mechanization of American life and architecture as reflected, for example, in the Woolworth Building and other "skyscrapers." A bitter blow was the 1906 murder of his friend and partner, Stanford White, in a sensational marital scandal. Beset as well by financial troubles, McKim withdrew in 1908 from the firm he had founded, retiring to the small Long Island cottage where he died the following year at the age of sixty-two.

As for Henry Lee Higginson, sixty-five years old when Symphony Hall was inaugurated, he as yet had barely passed the meridian of his service as founder, guarantor, and guide of what was already one of the world's great orchestras. Nineteen seasons of the Boston Symphony lay behind him, and in eighteen more to come, Boston would benefit from his leadership in the new home and the new century. In those years, the orchestra would attain still further heights of virtuosity, only to come within a hair's breadth of disaster amid the violence and cacophony of World War I. Not the least of Henry Higginson's services would be his steadfast and, for a time, successful insistence that national and personal antagonisms among the members of his polyglot ensemble must be subordinated to the higher artistic goals to which all of them were pledged.

Worn out at last by the struggles which ultimately forced his retirement in the spring of 1918, he never ceased to acknowledge the "great joy" that had come to him personally in discharging the responsibilities he had so boldly assumed in early middle life. Higginson's whole career, indeed, could have been read as a commentary on the Gewandhaus motto, *Res severa verum gaudium*: true joy is a serious matter.

THE DOCUMENTS

A NOTE ON SOURCES

Of the principal repositories on whose holdings this book is based — the Baker Library of Harvard Business School, the Boston Public Library, the Boston Symphony Orchestra Archives, the Harvard University Archives, the Harvard University Libraries, and the New-York Historical Society — no single one can be deemed preeminent since each possesses material indispensable to a reconstruction of the history detailed in the present volume. Each, moreover, has its own protective restrictions barring the improper use of its material, and the BSO Archives is grateful to all of its sister institutions for their generous assistance in interpreting and applying these requirements.

The Baker Library of Harvard Business School, as official repository of the papers of Henry Lee Higginson, is a major contributor in terms of the quantity and significance of the materials made available, which have been drawn exclusively from the Henry Lee Higginson Collection, Part II. This portion of the Higginson Collection is primarily correspondence to and from Henry Lee Higginson, relating to business matters, charities, and philanthropic ventures, including the Boston Symphony Orchestra.

Three Series (also called "Sections") within the Higginson Collection provide the material utilized in the present compilation:

- Series XII / XIII, Combined Correspondence Files (1869–1920);
- Series XIV, Special Correspondence Files (1900–19);
- Series XV, Letter Books (1893–[1919]).

Within each Series (or Section), the material is organized by Containers (or Cartons or Volumes), and, in most instances, by Folders or other appropriate subdivisions. Each document referred to in the present volume is accordingly cited in the form "Baker XII-2-53," giving (1) its Series or Section number (here, Roman numeral XII); (2) its Container, Carton, or Volume number (here, Arabic numeral 2); and (3) where appropriate, its Folder number or title (here, 53).

While the originals of all of the documents thus cited remain in the Baker Library, microfilm copies (and in many instances photocopies) are available in the BSO Archives, where they are subject to the same restrictions as the originals.

The Boston Public Library, whose Print Collection has provided a number of uniquely valuable illustrations for this volume, has also permitted reproduction of material from its Allan A. Brown Music Collection, particularly the invaluable series of Scrapbooks containing clippings, leaflets, and other ephemera relating to the Boston Symphony Orchestra and Symphony Hall. Cited in this volume as "BPL Scrapbook," the content of the BPL volumes is also available in microfilm in the BSO Archives (subject to the same restrictions as the originals). In addition, the BPL Microtext Division has facilitated access to some contemporary newspaper material which had escaped the vigilance of the BSO's clipping services.

The Boston Symphony Orchestra Archives, as the authorized repository of documents, photographs, recordings, and artifacts relating to the history of the Boston Symphony Orchestra, has provided indispensable source material through the microfilm collections already cited and through its own resources, particularly its extensive photographic collection and its unrivaled scrapbook series. The BSO Scrapbooks, a series of 130 bulky volumes running from 1889 to 1973, provide a staggering quantity of material from contemporary newspapers and other publications in Boston and elsewhere. These volumes — whose content from 1889 to 1908 is also available on microfilm — are cited in the present work simply as "Scrapbook," with volume and page number and date. Other types of documentation in the BSO Archives are cited in most instances by series number and by box number or title where appropriate.

The Harvard University Archives hold essential documents relating to such Harvard personalities as President Charles W. Eliot, Professor Wallace C. Sabine, and Treasurer Edward W. Hooper, and have generously permitted quotation of documents bearing upon these individuals' relationships to the Boston Symphony Orchestra. All such documents are cited in conformity with the practice of the institution.

The Harvard University Libraries, including not only the Baker Library but also the Harry Elkins Widener Memorial Library, the Fine Arts Library, the Loeb Design Library, and the Loeb Music Library, have generously assisted the author in the use of their abundant resources, which, though somewhat decentralized, are made readily accessible through the University's admirable electronic cataloging system.

Finally, the New-York Historical Society in Manhattan granted free access to its unique McKim, Mead & White Collection, which contains a wealth of indispensable correspondence relating to the work of architect Charles Follen McKim and his associates in the planning and eventual building of a "New Music Hall" for the City of Boston. All of the pertinent documentation cited in this volume — much of it reproduced in the Documents section — is drawn from a single invaluable folder in the Society's McKim, Mead & White Collection, designated Box M-10 Misc. Folder: Boston Music Hall.

(1) James R. Gregerson to Henry Lee Higginson, March 11, 1887, describing a plot of land at Huntington Avenue and West Chester Park (later Massachusetts Avenue) and enclosing a note from the owner.[245]

Office of Snell and Gregerson, Architects
Studio Building, Boston, March 11th, 1887
Henry L. Higginson, Esqr.

Dear Sir,

In examining Huntington Ave lands, I found a fine and what will be as soon as the bridge is built to Cambridge and the bridge built on Boylston St. to West Chester Park a central lot on a main thoroughfare.

The lot contains 33986 sq feet and belongs to Mr. Dexter he was in the office yesterday p.m. and I questioned him in regard to the sale of it for a church or other public building — I send you his reply to read.
Very truly yours,
James R. Gregerson

[ENCLOSURE]

2 Pemberton Square,
Boston, March 11th, 1887

My dear Gregerson
I find the land at corner of Hunt. Av. and W. Chester Park [runs?] like this

[SKETCH; SEE ILLUSTRATION ON P. 8.]

10 feet set back on Falmouth [later St. Stephen Street]
15 " " " " Hunt. Av.
Nothing on W. Chester Park
If any public building goes on to the lot it will be for ever regretted if the whole is not taken.

I am committed to no price to you. If a part only is wanted price must depend partly on how the remnant can be used.
Yrs
FGD [F. Gordon Dexter]

(2) Henry Lee Higginson to Charles F. McKim, October 27, 1892, broaching a plan to build a Music Hall in Boston.[246]

Oct. 27 '92 —
Knickerbocker Club
319 Fifth Avenue

Dear McKim,
This is a secret — please keep it absolutely —

Two or three of us have bot [sic] the only feasible lot in Boston for a Music-Hall — [southern?] corner of West Chester Park, Huntington Avenue & a good [small?] street — 34,000 ft. in a parallelogram —

No hall is intended yet, & perhaps never — but if a very good offer for the present hall comes we might have to decide in haste —

I know of no one, but you, to whom I should like to entrust the work — Possibly others are as good but not for me — nor do I know if Mr. [Stanford] White is as good — nor if you or he would touch the job.

Possibly you may have time to glance at the land, — then we will meet for discussion, if you choose — *I* can't give the work to any one without consultation, & I would not ask you to spend a minute on it, except just to look at the ground — which will take much more than a hall for 2500 people —

If anything is done, it must be at low cost — & *perhaps* a theatre might be better.

Now will you please keep this perfectly dark, else it would foil my plans in many ways — forgive the scrawl & the [word illegible]
Yorstry [sic]
H. L. Higginson

(3) McKim to Higginson, October 29, 1892, welcoming the Music Hall project.[247]

[No letterhead][248]

Dear Mr. Higginson:
I wired you last night from the train to say that I had received your letter at the moment of leaving and having to be here to-day was unable to remain over as I should have [word illegible] preferred to do.

We all feel that it is quite impossible to express the pleasure we have that you should wish to associate us with the development of your splendid idea for a Music Hall for the City of Boston; and that nothing more flattering or complimentary has ever happened to our office, and I must leave all that I should like to say unsaid, except that we shall do our best, when the time comes, to assist you to reach the result you desire. We fully appreciate the importance of keeping the matter dark until you give the word. Some time next week Mr. [William R.] Mead and myself propose to pay you a visit and look over the ground with you, and we shall endeavor to keep any appointment which may be convenient to yourself. I will only add that while our ambition will be to make the building representative of the purposes for which it is intended in the best sense, we believe that this is not inconsistent with the use of simple materials and economical construction.

Yours sincerely,

Charles F. McKim

(4) McKim to Higginson, November 10, 1892, reaffirming interest in the Music Hall project (excerpt).[249]

McKim, Mead & White,
No. 1 West 20th Street,
New York.
10th November 1892.

Dear Mr. Higginson:

★ ★ ★

I expect to sail by the City of Paris on the 23rd to be gone six or eight weeks. To-morrow I leave for Boston and thence for Chicago. I am very anxious to see you before I go. Please let me know if this reaches you in time whether you will be in Boston at any time on Friday, Saturday or Sunday. I leave by the nine o'clock train to-morrow. #9 West 35th St. will find me till 6:30 to-night.

Yours sincerely,

C. F. McKim

P.S. — — There isn't a day that I don't dream about that Music Hall. I am most anxious to see the lot and have your views, and a large part of the pleasure of my vacation on the other side will be studying a practical application of them from the best existing examples.

(5) McKim to Higginson, November 22, 1892, proposing to study the project while in Europe.[250]

[Letterhead]
22nd November 1892.

Dear Mr. Higginson:

I forgot to acknowledge the dimensions of the land you sent me while in Chicago.[251] I would like very much to have a survey of the plot if you have one to carry with me to the other side. It should show the relation of the adjoining streets to the land and each other, with the points of the compass.

If we should find that the development of the problem can be accomplished, as I believe, without injury, by the introduction of certain utilitarian elements which will help the investment,[252] I assume that you will not be displeased.

I expect to leave for Boston on Friday afternoon [November 24] and to be at the new [Public] Library building most of Saturday — this in case there is anything further to be said.

Yours, very truly,
C. F. McKim

(6) Higginson to McKim, November 27, 1892, presenting ideas and suggestions regarding the proposed Music Hall.[253]

[No letterhead]
Boston, Nov. 27th 1892.

Dear McKim:

Excuse the pencil, but I can write just now more quickly and easily to give you the letter for to-morrow.

The plot, &c. you shall have. Did you get certain papers sent to the library yesterday?

1st. The hall should hold about 2200 to 2500 people — not more; have an ample stage for an orchestra of 90 men and for a chorus of 300 singers if need be; two or three adjoining small rooms for tuning the instruments, for overcoats, hats, etc. and for the singers; have a good space for an organ which can be set into the wall. The hall must have ample exits — on several sides if may be — and ample corridors and staircases. It should be on the street level I think and have perhaps two galleries of small dimensions. I think that it should be lighted from the top only, i.e. from windows in the top or in the highest part of the side walls. I say all this on account of quiet — to keep out sounds from the world. Of course quiet — and then full and yet delicate effects of sound are essential. For instance, our present hall gives a piano better than a forte, gives an elegant rather than a forcible return of the instruments, noble but weak — I *want* both.

The land is 34,000 square feet. The present hall was about 16 or 17,000 square ft I think and certainly much under 20,000. The 34,000 ft cost $170,000. and will stand in at $200,000. before a hall can be built. I've no notion of the cost of a new hall. The present hall has a capital of $100,000. and a debt of $140,000. It has paid me *no* return since buying and using it, i.e. since '81. It was much out of repair, has called for electricity, ventilation and all kinds of things since then. With a new hall we might earn ten or twelve thousand dollars or less, and then more in due course; but much of present business would leave us for a time at least and perhaps for good. Possibly you may like to use a sounding board of some kind or a stage shut in by an alcove, rounded or angular. *The* authority on sound here — Prof. [Charles R.] Cross — tells me that an angular sounding-board is better than that of any other shape, and of as few angles as may be.

2nd. As I must bear the burden of the new hall, perhaps quite alone, and as I keep my purse fairly depleted all the time, I must not — cannot — spend too much money for a new hall. The present hall cost less than $200,000., [and] some two or three small buildings, used now as shops and rooms for study, have since been bought and paid for. Later on we paid a large sum for an entrance by Hamilton Place. You suggest that we may perhaps be able to use some of these 34,000 ft for other purposes. Of course I shall be glad if it is so, for all money sunk in land is lost to me. Perhaps you may like to work in a small hall — 700 or 800 seats — for chamber-music and lectures, &c. &c. The Viennese opera house is good for sound and for ventilation and I think the same is true of the music-hall of the Conservatory there — Gesellschaft der Musik-freunde. [Wilhelm] Gericke, [Julius] Epstein, [Hans] Richter, any of these men would help you to see any building, if you use my name.

The Leipzig Gewandhaus (new) is also said to be good — very good, but I don't know. I *think* that the Dresden opera house is good, and also that a new hall in Berlin has been built.

In England I know of nothing good and as to France I am ignorant. The old opera houses — Grand & Comique — were prime, as you know, and isn't the same true of the Italian opera house and of the theatre for the Conservatory concerts? But the French musicians would know well. The Baireuth [sic] Wagner opera house is built with enormous pilasters — almost side-aisles, and the effect is excellent. I think the ceiling is lowered from the original height or rather is a false ceiling of canvas. I've always thought our hall too high — just so much space to be filled to no purpose.

I've no present purpose of building but already hear an inquiry for the present hall. If a good purchaser were to arrive it might precipitate matters. As I understand it, we could not well have a hall before the fall of '95, eh? or still later? *Can you guess at the cost?*

I *like* round-arched Norman or Lombard architecture — like some of the handsome brick buildings in Italy, and I rather incline to brick and brick ornament. I always like the severe in architecture, music, men and women, books, &c. &c.

All of which is respectfully submitted. I'd have this typewritten but then might miss you. If you care for it you'll have it typewritten.

[Now?] tomorrow as a goodbye.

Yours,

H. L. H.

(7) McKim to Higginson, March 3, 1893, promising drawings and studies for a new Music Hall (excerpt).[254]

My dear Higginson:

The enclosed from [John Galen] Howard to-day is gratifying.[255] I will forward the drawings to you as soon as received. We shall send you also shortly studies for the development of the site based on both semi-circular and rectangular halls. The last one seems to give a great return of reliable space without losing its monumental character.

★ ★ ★

Yours sincerely,

C. F. McKim

(8) William R. Mead to Higginson, April 28, 1893, conveying an estimate of the cost of the proposed Music Hall.[256]

[Letterhead]

28th April 1893.

Dear Sir:

Mr. McKim went to Chicago yesterday and asked me to write you the result of an approximate estimate we had been getting for the proposed Music Hall. From the estimate submitted, I believe it can be built in the very simplest manner for three hundred thousand dollars ($300,000); but to do it in a creditable manner would I think require more money. This estimate contemplates a building devoted entirely to Music Hall purposes and from which no rent from shops would be received. It would contain the necessary vestibules and stairs, a large and small Music Hall, and certain rooms for instruction and administration.

When Mr. McKim returns from Chicago he will send you the sketches upon which this estimate is based.

Very truly yours,

William R. Mead

(9) McKim to Higginson, May 3, 1893, proposing a meeting to examine alternative plans.[257]

[Letterhead]
3rd May 1893.

Dear Mr. Higginson:

Returning from Chicago this morning my first question was in relation to the approximate estimate forwarded to you. In the past three months we have worked up a number of schemes, in Paris as well as here, of which the last has seemed to both Mr. Mead and myself the most practical, economical and desirable. Before proceeding further I should like to have the opportunity of going over the several schemes with you with a view to determining the policy which you intend to pursue. We can meet here or in Boston, as you prefer. I expect to be in Boston the early part of next week.

Yours, very truly,
Charles F. McKim

(10) Emergency fund-raising campaign: Statements to the press, June 14–20, 1893

(a) Statement by "several prominent gentlemen," June 14, 1893.[258]

The new rapid transit bill, which will become a law (in all probability) next autumn, destroys Music Hall, thus depriving the city of the only hall which can be used for concerts, public meetings, or festivals of any kind, always excepting Mechanics' Hall, which is too large for ordinary use. This loss will interfere with the concerts heretofore given at Music Hall, viz: those of the Handel and Haydn, Apollo and Cecilia societies and of the Boston Symphony Orchestra, as well as all occasional concerts.

The contracts for the Symphony Orchestra are now in process, and must be settled at once. If funds to build a new hall cannot be raised within ten days the concerts of that orchestra must be abandoned indefinitely.[259]

It is proposed to build a new hall or theatre, of which the plans will be put in the hands of a competent committee. An option on an excellent location at the corner of West Chester park and near Huntington avenue has been taken at a fair price.

To this end it is desired to raise $400,000, and subscriptions may be sent to the office of Mr. T.D. Boardman, Ames Building.

(b) Communication from the Committee for a New Music Hall, June 17, 1893.[260]

We have been asked to act as a committee for the building of a new hall for music in Boston, and also to receive subscriptions of money, and we shall attend to our duties in that respect. We have made Mr. T. Dennie Boardman of the Ames Building our agent, and are glad to answer any questions about the scheme. The hall will be built under an act of incorporation and shares of $100 each will be issued.

It is hard to find in Boston a square lot of twenty thousand feet which offers good exits, quietness and cheapness. The piece of land under option at the corner of Huntington av and West Chester pk combines all these points. We think it the best site. We beg to remind the public that great despatch in subscriptions is needed in order to keep the Symphony Orchestra together and in order to finish the new hall by Oct. 1, 1894, as before that date our city will be without a place for large concerts.
(Signed) Edward W. Hooper
Henry F. Sears
H. L. Higginson
Boston, June 17, 1893.

(c) Letter of H. L. Higginson to the editors of Boston newspapers, June 20, 1893.[261]

To the Editor of the Herald: In order to avoid any mistake in the minds of the public as to the new hall for music, of which you have so kindly spoken during the past week, and of my relation to it, I ask leave to make the following statement:

I must engage a conductor for the Boston Symphony orchestra, if at all, for five years, and before doing this must be sure of a hall in which to play. Still further, these engagements must be made at once, as the musicians cannot wait longer. In all probability the present Music Hall will be taken by the city within a year for the new street, and in any case it cannot be relied on for more than one season. There is no other hall in Boston which would fill the place of Music Hall for large concerts.

It has been a great pleasure for the past 12 years to plan for, to work for and to support the Symphony orchestra, which is the outcome of much artistic skill, knowledge and long and persistent work on the part of the musicians. No good orchestra can be got in any other way. I shall gladly carry on my work as regards the orchestra if a good hall be provided for it, but only on that condition.

The orchestra has this year reached a self-supporting stage, which it may or may not keep, for there is always a considerable risk each year as to the receipts. During these past years the total deficit has been large; but the expenses must always be met, and this risk falls on me, and may be fairly considered my share.

May I suggest that a new hall can readily and without much greater expense be built so as to be used for opera, and thus command a larger rental (it may well have open boxes, as in the Carnegie Hall in New York, and seats of various grades and at different prices). At the present time it is very difficult to get any theatre in Boston for opera or other large occasional entertainments.

Every considerable city in our country has some such hall, and it is for the citizens of Boston and its neighborhood to decide whether they care enough for music in its different forms to build this hall; and for them to decide at once if they wish to keep the orchestra. Money will be wanted for the building later in the year, but the promise of it is needed now.

The building must be ready for use, so far as the Boston Symphony orchestra is concerned, in October, 1894.

To sum up: The public may be sure that to make a good orchestra much work, much time and much expense are required. All these elements have been contributed, and we have the orchestra as it now stands. Shall we keep it, or lose it for want of a proper hall? The decision cannot be postponed beyond a few days. Unless within that time a new hall is assured, I must disband the orchestra, and finally abandon the Symphony concerts.

Henry L. Higginson

Boston, June 20, 1893.

(11) Organizing a Corporation: Circular letter to subscribers from the Committee for a New Music Hall, October 30, 1893.[262]

The undersigned committee have the honor to report to you that the total subscription for a new Music Hall in the city of Boston now amounts to a little over four hundred thousand dollars, and that, in consultation with experts, much time and thought have already been given to the preparation of plans and to other preliminary questions.

After full consideration as to possible sites, your committee have decided that the lot on the northwest corner of West Chester Park and Huntington avenue is the best lot available, taking into account location, shape, size and price. This lot was selected last year by two members of your committee and two of their friends, on the understanding that a new Music Hall would soon be a necessity, that it was the best lot to be had, and that it should be offered for the purpose at its cost, with interest and taxes. The whole of the purchase money was borrowed for five years at four and a half per cent. with an option to prepay the note, which was indorsed by the four persons above mentioned, who were to have the profit or loss of the purchase only in case the land should not be taken for a music hall within a reasonable time. Your committee think that the option to take the land for a music hall and to pay for it in full should now be exercised. For this purpose, for the cost of plans and other preliminary expenses, and for the further prosecution of the work, the committee ask each subscriber to pay one-half of his subscription on or before Nov. 15 next. A second instalment will not be asked for before May 15, 1894; but any subscriber can, if he prefers, now pay his subscription in full, and receive stock therefor. As soon as the sum actually paid into the committee shall amount to two hundred thousand dollars or more, a corporation will be organized and one share of stock issued for each one hundred dollars paid. When later instalments shall be called for, the capital stock will be increased to not exceeding five hundred thousand dollars, in accordance with the statutes. As stock cannot be issued for fractions of $100, each subscriber of an odd number of hundreds must have the option to make his first payment $50 less than his share of the first instalment.

When the corporation has been organized, the question of the purchase of land, as above proposed, will be submitted to the stockholders at a special meeting, and later the plans for building will be likewise submitted for approval.

If you will kindly send to Messrs. Lee, Higginson & Co., at No. 50 State street, on or before Nov. 15, 1893, one-half or more of your subscription, the receipt of the committee will be given therefor, until stock of the corporation can be issued to you.

Yours truly,

Edward W. Hooper.

Henry F. Sears.

Henry L. Higginson

(12) McKim to Higginson, July 5, 1893, promising plans and elevations of proposed Music Hall (telegram).[263]

Letter and despatch just received. Look for plans, sections and interior perspective at quarter scale by Thursday's express, elevation and exterior perspective by Saturday's express.
C. F. McKim

(13) Edward W. Hooper to McKim, September 1, 1893, authorizing preparation of a model of the proposed Music Hall.[264]

50 State St. Boston
Sept. 1, 1893.

Dear Mr McKim
Your first letter about model for the Music Hall came too late to be answered before I went off for vacation.

I have to-day consulted with Mr Sears and Mr Higginson about the matter, and we agree that you may spend on our behalf not exceeding twelve hundred dollars ($1200.) for such a model as you think it important for us to have. As we have no money to spare, and do not wish to squander any of yours, we advise that no costly detail, merely for looks, be provided. If we can be sure that the general scheme is sound, there will be no trouble about the ornamental detail. We hope to prove that your plan as it is, or with slight modification, is the best possible plan.
Yours sincerely
E. W. Hooper

(14) McKim to Hooper, September 2, 1893, welcoming authorization to prepare a model.[265]

[Letterhead]
2nd September 1893

Dear Mr. Hooper:

I expected on opening your letter that its tone (musically considered) would be "deaf" to my entreaties for a model, but when read aloud it produced the effect of a whole orchestra on the feelings of this office; and I write to say that the order to go to work has been given today to a man named Hall, who will have five assistants, and who will continue steadily upon the work until it is done.

We are very much obliged to you all, for consenting to spend twelve hundred dollars at a time when twelve hundred cents becomes a considerable sum; but we are especially obliged to you for this vote of confidence in the plan as it stands. As the model proceeds it may be desirable to make changes in it; if there should be any such I will notify you promptly.

In regard to the cost of the model, as we should probably, in any event, have undertaken it for our own satisfaction, I do not feel that it is right to charge you with more than half the amount and only suggested your bearing a part of the expense because models are (the more's the pity) unusual luxuries.

Yours sincerely,

C. F. McKim

P.S. You might mention to Mr. Higginson, in case you think of it, that I refrained from answering his last note to me on the subject of leaky vessels (premature reports on the subject of Music Hall).[266] He states that although born in Amity Street he is partly Yankee and good at guessing. Now, we Quakers from Pennsylvania guess also and are guilty of some other very gross things, but *we never suspect*!

McK

(15) *McKim to Hooper, December 21, 1893, commenting on matters relating to the Music Hall model.*[267]

[Letterhead]
21st December 1893.

Dear Mr. Hooper:

Ever since we received authority to make the model, the work upon it has progressed without intermission, and after many perplexing moments [it] will soon be ready for the inspection of your Committee.

After consulting with you and by permission of the trustees of the Library, the model will be placed in one of the rooms of the new building unless for any reason you should prefer to have it elswhere. In this case will you please at once advise our superintendent, Mr. G.E. Wolters, at the library building, what disposition you wish made of it.

The plan seems to us to sustain itself in its structural and architectural possibilities, and as regards acoustics, we believe that the wedge-form stage walls and the succession of rising concentric arches immediately behind and above the orchestra offers a series of sounding boards of the best.

Yours sincerely,

C. F. McKim

P.S. The James T. Hall Co., have asked us for a payment of $750 on account of the model. If this is satisfactory will you send us a check drawn to their order for this amount.

(16) *Typical description of the model on view at the Boston Public Library January 8, 1894: from* Boston Daily Advertiser, *January 9, 1894.*[268]

THE NEW MUSIC HALL
The Model at the Public Library Satisfies All Critics
If Accepted, Boston Will Have Most Beautiful Hall in the World

The model of the proposed new music hall was exhibited yesterday morning to the directors of the enterprise and members of the press at the new Public Library building, and it is not too much to say that if the design is followed Boston will possess the most efficient and beautiful structure devoted to music in the world. It seems to meet with the enthusiastic approval of the committee in charge.

The hall was designed by C.F. McKim, who made a special trip to Europe last summer and inspected every music hall of importance on the continent. In this production he thinks that he has combined the best features of all and eliminated much that is faulty and unsatisfactory. It most resembles the music halls of Vienna and Leipsic, which are considered to be among the finest in existence.

The entire seating capacity is 2500. The gross dimensions of the interior of the building are 150 feet in length, 143 feet in breadth and 83 feet from the floor to the highest point of the ceiling. It will be made as nearly fireproof as human ingenuity and experience can devise with solid brick walls, iron beams, brick arches and fibrous plaster on the ceiling. All the lighting, ventilating and other appliances will be of the best sort.

The hall is patterned on the Greek theatre, and there is no such thing as an angle or overhanging balcony in the house. Its general shape is that of the toy magnet with which every boy is familiar, the seats for the spectators occupying the central and curved portions, and the musicians' stage being placed across the two ends. All the seats focus on the platform, and the view of each and every spectator will be uninterrupted.

The centre of the floor is occupied by what in the old theatres was called the "pit," corresponding to the "orchestra" in the modern. Rising from this on all sides in sweeping, amphitheatrical series, are the great body of the seats. Their wide, easy curves, with the Ionic pillars which support the gallery at the rear, the hollow, domelike ceiling and the ample scale upon which everything is designed gives a classic air to the impressive interior.

The stage is semi-circular, occupies almost the entire width of the building, and has a double break, which insures most perfect acoustic properties. It is 72 feet wide and 30 feet deep in the centre, and rises in concentric, broad steps from the front. It will seat 120 members of the orchestra and 350 singers.

Passing through the main entrance, one comes at once into a stately, curving "Ambulatory," as it is described in the architect's plans. It is a corridor which follows the curve of the raised seats, passing underneath them and terminating in two large lobbies on either side, nearly opposite the extremities of the stage. The ambulatory is 18 feet wide, and from it all the stairways, entries and exits, cloakrooms, smoking and toilette rooms are reached. [W]hen completed it will be ornamented with statuary and carving.

Every part of the auditorium is accessible with extreme ease, and in case of a panic or other emergency the hall could be emptied without the slightest danger, in a very few minutes.

The cloak rooms are immense. It is evidently the intention of the managers of the new hall to encourage the evening dress idea as it never has been before at concerts. No man will be encouraged to hang his ulster over the back of his seat and hold his hat between his knees throughout the performance.

An examination of the stage shows that it is virtually a system of double sounding boards. It is closed by a segmental arch and half dome and beyond this the proscenium arch is not flat but opens like the mouth of a trumpet. All the vibrations of sound are thrown as from the mouth of the trumpet directly at the audience.

Yet another point of interest is the arrangement of the lights. They will be so placed as not to interfere in the slightest degree with the view of the stage. There will be one strong light directly overhead in the dome of the ceiling. All the other lights will be placed along the gallery, which runs at the back of the amphitheatre, and is supported by graceful Ionic pillars.

If work on the new structure were to begin at once, the building would probably be completed for the concert season of 1895. The lot selected for the site is the westerly corner of Huntington ave. and West Chester Park. The left side of the hall is to be parallel with West Chester Park, with the main entrance on Falmouth [now St. Stephen] st. and side entrances on West Chester Park.

(17) *Higginson to McKim, April 23, 1894, deferring action on the proposed Music Hall.*[269]

Boston April 23d 94

Dear McKim,
Your two kind letters should have had a reply ere this.

We both were very sorry not to dine with you & not to see Mr. & Mrs. [Theodore?] Thomas & to hear their views on the Hall —

I shall try to see the changes about the stage when next in N York —

Meantime it has seemed to me best to wait awhile before building — No one cares to put out fresh money, no one knows about the plans of transit — or can guess at the future — therefore we should wait — Edward H[ooper] & I agreed as to this point before his sailing.

One word as a [word illegible] is large, & valuable — & musicians must decide the point, eventually, but can any of them know except by the ear [?]

I always feel like hearing their opinion most respectfully & then deciding — Blakes' [?], & Cross's opinions *seem* to me better —

I hope you are well & busy — I liked the great Clubhouse very much — It needs only men (& women) to make it delightful.

Yorstry

H. L. Higginson

(18) McKim to Higginson, April 26, 1894, acquiescing in the postponement.[270]

[Letterhead]

26th April 1894.

Dear Mr. Higginson:

I have received your letter in regard to the Music Hall, and while I regret that it is not likely to be pushed through to completion this summer, as we had hoped, I recognize that once built it must stand for success or failure, and am therefore quite willing to regard the necessity as fortunate which forbids its immediate construction.

Yours sincerely,

C. F. McKim

(19) *McKim to Hooper, July 9, 1894, referring to disposition of the model and sig-
nifying continued attachment to the Greek theatre concept.*[271]

McKim, Mead & White,
160 Fifth Avenue,
New York
9 July 1894.

Dear Mr. Hooper:
I hear from [John] La Farge (whom I have not yet met) that you have both
returned, and shall hope to see you soon in Boston. Meanwhile the trustees
are expected to open the Public Library Building for use in September, and
this morning I am notified by our superintendent that they desire, as soon
as convenient to you, to have the model of the Music Hall removed. If it will
be any relief to you to have it undertaken by us we will gladly attend to it;
otherwise will you please entrust the work to someone familiar with plaster
construction.

I daresay you have returned [from abroad] with models in your mind's eye
newer and fresher, but until I know positively from you that the form of the
Greek theatre must go, I propose to cherish my faith in it.

Mr. G.E. Wolters at the New Public Library will act or co-operate with
anybody you may send.
Sincerely yours,
C. F. McKim

(20) *Report to stockholders of the New Boston Music Hall, November 17, 1894,
recommending a further postponement of construction.*[272]

To the Stockholders of the New Boston Music Hall — In accordance with the
votes which were unanimously passed at the last stockholders' meeting on Jan.
6, 1894, your directors at once bought and paid for the lot of land on the corner
of Huntington and Massachusetts avenues, and afterwards submitted for your
consideration and criticism the model which had been prepared by the architects, McKim, Mead & White, as a suggestion for the new Boston Music Hall.
Although your directors have during the past year given much thought to var-

ious matters connected with the new hall, they have been and still are unwilling, for business reasons, to advise you to adopt a plan and begin the building.

When your subscriptions were made in the summer of 1893, it seemed to be certain that the old Music Hall would shortly be taken by the city of Boston for its rapid-transit scheme. But for your generous and prompt subscription of $400,000 to build a new hall, the Symphony Concerts would have been at once permanently abandoned by Mr. Higginson. When, a few months later and after the failure of the rapid-transit scheme, you authorized the purchase of the new lot, it was well known that the old Music Hall was for sale, as Mr. Higginson and other owners of its stock were unwilling to maintain it much longer as a public hall. During the year 1894 the owners of the old hall gave an option on the property for conversion into an arcade with shops; but existing business conditions were unfavorable to the scheme, and this option expired on Sept. 25, 1894.

After careful inquiry, your directors are satisfied that so long as the old Music Hall is used as a public hall the income from the new Music Hall would not be sufficient to pay even its current expenses for taxes and administration. They therefore have been unwilling to advise you to build until the fate of the old Music Hall shall be settled. At the annual meeting next February, if not sooner, all questions relating to the new hall should be carefully considered by the stockholders, and such action should be taken as they may then think fit. In the meantime the stockholders should remember that their subscriptions have already done much good by preventing the breaking up of the Symphony Orchestra last year and by providing a suitable lot of land for a new hall.

Mr. Higginson wishes to thank you for your generosity which carried the orchestra over a crisis and kept it alive.

All your directors believe that a new and better Music Hall will soon have to be built in the interest of music in Boston, and that the land now owned by you is the only available lot in the city which is adapted to your purpose.

(Signed) Henry L. Higginson

Edward W. Hooper

William Sturgis Bigelow

Henry F. Sears

Charles E. Cotting

(21) Hooper to Higginson, October 22, 1898, recommending McKim be asked to implement a simplified Music Hall plan.[273]

50 State St., Boston
Oct. 22, '98

Dear Henry,
Since our last Music Hall meeting I have given much thought to the question of an architect, and I am decidedly of the opinion that it is unwise as well as unfair to employ anyone except McKim, if he consents to abandon his old scheme, & take up cheerfully our new plan, at a cost not to exceed two hundred thousand dollars (exclusive of furniture). This would mean either more subscriptions or a small mortgage debt. John [Quincy] Adams [II, 1833–94] and I built Sever Hall and Austin Hall [at Harvard], with Richardson (and Norcross). We had no trouble that was serious, and hardly any extras. Sever, of brick, cost eight dollars a foot, and Austin, of stone, ten dollars for 14,400 feet (four faces of stone work). We ought to cover 25,000 feet, with a simple hall & entries, for $200,000 even allowing for piling. Sever had four floors above the basement and was much cut up —
Yours always
E. W. Hooper

(22) Higginson to McKim, October 27, 1898, explaining current financial constraints and asking his reaction.[274]

[No Letterhead]
October 27, 1898.

Dear Mr. McKim:
The old Music Hall has been sold and is to be vacated by April 1, 1900, so the time has come when we must build our new Music Hall. We, the directors, have been discussing the matter for some time among ourselves and, considering that the money subscribed belongs to so many people, we feel afraid to try any experiments. While we hanker for the Greek theatre plan, we think the risk too great as regards results, so we have definitely abandoned that idea. We shall therefore turn to the general plan of our Music Hall and of the halls in

Vienna and Leipsic, the latter being the best of all, and Mr. Cotting will ask for a plan on those lines.

We have 18 months in which to complete our work, and we have, at the outside, $200,000 (probably somewhat less) to spend. With the slender income which this new hall will give us, we must keep within that sum so as to incur no debt. We therefore hesitate as to whether this scheme, devoid of poetry and charm, will have enough interest to bring you in person over here and give your own thoughts and time to the completion of the work. Will you kindly tell us your wishes in the matter? We are all greatly obliged to you for the beautiful plan, which we should much like to use if we dared to run the risk. All this must seem very stupid to you, but we cannot help it.
Yours truly,
H. L. Higginson

(23) *McKim to Higginson, October 28, 1898, offering either to withdraw or to complete the project under the new conditions.*[275]

[Letterhead]
Oct. 28, 1898.

Dear Mr. Higginson:
I am in receipt of your favor of yesterday, in relation to the sale of the old Music Hall and your intention to build the new one, under altered conditions of design, time and money. It was very kind of you to write us, explaining the circumstances, and while we regret the necessity which compels you to depart from the form of the Greek Theatre, we fully appreciate your position.

As for an expression of our wishes, which you are good enough to ask for, and as regards the design for the new Hall, under the altered conditions, let me say that if you feel it will be to your interest, and that of the Directors, to do so, please eliminate us from further connection with the problem. On the other hand, having, as you will recollect, studied the Leipsic plan, and having met Lamoureux, in Paris, and Richter and Gericke, in Vienna, at your instance, I naturally feel great interest in the final development of the scheme, whatever form may be adopted, or however inexpensive or simple its character, and should be glad, if desired, to submit a proposition, along the lines which you now propose to carry into execution. Given the necessary data and requirements, and with the collaboration of such a builder as Norcross, we could submit a proposition which would meet your views as nearly, I believe, both as to arrangement, cost and design, as anybody. Should this meet with your approval, we would immediately send our Mr. Wolters, a thorough man of business, and our superintendent in the construction of the Rhode Island State Capital [sic], at Providence, to you for a preliminary interview, and who could then place us in possession of the data necessary for a preliminary sketch, to be made at once; but, as I have said before, if you prefer to work independently of us, for reasons, whatever they are, we shall entirely understand it.

Very truly yours,

Charles F. McKim

(24) *Higginson to McKim, October 31, 1898, welcoming his availability and outlining present requirements.*[276]

Lee, Higginson & Company,

44 State Street,

Boston,

October 31, 1898.

Dear Mr. McKim:

I have your letter of the 28th inst. for which I desire to thank you. The letter has been read to the four other directors of the new Music Hall — Messrs. Hooper, Bigelow, H.F. Sears and C.E. Cotting. It is very satisfactory to the directors. We wish you to take up the matter of the Music Hall and are very glad that you are willing to do so. We do it, because we think you can give us what is needed better than anybody else.

We should be glad to see Mr. Wolters or anybody that you choose to send, next Monday morning, the 7th of November. Mr. Cotting is very busy until about that time, but asks that Mr. Wolters shall come to his office, 9, Tremont Street, Boston, when he will show him the lot of land (It is the same as before — on Huntington Avenue); and also show him the present Music Hall, as well as the plans of the Leipsic Music Hall, which we have here. Mr. Cotting will endeavor to tell him what spaces are essential to our work. Our lot is 150' x 225', the length of 225' being on Massachusetts Avenue, and the 150' being on Huntington Avenue and Stevens [sic] Street. The fourth side is on a passageway, with a blank wall, against other buildings — not yet erected — we having the rights on [?] the passageway.

Our chief object is a music hall which will hold 2400 or 2500 people. We think our present music hall too wide and short. Of course our present hall is very insufficiently provided with corridors and exits, so that it is really dangerous. We wish the hall to be on the level with the streets, or thereabouts. We will endeavor to tell you about the size of the stage needed, as well as the anterooms for musicians and the like.

These few facts will be of little interest to you perhaps, but they will certainly do no harm. As you know, we have very little money to spend and shall have to ask for an exterior as plain as possible. I have just been looking at the Radcliffe Gymnasium, which I like very much, and I often look at Sever Hall, Mr. Richardson's work, which is, of it all, the best looking building in the possession of the College and which has no ornament whatsoever.

Will you allow me to say that it gives us very great pleasure to go on with you. Our doubt has been to ascertain whether you cared to do the work or not, and your reply made it very clear.

I am,

Very truly yours,

H. L. Higginson

(25) McKim to Higginson, November 5, 1898, suggesting a plan of operations.[277]

[Letterhead]
Nov. 5th, 1898.

Dear Mr. Higginson:
We are in receipt of your kind letter of Oct. 31st, and have instructed our Mr. Wolters to communicate with Mr. Cotting, at 9 Tremont Street, Boston, on Monday, the 7th, as requested by you, to go over with him the question of the Music Hall requirements, and to collect all data necessary for a preliminary sketch plan.

In order to make time, after taking only that sufficient for the working up of your scheme, we should propose to provide you, at first, with plans explanatory of this, however rough and incomplete, upon which any changes desired can be worked out.

Thanking you again for your expressions of confidence in this office.
Yours very truly,
Charles F. McKim

(26) McKim to Higginson, November 23, 1898, reporting on current consultations.[278]

[Letterhead]
Nov. 23rd, 1898.

Dear Mr. Higginson:
I had an unlooked for, but most pleasant visit from Mr. Hooper on Monday, who stopped in, on his way to Washington, and to whom I showed the schemes referred to in my despatch to you. Without going into any very careful scrutiny, one of them appeared to him, as to us, obviously more promising than the others, because of its greater compactness, simplicity, and economy. When I telegraphed you,[279] I entirely overlooked the fact that this is Thanksgiving week, and that tomorrow is Thanksgiving Day, and I therefore suggested to Mr. Hooper, with his approval, that it would be wiser for us to take a little more time, in order to be able to submit our plan to better advantage, setting the day on to next week, (he suggested Thursday afternoon, or Friday). Since Wolters' return, we have been hard at work on the problem, and have not lost a minute.

Norcross's visit was very satisfactory, especially his concurrence in the buildableness of the plan above alluded to, and which, in its proportions, most nearly resembles the Leipsic hall. If Thursday afternoon would be as convenient to you as Friday, I will meet you, at that time, in Boston, but any day, after Wednesday, will be agreeable to me, if you will appoint time and place in advance.

Thanks for your note. Although not yet strong, I am gradually picking up my strength again, after a year of infernal dyspepsia!
Sincerely yours,
Charles F. McKim

(27) Conference in Boston: Report of the Boston Herald, *December 2, 1898 (excerpts).*[280]

One more step was taken yesterday toward the creation of a new music hall. Architect Charles F. McKim brought over several sketches from his New York office, for the consideration of the board of directors. There was long discussion, lasting over three hours, and as a result one of the sketches was provisionally accepted. Mr. McKim is to make a relatively elaborate and careful plan for submission later, when the time for final decision on building the structure comes.

★ ★ ★

The general idea of the latest plan is founded on the best German music halls. The German auditoriums found best adapted to orchestral concerts are halls about twice as long as they are wide, and this idea will be followed in the main here. The stage will be at the end, and there will be little else, [such] as ante-rooms, foyer, etc., for the public. Two galleries are contemplated here, a departure from the German plans, where a lower hall for lounging and ante-room purposes is provided, in addition to the concert hall proper. The building will be a modest one, as it must be fireproof and cost only about $10 a square foot — on 34,000 feet of land.

(28) Charles A. Ellis, Manager of the Boston Symphony Orchestra, to Charles E. Cotting, Clerk of the New Boston Music Hall, from Washington, D.C., January 6, 1899, commenting on architects' plan for the new Music Hall.[281]

Washington, D.C., January 6, 1899.

Dear Mr. Cotting:

I beg to apologize for so long a delay in writing to you. LaGrippe is epidemic in Philadelphia and we have had much sickness among the singers. This has made it necessary to find a good many substitutes and to change the bills frequently at short notice and it has given me so much extra work that I could hardly get through it, but the situation seems to be improving. I have looked over the plans of the new hall; it is my opinion that the rows of seats on the floor should be slightly curved, as is usual in the theatres and not perfectly straight as shown on the plan. This arrangement enables persons sitting at the extreme side of the hall to see the centre of the stage without turning in their seats, and also enables the audience to see each other, which I think is agreeable for them and it also gives the audience a finer appearance.

I agree with you that the artists' rooms on the Massachusetts Avenue side of the building should be placed up one flight, the stairway moved back, and this space utilized for the principal box offices and the business offices.

If I understand the plan rightly the proposed arrangement of the vestibule on the Huntington Avenue side is bad. The box office is in the centre of the vestibule, and in case of a rush a long line of ticket buyers would be apt to extend across the vestibule, and persons holding tickets would be obliged to break through this line to enter the hall. Two of the doors leading from the lobby to the vestibule and from the vestibule to the street are on direct lines, and when the doors are swinging there would be drafts of cold air. Then there seems to be six different entrances from vestibule to lobby and six ticket takers would be required. I think it would be an improvement to have a wide entrance from vestibule to lobby in the middle (where the box office is now indicated) with a brass rail so divided that two or three ticket takers could work at the same time, and by placing the box office at one side, or having one box office at each side all blockades would be avoided. It would probably be necessary to have one entrance to the lobby on each side of the vestibule, but at most not more than four ticket takers would be required. It might be well to remind the Architects to make one door at the rear of the building and the passage from it to the stage wide enough to allow the movement of a piano of the largest size. I am told that this was forgotten when Carnegie Hall was built and pianos have to be carried in at the front entrance. These are all of the suggestions I have to make and I offer them for what they are worth.

I expect to be in Boston next Sunday, and if you care to see me send word to "The Ludlow" and I will call on you.

I return the plans to-day by Adams Express.

Yours sincerely,

Chas. A. Ellis

*(29) Higginson to McKim, January 26, 1899, conveying views of Professor Wallace
  C. Sabine on acoustical aspects of the Music Hall plan.*[282]

[Letterhead]
January 26, 1899.

My dear Mr. McKim:

I have your letter this morning and will send you the facts about the wire
screens.

Mr. Hooper and I had yesterday a long talk with Professor Sabine, who has
studied your plans for some days and who likes them very much in some
respects.

Professor Sabine is a physicist at Cambridge who has studied acoustics and
ventilation with great care for some years and who is accounted here the best
authority. He is a very pleasant, intelligent and broad minded man, most
cautious in his statements and much interested in our hall. He has studied all
the halls which he could see, proposes to go to New York to see Carnegie Hall
and to Baltimore to see the music hall there, which our people think the best
they have encountered. (I may say in passing that our people all think Carnegie
Hall horrible. Very noisy music produces considerable effect, but the moment
an orchestra plays the older music and relies on delicate effects, everything is
gone. I have always disliked the hall very much, and I expected to like it very
much before trying it.)

Professor Sabine likes your low ceiling. He likes very much the rising floor.
He says the pitch should be as much as we can stand. He says the galleries
ought to pitch rather more than less, that is, have the pitches both at the sides
and back as much as can be. He suggests that about half of the outside sections
on the floor of the hall should be raised, that is, the five or six seats nearest the
side walls should be a step higher than those further in. He objects to anything
on the stage whatsoever in the way of a box or furnishings (drapery) of any
kind. He thinks the stage should perhaps be rather smaller, — that is, narrower, — than at present; that the top should be lower and should be covered
by a slanting sounding board, as in our present hall. He does not mean that a
sounding board should be put in but that the room in which the orchestra
plays should be with such a ceiling as would throw the music out into the hall,
— one of your objects in the construction of the hall.

About the height of the stage from the floor of the hall, he has nothing to
say, and that is a matter easily settled between you and me.

Professor Sabine thinks the hall altogether too long. How long it should be he does not venture to say, considering that partly a matter of experiment and partly a matter of calculation, which he has not yet reached, but he is very much afraid of the long tunnel which we have laid out. In this I entirely agree with him and so does Mr. Gericke. He thinks the hall will be the better for the first tier of boxes which you planned for half way down the hall from the stage. From there he would run a small second gallery, shallow at the sides and possibly a little deeper at the back. He does this to prevent an echo, thinking that part of the hall particularly should be guarded from echo. He does not think the protrusion of the boxes beyond the wall (which, as I understand it, is a new feature) will hurt the sound at all. He does not think the upper tier of boxes would be useful, because they would be so high. He thinks the second gallery coming over the first gallery and the first gallery coming over the floor will work very well. He thinks the stage should be nearly level for the sake of the piano standing even and the instrument stands as well and that we could use boxes or steps on which the men could stand or sit, just as we do now. That is in effect what you already have, but possibly your stage slants a bit too much. He does not think any boxes should be at the back of the hall.

Professor Sabine lays stress on the pitching because of the sound and because of the sight. People can see more easily if the galleries are well pitched.

I asked Professor Sabine about a row of boxes all around the first floor, just as they have in Vienna, as you may remember. He thought that would be very well, but he rather thought that raising the seats on the sides of the hall for five or six seats in as above described would be better. That leaves room for people to stand around the hall as they do now. He would like to have the space under the stage hollow. Under the floor of the hall he would like to have two or three chambers, in which should be exhaust fans. He would like to make the floor of iron grating and cover it with Manila matting of some sort. Heat the air above and draw it down through this floor, thus carrying off all dust from the hall and making the temperature even, as far as it may be so. So far as the effect on the music goes, he thinks this will be good; a strong upward current or draught carries the music away from the audience; if it is a downward draught, whatever there is in the theory, it will bring the music to the audience.

These are Professor Sabine's views. He is going to look at that Baltimore Hall of which Mr. Gericke spoke yesterday in the highest terms as giving the best possible effects. In fact, Mr. Gericke said he had never heard our orchestra play and sound so well as it did in Baltimore during the last trip, and he never heard it sound worse than it did in Carnegie Hall the other day. Around this Baltimore hall are the boxes as in Vienna on the lower floor. I confess that I see no particular advantage in them. People will not pay for them any more than they will on the floor. They will cost something and take up some room and may mar the acoustic effect. Certainly I think they would mar the hall in appearance.

I give you all these facts for what they are worth. We here have considerable opinion of Professor Sabine.

I venture to speak to you one word about the size of the hall, of which I spoke to Mr. Mead or Mr. de Gersdorff the other day. Our present hall, from the front of the stage to the back wall is 97 1/2 ft. The new plans make the distance on the floor, from the front of the stage to the back wall, 121 ft. 8 in. The additional space of almost 40 ft. is above in the galleries. That is, from the front of the stage to the back wall of the galleries is 160 ft. I believe that size altogether too much. Perhaps we can venture with a hall of 120 ft., but I should think that was the extreme. Mr. de Gersdorff said he could put in 175 more seats or thereabouts by placing the seats in the new hall as near as they are in the old hall. That is to say, the seats in the new hall were planned to be five inches further apart, back to back, than they are in the old hall. That is very agreeable but not at all necessary.

I shall be very glad to show what you have to Mr. Ellis and hear his objections (comments) as to the economy of the hall, that is, the service rooms, etc. The room itself I think we can settle between your office Professor Sabine's office and our office; in fact, we shall have to do so. I am quite ready to go to New York next week with Professor Sabine and see you.

I have telegraphed you today as follows:

"It may be wiser to await important letter going tonight before more work on plans."

Yours truly,

H. L. Higginson

[Handwritten postscript:]
We will have a perfect hall under your guidance.

(30) Sabine to Higginson, Cambridge, Massachusetts, February 26, 1899, reporting on an interview with McKim.[283]

Feb 26 1899
Cambridge
Mass

Dear Mr. Higginson;

Mr. McKim feels that he has evolved a beautiful and artistic plan in spite of, or rather, as he puts it, with the aid of the second gallery, and apparently takes pleasure and interest in the architectural problem because of the difficulties and restrictions to be overcome.

It is not his intention to lengthen the hall beyond the dimensions shown on the plan already submitted to you.

He strongly favors the three and two row galleries and I could do but little more than urge, in accordance with your note of Friday, the consideration of the increased seating capacity of the four and three row galleries.

The interview yesterday was both pleasant and satisfactory.

Very truly yours,
W. C. Sabine

(31) McKim to Higginson, February 27, 1899, requesting authorization to proceed.[284]

[Letterhead]
Feb. 27th, 1899.

Dear Mr. Higginson:

Professor Sabine appeared, from Boston, on Saturday morning last [February 25], at 11 o'clock, and passed the next two hours here, in going over the plans, and in a thorough consideration of the unsettled points. I was as much impressed by the force and reasonableness of his arguments, as by the modest manner in which they were presented, and have confidence that the acoustics of the hall will have greatly benefitted by his counsel and advice. The points in doubt having been removed to his satisfaction, I write to ask if we may now regard this as the official plan, upon which to base and complete our construction drawings, which we do not wish to commence, both on account of the expense and the loss of time involved, until the plan receives your official acceptance, and is not likely to undergo further change. In view of the very short time remaining at our command, for purposes of construction, and taking into consideration the time necessary for the proper development of the working drawings, it is very important that a decision should be reached at the earliest moment.

Very truly yours,

Charles F. McKim

(32) Higginson to McKim, March [5?], 1899, approving McKim's plans.[285]

Boston — Mch. [5th?] '99

Dear Mr. McKim.

What reply can I make to you? I've been filled with admiration at your self-abnegation even more than your knowledge & ingenuity & skill —

We will call it square — to go ahead — That row costs *me*, about $2000 yearly — one hundred [teachers?] in seats twice a week — but still I think it best, as you have made it — Remember each seat on the floor relieves me of about $50 deficit yearly — therefore 100 seats there means $5,000 yearly —

I did specify 2500 seats, but did not wish to make that a limit —

Of course these arrangements apply to the price of the hall for other [word illegible] —

But the wise man considers all these points and [delivers?] the best result under *all* the circumstances —

I simply state to you this wish — reminding you that *I cannot* raise prices — & am quite ready to pay the needed bill.

Mr. de Gersdorff spoke of [using?] a little more space for seats — & the point above is to be remembered in settling that minor question.

I accept your decision as to the galleries & am sorry to have interfered at all with your ideals —

I've asked Hutchings to see you at once about the placing of the organ — The pipes of the organ should be within the hall — but they may be widely distributed — bunched, spread — almost anything — The machinery can be put anywhere & the seat also — moveable in any case — When you've seen him,

we (you and I) will talk & the sooner the public can see the plans, the sooner
we can ask for money to make a start — With many thanks
I am Yorstry
H. L. Higginson

(33) McKim to Higginson, March 10, 1899, reporting drawings are on the way.[286]

[Letterhead]
March 10th, 1899.

Dear Mr. Higginson:
In order to make sure of the delivery of the drawings to you on Sunday
morning [March 12], we shall send them to you by special messenger, (Mr. de
Gersdorff) who will carry them with him on the midnight train, on Saturday,
and will remain in Boston over Sunday, and, if necessary, Monday, in order to
explain any points, and answer any questions which may arise, should you so
desire. On reaching Boston, early Sunday morning, he will deliver the drawings at your house, where he will return again later in the morning, for the
purpose of going over them with you.
Very truly yours,
C. F. McKim

(34) New plans submitted March 12, 1899: Descriptive article in the Boston Transcript, *March 13, 1899.*[287]

NEW MUSIC HALL PLANS
They Arrive in This City Sunday
And Are Exhibited in the Tremont Building
General Style of Building Is to be Classic
It Is Longer, Narrower and Lower Than Old Hall

Plans for the New Music Hall, to be located at the corner of Massachusetts and
Huntington avenues, arrived in this city Sunday morning [March 12, 1899] from
the New York offices of the architects, McKim, Mead & White, and at present

they may be seen in room 314 of the Tremont Building. The building committee of the New Music Hall corporation is to consider these plans before their acceptance, and it is possible that a number of alterations will be suggested; therefore as they are drawn at present they are not deemed to be final plans, but rather preliminary. There are eight plans in all; one is colored and represents the exterior of the building, while the others show longitudinal and transverse sections, the elevations on Massachusetts and Huntington avenues, and plans of the basement, the floor and the first and second balconies. It is understood that the material to be used will be brick, probably red, and stone. The main entrance, on Huntington avenue, has an Ionic portico, with eight stone pillars; the main hall, or what better might be called the hall proper, rises higher than the rest of the building, with a pediment at the top; what seems to be a harp is the crowning glory of the roof front. At either corner of the front section is a pavilion which runs into a wing extending the length of the building, with a pediment at the top; overlooking these wings in the main hall are clere-windows. On the Massachusetts side is a vestibule which if followed up makes a straight line through and across the hall interior; protecting this vestibule is a marquise, on the lines of that at the Thirty-fourth-street entrance to the Astoria in New York. The building will completely fill the lot purchased for it, and consequently will have a frontage of 150 feet on Huntington avenue and will extend 210 feet on Massachusetts avenue. It is notable that the plan measurements give no figure for the height of the building, but it would seem to be between seventy-six and eighty feet.

No estimate of the cost of the building, of the material to be used, or of the quality or degree of interior embellishment, has been made by the architects. They took into consideration solely general arrangements, such as seating capacity, offices, and incidentally acoustic properties. No one concert hall, either at home or abroad, has been taken as a model or as a basis for these plans; they stand as the results of original ideas, intended to meet the rather peculiar requirements of the builders. It is true that some conception of the ultimate exterior appearance can be had from the colored plan; at the front, on either side of the portico, stands a niched statue, while on the Massachusetts-avenue side a similar statue stands at each corner. Over the portico is a space reserved for appropriate inscription, while a smaller space is left, in the form of a square, at either end, about on a line with the larger space. As to the interior, the present plan allows for several statues along the walls; the windows, now drawn as full windows, may be cut down, giving an upper curved half only. The distinguishing features of the new building are that it is longer, narrower and lower than the old Music Hall.

While naturally there will be much vacant space in the basement, allowance has been made for a baggage-room, 54x29 feet; a carpenter shop, 17x20 feet; a kitchen, 17x27 feet; a serving room, 10x18 feet; a large boiler room with two boilers on one side and one boiler on the other; space for smoke and for foul-air exhaust, coal storage and heating and ventilating machinery. It has not been decided whether an electric-light plant will be established in the building, but the architects have kept such a possibility in view. The floor plan shows a main vestibule, 28x76 feet, from which entrance by two doors is made into a lobby seven feet wide at the front and fourteen feet wide on either side of the auditorium, which, by the way, is walled off from these lobbies. To the right of the vestibule come in succession a cloak and coat room, ladies' toilet, ladies' reception room, 16x24, a side vestibule opening on Massachusetts avenue, 17x37 feet; a ticket office, and offices for Mr. Mudgett, a bookkeeper, Mr. Comee and Mr. Ellis. To the left on entering are a coat room, gentlemen's toilet room, a boiler room, 18x72 feet, and a serving room. The stage, which is 60x32 feet, has at the right an artist's room and a dressing room, and at the left a tuning room, 33x37 feet.

The first balcony will also have a continuous lobby seven feet wide at the front and eight feet wide on the sides, with two large oblong lobbies, 14 by 20 feet, at the immediate right and left of the entrance. The libraries of the Symphony Orchestra and of the Handel and Haydn Society are to be on the right. Two artists' rooms are at the stage right, while corresponding to the tuning-room below is a large chorus room. The second balcony will have a foyer 75 by 28 feet, with two oblong lobbies at right and left of entrance, while the side lobbies will correspond in width with those on the first balcony floor.

The total seating capacity of the new Music Hall will be 2630, against 2397 in the old hall. The floor capacity will be 1511, that of the first balcony 608 and that of the second balcony 511, against 1251, 680 and 466 for the old hall. This is a net gain of 233 seats, while the space available for standing room will be on each side of the auditorium thirty feet more than that in the old hall. All seats are to be larger and presumably more comfortable than those which have been in the old hall since it was built. There will be only two rows of seats in the first balcony, whereas there are three in the old hall. The new hall has an interior length of about 140 feet and a width of 75 feet, while the old hall is 97.6 feet long and 77.6 feet wide. The main ticket office will be on the Massachusetts-

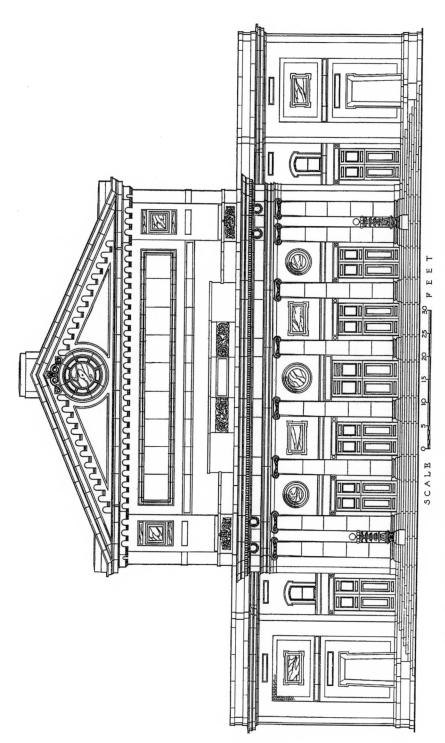

SCALE 0 5 10 15 20 25 30 FEET

Selected architectural drawings for "The Boston Music Hall," by McKim, Mead & White, 1899–1900. (above) Front elevation.

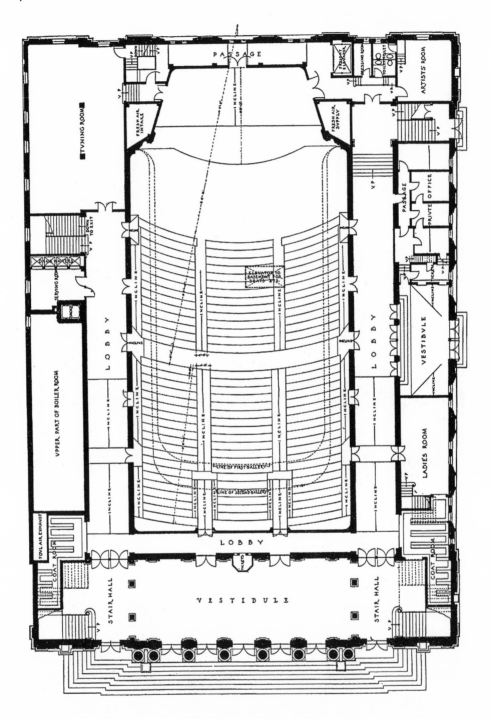

Original ground floor plan.

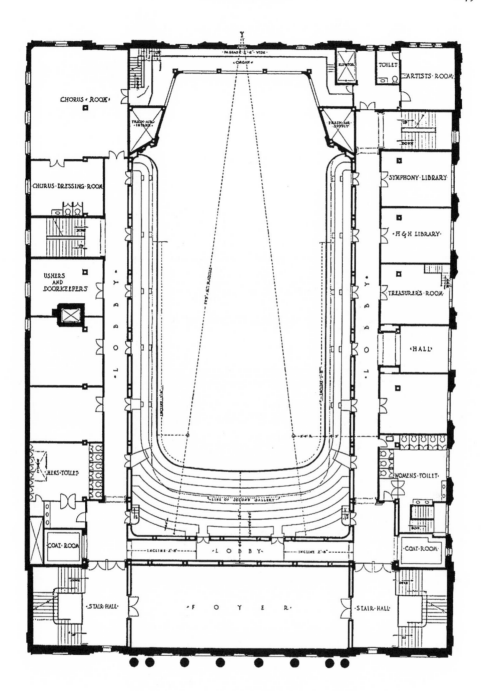

Original second floor plan.

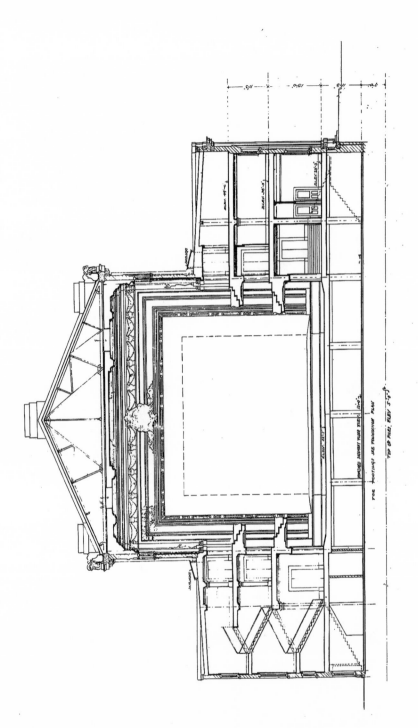

THE·BOSTON·MUSIC·HALL.
MC·KIM·MEAD·&·WHITE·, ARCHITECTS.
160 FIFTH AVENUE.
NEW YORK.

Transverse section looking north.

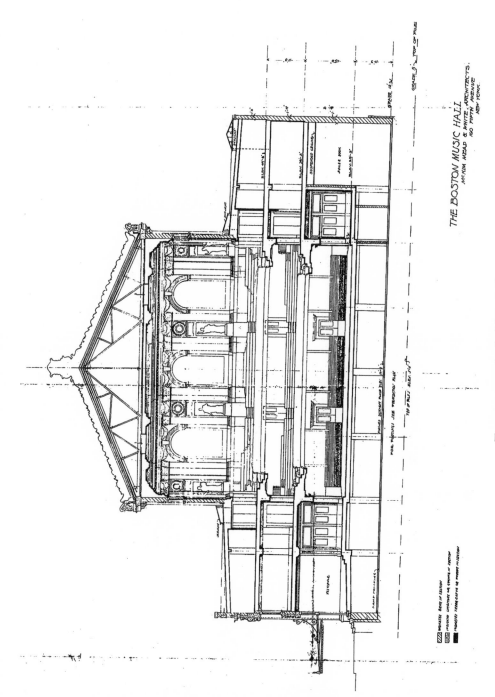

THE BOSTON MUSIC HALL

McKIM, MEAD & WHITE, ARCHITECTS.
160 FIFTH AVENUE
NEW YORK.

Transverse section looking south.

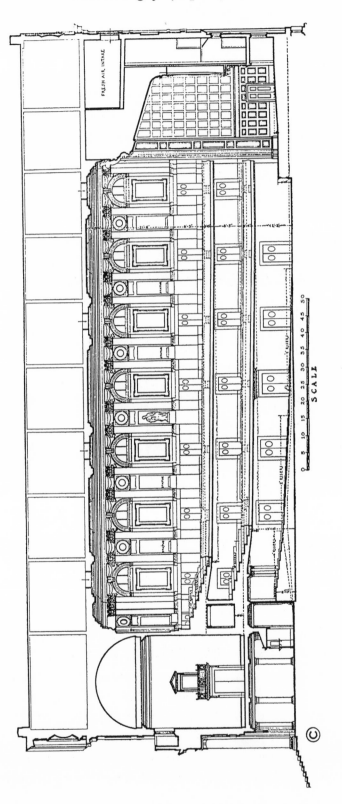

Longitudinal section.

avenue side, and that at the main entrance will be used only prior to and during performances. The long standing complaint of draughts in the old hall will have no ground to stand on in the new hall, for it is proposed to close the two inner doors leading directly to the auditorium, and to send people round to the right and left to doors large enough to make congestion impossible. The two doors in question open directly on the two aisles, there being no centre or main aisle. It is estimated that, if necessary, the entire audience, assuming that the floor is filled, can be turned into the broad lobbies which encircle the auditorium.

In the old hall two sections of seats in the first balcony overlook the stage; in the new hall not a seat throughout will be over the stage. There should be an abundance of coatrooms, since there are to be two on the first floor and two more on the second floor. The balcony will have four entrances. The corridors on the floor conform to the pitch of the floor itself, and there are no steps. In the summer when the chairs and other appurtenances are removed the floor can be made level. Taken all in all, it can be seen that the plans include many improvements over the old hall's arrangement, and promise to yield a structure which will be desirable and satisfactory both as a whole and in detail.

(35) McKim to Higginson, March 17, 1899, noting issues to be resolved.[288]

[Letterhead]
March 17, 1899.

Dear Mr. Higginson:
Yours of the 15th received yesterday, and we are glad to know that changes likely to be made will be confined to those mentioned by you, as any changes, involving the alteration of centres, would oblige, practically, a re-drawing of the plans. We have gone carefully over the question of the widening of the foyer into a smaller Hall, by a reduction in the length of the large Hall, and find that it can be accomplished, without materially affecting the plans already drawn. As I have already written you, it will be no improvement to the proportion of the large hall to cut down its length, but if, acoustically, you consider that you have reason to believe that it will be better, we shall not oppose, provided such reduction does not exceed seven feet. If it is determined to make

this change, and to increase the foyer into a chamber music hall, sufficient to seat 450 to 500 people, then we should advocate the lowering of this hall from its present level (on the line of the second gallery) to the line of the first gallery, for although the lowering of the hall to this line would involve a considerable loss of height to the entrance vestibule, it would render the hall much more accessible from the ground floor, and I think we shall find a way to treat it, so that its apparent height will be sufficient. Moreover, at times when the hall is not used for chamber music, it would become an admirable foyer or banquet hall. Although, from the point of view of proportion, we are opposed to curtailment in the length of the large hall, no doubt the acoustic reasons which actuate you, justify this decision.

We expect to have a copy of the specifications ready for approval by the 25th, and, on the same day, a set of drawings, for estimates. Allowing a week for the study of the question, with Norcross, we should be able to report to you, by May 1st, and to submit to you a reliable approximate estimate of the cost of the building. If satisfactory, a piling and foundation contract can be let, in advance of the closing of the general contract, in this way saving much time, and affording us an opportunity to complete our drawings at all points, without delaying the progress of the work.

The question of heating and ventilation should receive immediate attention, as the boiler room forms a part of the foundation plan, and should be started as soon as possible.

Yours very truly,

Charles F. McKim

(36) Higginson to McKim, March 24, 1899, conveying views of Professor Charles R. Cross and Mr. Cotting.[289]

[Letterhead]
March 24, 1899.

Dear Mr. McKim:

I saw Professor Cross of the Technology yesterday and had a long talk with him. He had studied the plans with a good deal of care. His opinion and that of Professor Sabine coincide almost entirely.

Professor Cross suggests that pilasters, or some roughness on the walls of that nature between the galleries, and indeed the lower gallery, if quite convenient, would help the sound, — that is, would prevent an echo. Will you kindly think of this?

He would be glad to see the hall a few feet lower, if possible. He would not wish the roof of the stage too high. He would line the stage, above and below, with wood set off from the plastering an inch to three inches, and he would line the whole hall in the same way, if possible. On this last point Professor Sabine has reserved his opinion and will give it a little later, as he is making experiments. Professor Cross declined glass absolutely as being too hard a material.

Professor Cross thinks highly of the plans. He would avoid drafts of cold air and hot air and, without expressing an opinion on the system of ventilation, in a general way, likes it. He expressed the belief that many halls where the sound was bad suffered from using the wrong material for the walls. This talk was very complimentary and satisfactory to me, and he is an absolutely simple, straightforward man, very intelligent and very well educated — the man upon whom Mr. Storrow of the Bell telephone relied more than upon anybody else as a physicist. I think we are right on this side.

As to boilers, — the boiler room is in the right place and is none too large. The coal bin is in the wrong place, as it should be on the alley and near the boiler. Mr. Cotting is studying that question and will report, but we do not want it on Commonwealth [sic] Ave. Mr. Cotting will remind you once more that the basement of the hall will be very low, as we can go down but a little distance on account of tide water, therefore the space under the floor will be small. This is said in relation to a place where we may put the benches etc. from the stage. Mr. Cotting is studying that question also, but does not see any reason for keeping back the plans on that account.

Mr. Cotting and I both think that the elevator should go to the upper story. When the building is in hand Mr. Cotting proposes to use such space for these platforms etc. as he has.

We hold our stockholders' meeting Tuesday and shall be glad to say that the working drawings are all in order and the specifications made. We really ought to break ground at the earliest possible moment.

I think of nothing more to add tonight.

I have said several times, and repeat, that, if it will hasten matters, I am ready to go over to New York on Monday afternoon or later. We think we have done all the talking we can on this subject and now need to act, and I would not keep you back one moment.

Yours truly,

H. L. Higginson

(37) *George B. de Gersdorff (McKim, Mead & White) to Higginson, March 31, 1899, describing minor changes in the plans.*[290]

[Letterhead]
March 31, 1899.

Dear Mr. Higginson —
We send you tonight by special two drawings showing the Basement and First floor plans [rearranged?] in accordance with the ideas discussed at your visit to the office on Wednesday.

We have increased the size of the tuning-room so that it now measures 33' x 57' and at the same time we have enlarged the serving room and placed the coal entrance on the alley way. To do this we have sacrificed the Men's toilet room on the First floor and have placed it in the Basement, and arranged a stairway under the main stairs on the Mass. Ave side.

We have also shown the vestibule on Mass. Ave. enlarged to 17' x 48', with three doors instead of one as formerly. This [however?] necessitates the placing of the Ladies' toilet room in the Basement, reached by a special stairway from the Ladies' Reception Room; and also the loss of one of the Office rooms (that formerly marked "Mr Ellis") which we propose to place either on the second floor or in a Mezzanine story, reached in either case by a small staircase shown on First floor plan.

Your approval of any or all of these changes would help us in completing our working drawings. Will you kindly return the tracings when you have finished discussing these questions as we have taken no copies —

Very truly yours
McKim Mead & White
per G.B. de Gersdorff

(38) Financial adjustments: Open letter of Major Higginson to the people of Boston, June 5, 1899.[291]

Henry L. Higginson, president of the Boston Music Hall corporation, has issued the following letter to the public of Boston:

For many months the directors of the New Music Hall have studied the various questions concerning its construction under the advice and with the help of the architect and of other experts, and have tried to secure the essential points of a successful hall. These points are excellent heating and ventilation, good light, safety from fire and from fright, and finally strong and fine sound through the hall. Beauty of form and of ornament are also desired, and of these the directors have got much. But the essential points are very costly. It is not easy to keep twenty-five hundred people comfortable in a great room (each person being a small furnace of a different temperature) and to supply constantly their lungs and brains with fresh, warm air, and at the same time to avoid ill effects on sound by currents of air. Safety enough for . . . [sic] and for imagination is less difficult, if the purse is fairly long.

As to acoustics, the directors have had the best advice obtainable, and believe that much of this science has become known through late studies and experiments. The directors were fortunate in the purchase of land which today, even if obtainable on that spot, would cost $120,000 more than the price paid — and elsewhere a much higher figure. The total cost of the hall inclusive of organ and seats, and exclusive of the land, will be about $500,000. The directors have kept the contracts at the lowest point and have scrupulously turned away from reasonable wishes and suggestions of the architects, who on their side have striven to secure the essential points and to keep the artistic side subordinate.

At the present time the treasurer of the hall has $166,000, he having spent the rest of the receipts — about $200,000 — for the land, taxes and expenses. Before signing the contracts he should certainly have $300,000 cash. Even then a mortgage of $200,000 will be necessary.

It is expected that I should lease the building for ten years, agreeing to pay the taxes, the cost of administration and the interest on the mortgage — probably $40,000 in all yearly — and to pay to the stockholders of the hall any earnings beyond these above expenses. This lease I am ready to make. Thus the stockholders are for ten years at least free from possibility of loss, except that of interest on their investment, and they may enjoy an increase of value.

I venture to lay these facts before a public which has been for eighteen years invariably kind and generous to me, and to add that my share of the musical enterprise during all this period of time has been heavy and can never be light. The invariable experience of the world has been that artistic or educational undertakings of a high order cannot succeed without subsidy. Of this I was sure eighteen years ago, and am quite content with the results gained. The old hall is entirely unfit for its uses, and a new hall must be built at once or music be without a home in Boston.

I heartily thank my fellow citizens for their generosity in the past, and earnestly ask them to raise the sum in the treasurer's hands to $300,000 at least. Today the contracts are awaiting execution, and as the new hall must be in use April 1, 1900, no time is to be lost. Subscriptions may be sent to Mr. C. E. Cotting, 9 Tremont street, who will issue the shares of the company.

Henry L. Higginson

(39) *McKim to Higginson, November 3, 1899, urging prompt settlement of "the organ question."*[292]

[Letterhead]
Nov. 3rd, 1899.

Dear Mr. Higginson:
We have been waiting for the settlement of the organ question, upon which depends the design of the wooden panelling called for around the stage. We are now far advanced, and shall soon be without other work. Cannot this matter be taken up and settled, so that we may not be delayed in the completion of the interior design, which, by the way, promises to be more successful than some people might think!
Yours very truly,
Charles F. McKim

(40) *George S. Hutchings & Company to McKim, Mead & White, November 7, 1899, reviewing past understandings regarding the "organ space."*[293]

Boston, Nov. 7, 1899.

Gentlemen:

Replying to your favor of Nov. 3rd would say, that I had an interview yesterday with Messrs. Higginson and Cotting, both of whom are very much disappointed and disturbed at the present condition of affairs regarding the organ space at Music Hall.

Now you will no doubt remember that I visited you in New York at the request of Mr. Higginson to determine the space required for the organ. You will no doubt also remember that I told you it would be an impossibility to get an organ into the space retaining the two passageways, one each on a level with the first and second balcony. You stated that these were unimportant and could be dispensed with, and while Mr. Cotting is disappointed at the loss of them, still I think he would accede to the requirements of the instrument.

The raising of the ceiling of the stage portion of the wall they both objected to, as they think it will destroy the acoustic properties of the house, and while I do not agree with them in this, still it would be very difficult to make them look at the matter as I do.

I had supposed when I left you that the entire matter was settled, as you will remember you gave orders to your two assistants, who were working upon the plan, to change the plans omitting the two passages, and I have a tracing showing this. Then you will no doubt remember that you made the suggestion of carrying up the ceiling by omitting the splayed cornice at the top, carrying the perpendicular mouldings straight up to the ceiling, thus giving a greater amount of height. I have gone ahead upon these lines and laid out my work and have it well in hand, so something must be determined at once.

Very truly yours,

Geo. S. Hutchings & Co.

(41) *McKim to Higginson, November 8, 1899, pressing for firm instructions regarding the organ matter.*[294]

[Letterhead]
Nov. 8th, 1899.

Dear Mr. Higginson:

In reply to yours of Nov. 6th, and in relation to Mr. Hutchings and the organ, let me say that beyond a single visit from Mr. Hutchings some months ago, during which we conversed in a general way about the subject, I have not seen him since, the questions involved being referred back to the Committee, whom he was to see, and whose conclusions, with his, we were to embody in the plan. Since then, the matter has been allowed to rest. From an architectural point of view, we should naturally be glad to have as much height as possible, but recognizing that the question was primarily one of acoustics, I advised Mr. Hutchings that any change of height, or other alterations, must be determined by the Committee. Under these circumstances, why he should quote me, as proposing to increase the height of the stage 8 feet, I cannot understand, and such a statement is unauthorized. We are not giving any advice as to the treatment of the organ, nor the height or other dimensions of the stage. What we want are instructions on the subject. We need this data to enable us to proceed with the design of the surrounding panelling.

As to the passages behind the organ, on the level of the first and second galleries, connecting one wing of the stage with the other, they may be retained or omitted as you may consider advisable. If required for pipes, direct access, from one side of the house to the other, can be had only by descending to [the] passage on stage level and ascending on the other side.

Awaiting your decision,

Yours very truly,

C. F. McKim

(42) Sabine to McKim, November 12, 1899, proposing a solution to the organ difficulty.[295]

Jefferson Physical Laboratory,
Harvard University,
Cambridge, Mass.,
Nov 12, 1899

Dear Mr. McKim:

I spent Saturday afternoon with Mr Hutchings. I think he is persuaded, although no final decision has been reached, that the best result, best even from the standpoint of his organ, would be an open grill, similar to that which you are placing in several sections of the ceiling, forming a strip along the sloping ceiling in front of the organ and reaching across the whole stage [see sketch on p. 80]. I should like to inquire whether this will be architecturally possible. I feel very sure that it will furnish more of an outlet for his swell and pedal organs than would the display pipes even if the ceiling were raised, as he wishes it, eight feet. I feel very sure, also, that Mr Hutchings will agree with this after he has thought it over, but whether it is architecturally possible or artistically desirable is another matter, and I do not want to urge it except with your entire agreement. If you would like to have me, I shall be very glad to come down to New York to talk it [and?] any other points that may have come up.

When you have the details of the hall finished I should be very glad if I could get at them for use in preparing an illustration for an article on acoustics. I should like to make the drawing as complete and more attractive than that of the Leipsic Gewandhaus which I have. I should also want to submit the article to you before publication, in as much as [it] would concern one of your creations. [See Appendix A.]

Very truly yrs

Wallace C. Sabine

*(43) McKim to Higginson, November 15, 1899, asking preparation of inscriptions
     for the front and side panels.*[296]

[Letterhead]
November 15th, 1899.

Dear Mr. Higginson:
In order to avoid delay, and because the question of inscriptions, as we have
found it, at Harvard, Columbia, the Shaw Monument, the Public Library,
and elsewhere, is a serious one, requiring time, I write to ask if you will not
compose, or cause to be composed, the inscriptions indicated on the accompanying memorandum, namely that of the main panel, over the portico; also
that in the panel over the side entrance, both included in the contract, and
for which the contractor is now crying out, in order that he may be ready with
his work when the time to set it arrives.

    We feel that nothing imparts such dignity and scholarly character, as the
wise use of inscriptions, and are depending largely, in the case of your Music
Hall, upon their use. They may be either commemorative, or express the
value of Music in some great sentence — which, however, please note, must
fall within the number of letters specified. The number of these letters is determined by their size, which has been made to be legible, as seen from the
opposite sidewalk.
Very truly yours,
Charles F. McKim

[ENCLOSURE]

November 15th, 1899.
Memorandum concerning Inscriptions, Boston Music Hall.
Exterior Panels, bearing Inscriptions:
Main Panel over Portico. Letters varying from 10 to 14 inches in height. 79 let-
ters contracted for. Can be increased up to 118 letters. Additional letters, say
$2.50 each.
Side Elevation:
Panel over side entrance. 31 letters, 4 to 6 inches in height. Included in contract.

(44) McKim to Higginson, December 1, 1899, with further suggestions regarding inscriptions.[297]

[Letterhead]
Dec. 1st, 1899.

Dear Mr. Higginson:

I send you the accompanying photograph of the Fountain of POPE PAUL V, for the sake of the great panel which surmounts it, and from which that on the South front of the Music Hall was based. While, of course, our panel is but a reflection of the Roman example, it is of sufficient importance in the scale of the Music Hall to make its inscription of great consequence.

Since writing you the other day, I feel that the most dignified thing to do, in view of its size, would be to make the inscription rather a page out of the history of the Institution, as at Columbia, and referring, or not, as may be thought best, to the public spirit and munificence of the promotors, rather than any sentence or quotation taken from however great a source. The idea of the foundation of a permanent Orchestra for the Advancement of Music, seems text enough for an inscription that would justify three times the space at our command. However, we are only entitled, under the contract, to 79 letters, but this can be increased, without crowding the panel, to 118 letters, as stated to you in my letter of Nov. 15th.

I have today received from Mr. Hooper the form of date used in the Harvard College Commencement programme, for 1899.[298] In acknowledging his letter, I have posted him a little as to the subject of the main inscription.

Hoping that you will be able to furnish us with the inscription as soon as possible, in order that the work may not be delayed,
Yours very truly,
Charles F. McKim

P.S. The enclosed photograph of the Portico of Columbia College Library shows the university inscription, written by President [Seth] Low, and approved by the Trustees. An enlarging glass will make it clear to you.

All those who visited the Fair will remember [Harvard] President [Charles William] Eliot's splendid inscriptions, upon the Arch or Watergate opening to the Lake from the Court of Honor.

Please have the photographs returned to us when you are through with them.

(45) *Hooper to McKim, December 19, 1899, offering suggestions relative to the proposed inscriptions.*[299]

50 State St. Boston
Dec. 19' 1899.

Dear Mr McKim

I have just received yours of Dec. 18' about Music Hall inscriptions. Since I received your letters of Dec' 1' and 8' I have given much thought to the matter, and have consulted many judicious persons about it, with little result. Substantial objections have been made to every suggestion of a commemorative sort. The old Music Hall was built by a joint-stock company, which has been dissolved, after paying its stockholders their money with fair interest. The new hall is also built by a joint-stock company with a fair chance of a like ending within fifty years, or less time. The old hall now belongs to speculative people who may for years use it as a public hall under the name of "Boston Music Hall." To prevent confusion, while the old hall is used, the word "New" must be part of our title. Is it then best to cut now any title on our hall?

The new hall is built primarily in the interest of music, but it is not a gift to the public, as a matter of form. The Boston Symphony Orchestra is not as yet endowed as a permanent body, and it may hereafter change its name. On the whole, it seems to me best to leave your panels (except the date) blank rather than to cut now a commemorative inscription.

In your letter of Nov' 15', to Mr Higginson, you suggested that the inscriptions might "be either commemorative," or "they may express the value of music in some great sentence" — Mr Higginson turned over the whole matter to Dr. Bigelow and myself, and we sent you the quotations from Shakespeare, as suggestions which seemed to meet the approval of some of our critical friends. If used on your large panel as two separate quotations (with the same idea of the charm of music) they may give as much satisfaction as anything else would.

> *Here will we sit and let the sounds*
> *of music creep in our ears.*
> *Let rich music's tongue unfold*
> *the imagined happiness*

Whatever we do, it seems to me much safer not to cut anything until the stones are in place. Then any proposed inscription can be drawn on the stone in chalk, and its effect discussed before it is too late to change.

I find that neither Mr Cotting nor Mr Norcross cares whether we cut the inscription now or afterwards.

As to your panel for the date there will be no trouble, if we use the date *1900* in the form of the Harvard Commencement programme.

Mr Higginson leaves the old hall for the new in 1900.

I am not "telling" you. I am only "arguing" with you.

Yours sincerely

Edward W. Hooper

---

(46) *McKim to Higginson, December 29, 1899, urging prompt settlement of the inscription matter (excerpt).*[300]

[Letterhead]

December 29, 1899.

Dear Mr. Higginson:

★ ★ ★

In relation to the inscription, over the main entrance of the Music Hall, should you decide to consult with President Eliot, as you intimated yesterday, would it not be well to let him see the design of the PAULUS V FOUNTAIN, (photograph of which I sent you recently) as showing the style of lettering which we are anxious to suggest, and furnish him at the same time with the number of letters possible, indicated in the memorandum sent you? Buhler, the contractor, hopes to complete his contract, except the lettering, by January 25th, weather permitting, and if the interval between now and then can be employed to settle the question of the inscription, he will not be delayed, and it will enable us to remove the scaffolding in front of the building within the shortest possible time. Norcross told me that he would be as glad as we to have the scaffold down and out of the way.

Forgive me for adding to your cares.

Very truly yours,

C. F. McKim

(47) Higginson to McKim, Mead & White, January 18, 1900, urging an additional aisle in the new hall.[301]

[Letterhead]

January 18, 1900.

Gentlemen:

The arrangement of the seats on the floor of the New Music Hall indicated on your plan gives four aisles running the length of the room. The men who have had long experience in selling tickets and seating audiences in the old hall strongly urge the necessity of a fifth aisle in the centre, to make shorter rows of seats. They tell me that it is very difficult to get people to buy seats in the middle of a long row on account of the inconvenience of reaching them, and, in their minds, no row should contain more than 10 seats. They also remind me that practically the entire audience at the Symphony concerts expects to be seated in six or eight minutes and that it is impossible to do this with long rows of seats and only four aisles.

It is also suggested that, as the side exits to the lobby will be fewer than in the old hall, the number of aisles should not be less. The aggregate width of the four aisles shown on your plan averages about 14' 8". By making five aisles, each 3' or 3' 6" wide, we should not lose many seats and the public would be better accommodated. Apart from the loss of the seats, is there any objection to running a middle aisle the length of the hall, or at least as far back as the first cross aisle?

Very truly yours,

H.L. Higginson

P.S. The longest row on the floor of our present Music Hall contains 10 seats only; the Metropolitan Opera House 10 seats, and in Carnegie Hall 9 seats.

(48) de Gersdorff to Higginson, January 19, 1900, defending present disposition of aisles and exits.[302]

[Letterhead]
January 19, 1900

Dear Mr. Higginson —

In answer to your letter in regard to the number of aisles in the Music Hall we wish to state that it will be very difficult, if not impossible, to make a change in the rear of the hall, that is, back of the cross aisle, as the columns under the balcony and all the [word illegible] of openings in the lobby, vestibule and part of [two words illegible] depend on the position of these aisles. The longest row in this part of the hall contains 12 seats, so that no person has more than 5 seats to pass by to reach an aisle.

In front of the cross aisle we have, in the center, rows of 13 seats. At the sacrifice of a considerable number of seats we [might?] introduce another aisle forward of the cross aisle, but such an arrangement would be much less economical of space.

As to the number of side exits to the lobbies, there are now five doors shown on each side in our present plans, which we believe to be the number in the old Music Hall. There are in addition to these side doors two doors at the back.

Mr. [Thomas A.] Fox[303] is expected here on Monday and we should have an opportunity to go over this matter with him and he will see you about it when he returns to Boston.

Yours respectfully,
McKim, Mead & White
per G. B. de Gersdorff

(49) *Sabine to Higginson, March 8, 1900, discussing various acoustical matters.*[304]

[Letterhead]
March 8th 1900.

Major H.L. Higginson,
Dear Sir:
Wood lining for the stage is desirable but with the organ occupying the whole of the stage at the back, only the aisles and roof remain for consideration, and the gain to be made here is really slight; so that if for any reason wood is undesirable, through danger from fire or architecturally, it ought not to be insisted upon. Were the whole hall to be finished in wood I should be more actively interested, but the amount under consideration is small, and I am willing to take the responsibility of leaving it off, though subjectively even this small display of wood will increase the acceptability of the hall to the public by gratifying a long established — and not wholly unreasonable — prejudice. Should you use wood, the lightest would be the most desirable, and an inch clearance sufficient.

Should the hall at any time fail of an audience — of a full house — the kind of seats put in will make a great deal of difference. I hope that they may be upholstered at least as well as in the old hall. With a full house this of course makes no difference.

May I take this opportunity to suggest that in order to compare the two halls it would be well if the first of your concerts next year should be of music that had been heard in the old hall. I am anxious that the comparison should be a decisive one and such comparison would be the more close on strong and well liked music.

I wish that I might have heard the concert in Carnegie Hall to which you refer and indeed that I might hear the orchestra in a consecutive series of concerts on one of its trips, I may perhaps find it possible to do so.
Very truly yours,
Wallace C. Sabine

(50) *Thomas A. Fox, Boston architect, to Higginson, March 20, 1900, assuring him the work is progressing well.*[305]

Thomas A. Fox
Alexander S. Jenney
Edwards J. Gale
ARCHITECTS
Phillips Building, 120 Tremont St.,
Boston

Henry L. Higginson
Dear Sir,
I have just talked with Mr. McKim on the long distance telephone. He says the drawing for the organ front will be here tomorrow. This will clear up the last architectural matter of importance. In spite of appearances to the contrary I think the work is progressing well and as soon as a start is made in the plastering which will be within a day or two things will seem to move much faster than they have been. I see no reason why the work should not be practically finished at the time set. If you go to the building often I should like to meet you there and if there is any way in which I can help matters along I shall be pleased to do so.
Yours truly,
Thomas A. Fox
Mch. 20. 1900

(51) *Sabine to Ellis, March 22, 1900, reporting on discussions with McKim in New York.*[306]

[Letterhead]
March 22, 1900.

Dear Sir: —
I received your letter yesterday just before the beginning of the concert in Carnegie Hall. I had already seen Mr. McKim in regard to the new Music Hall, talking over with him all the questions that apparently remained. He and I agreed that pine would probably be the best. It is the material, which I

had in mind when I wrote to you. Other soft and light woods *might* serve the purpose and would be a little less expensive, but would be more liable to warp and check.

The trip proved profitable and very encouraging in regard to the new Hall. I desire to thank you and Mr. Higginson for the courtesies shown me on the trip.

Very truly yours,

Wallace C. Sabine

(52) McKim to Higginson, March 26, 1900, commenting further on the proposed inscription (excerpt).[307]

[Letterhead]

March 26th, 1900.

Dear Mr. Higginson:

I was very glad to hear from George de Gersdorff this morning, that the question of the inscription, upon which the success of the front of the Music Hall, on Huntington Avenue, depends so much, has again come up, and that you have decided to take counsel with President Eliot. We sent you recently a photograph of the PAULIST VTH[308] Fountain in Rome, with a similar panel of inscription, showing the arrangement of lines and lettering, from which I am anxious to type that of the Music Hall. If this commends itself to you, please have the photograph sent to President Eliot, with a request that he return it to us when through with it. De Gersdorff will send you the number of letters, (maximum and minimum,) adapted for the space.

    ★ ★ ★

I was sorry to have been out when you called last week.

Very truly yours,

C. F. McKim

*(53) McKim to Higginson, April 14, 1900, discussing several matters of
decoration.*[309]

[Letterhead]
April 14th, 1900.

Dear Mr. Higginson:

Referring to your despatch as to the models, we telegraphed you yesterday
stating that the models were packed and shipped on Wednesday, as previously
stated. Before the despatch left this office, and on communicating with Buhler,
the contractor, we found that the models had been actually shipped on Tuesday, the day before. Since that time, three additional consignments have been
shipped, and, as Mr. Fox, who was here yesterday, informs us, Mr. Monroe, the
contractor, has not been delayed for a moment.

Mr. Monroe has just completed for us, in the Capitol at Providence, the best
piece of plain & decorative plaster I have ever seen, and may be relied upon to
make a perfect success of the Music Hall work. Without good models, this is
not possible, and it was for this reason that we insisted on having the models
made under our own direction here in New York, where they could receive
constant superintendence.

Full size details of the organ front have been sent to Mr. Fox, who will carry
them to you for approval. They conform with the 3/4-scale smaller drawing,
which you have already seen.

In regard to the color decoration, and referring to yours of the 10th, we are
making a scheme, which will be explained to you by Mr. Fox, through whom
it will be sent. It provides for a maximum of water color and a minimum of oil
paint, in order to save expense, and while the term "Decoration" can hardly
be applied, we have proposed the least which will, in our judgment, enable you
to make a respectable opening of the building.

Very truly yours,

C. F. McKim

(54) McKim to Higginson, April 20, 1900, pressing for text of the inscription (excerpt).[310]

[Letterhead]
April 20th, 1900.

Dear Mr. Higginson:
I find the enclosed on my desk, in relation to the Music Hall inscription. Norcross was here the day before yesterday, and is anxious to satisfy his sub-contractor, Buhler, who is to carve the inscription, and has otherwise completed his work. Mr. Norcross says he is very anxious to get the scaffold down. Please furnish us with the inscription as soon as you can.
★ ★ ★

Very truly yours,
C. F. McKim

(55) McKim to Higginson, April 24, 1900, stressing importance of the inscription and discussing interior decoration.[311]

[Letterhead]
April 24th, 1900.

Dear Mr. Higginson:
We are all disappointed about the inscription on the Huntington Avenue front. The panel designed to carry it, and supported in arrangement by the columns below, forms an important part of the whole composition of the front (already sufficiently denuded by Mr. Cotting's ruthless economies), and if the inscription is now also taken away from us, in addition to the loss of the Cotting details above alluded to, I fear the building will look, when it is finished, more like a deaf, dumb and blind institution, than a Music Hall. But I am not so unreasonable as this sounds. I recognize the difficulty of getting what you want, so I suppose we must be content to wait until you can agree as to what is best to put there; but I urge you solemnly not to abandon the inscription, without which the panel intended for it will be meaningless, and the facade on Huntington Avenue unintelligible.

As to the color scheme, we are glad that you approve of the general proposition of the use of water-color and oil color, and will now go forward and
prepare such specifications as may be necessary to get estimates and carry it
out. While this does not pretend to be a work of permanent decoration, it
becomes all the more important that it should be carried out under the daily
superintendence of a competent eye. In the interest of the result, therefore we
would propose, in addition to our own superintendence, the employment of a
man appointed for this purpose. We know such a man, whom we would like
to name, who would live on the job from the start to the finish, and whom we
could trust from experience to carry out our directions. Mead agrees with me
that this would be an economy to you, and a safeguard for the result. We could
probably agree with Mr. Lawrence (the man referred to) upon a small lump
sum, including the cost of his board and travelling expenses while the work
was being done. Let us know how this strikes you, and meanwhile we will proceed with detail specifications.

Fox has rather a sleepy way about him, it is true, but he stands for good
work, and is a reliable man. I have given him a friendly blast this morning.
Yours very truly,
C. F. McKim

(56) *McKim, Mead & White to Higginson, April 28, 1900, discussing status of
balcony rail and staircases, and painting.*[312]

[Letterhead]
April 28th, 1900.

Dear Sir:
In reply to yours of the 26th, and in relation to the balcony rail and staircase,
all possible pressure is being brought to bear to get this work through. It is
being turned out as fast as is consistent with good workmanship, and the
Hecla Company is fully cognizant of the importance of its being shipped at
the earliest moment.

If you will kindly send the enclosed letter to Messrs Norcross Bros., in
reply to theirs of the 24th, (appended) with the assurance that we are bring-
ing daily pressure to bear, it may relieve their minds.

We see no reason why the Hecla Company's contract should not be carried out, without delaying the work. Norcross is naturally anxious, with a limited time, but the Hecla Company are amongst the most responsible contractors in this city, and, as you will observe, Norcross expresses full confidence in them.

In regard to the superintendence of the color decoration, Mr. Lawrence is a practical decorator himself, upon whose taste and discretion we can rely in the mixing of the colors. Much depends upon the success of this part of the work, which cannot be left to a contractor.

Hoping to meet you on Tuesday, when we will have the painter's specifications ready for estimate, and in order that we may be able to settle all details, Yours very truly,

McKim, Mead & White

[ENCLOSURE][313]

Apr. 27th,

Messrs. McKim, Mead & White, Archts.,

#160-5th Ave., New York, N.Y.

Gentlemen, —

As to the stairs and gallery railings we are making for Norcross Bros. would state that we lack no information or are we detained in any way by you in completing this work. It is being pushed as fast as it is possible to make it. Parts of the gallery railings had to be cast so that the ornamental figures could be modeled on them. Owing to the many hands this work has to pass through a certain time has to be allowed to complete it.

On Tuesday next we will ship some of the stair work and in a very short time thereafter the marble treads can be fitted and the plastering be done around the stairs. In the course of a week we can commence shipment of gallery railings, and expect to complete in three or four weeks.

Yours very truly,

Hecla Iron Works

(57) McKim, Mead & White to Higginson, May 18, 1900, reporting on painting arrangements and stage lighting.[314]

[Letterhead]
May 18th, 1900.

Dear Sir:

We are expecting the estimates for the painting of the interior of the Music Hall at any moment, and as soon as received will forward the same to you.

Mr. H.M. Lawrence, concerning whom we wrote you recently, in connection with the above painting, has made a careful study of the work to be done, and we are very glad to be able to write you that he agrees if desired, to undertake the charge of it, at a cost of $500, with $100 for travelling and expenses, added. We estimate that the work ought to be completed within six weeks from the time the contract is let, and Mr. Lawrence has made his estimate upon this basis. We are prepared, however, in the event of any further expense attaching to Mr. Lawrence's employment, to assume it ourselves. We hope that this will be satisfactory to you. We feel that this will assure the execution of the work in a manner that will be creditable to all concerned.

With this, we send you by express today, drawings showing a proposition from Mr. E.F. Caldwell, who is now engaged upon the contract for the light fixtures for the hall, for a pair of bracket lights, for the illumination of the stage, placed behind and immediately above the musicians, and sufficient in power to properly illuminate the stage. The present wiring, behind the projected moldings of the proscenium arch, calls for no fixtures, and none have as yet been provided upon the stage.

The enclosed letter from Mr. Caldwell [not in file], provides for the number of lights mentioned, massed at two points, and wherever they are essential to the proper illumination of the stage. Each projects 6 feet, and is made up of 24 lights. The small scale drawings of the stage show the position of the lights; the working drawing shows what is proposed, in full detail. The price is reasonable.

Awaiting your instructions,
Very truly yours,
McKim, Mead & White

(58) McKim to Higginson, from Boston, June 15, 1900, reporting impressions of interior decoration.[315]

Norcross Brothers,
General Contractors,
New Music Hall Building.
Boston, Mass.
Friday m[ornin]g June 15 [1900]

Dear Mr Higginson,
The walls and ceiling are beginning to have some relation — & enough of the ground tones of the first, are now determined to make it safe to go forward with the finish work [?] of the ceiling, commencing today — and the contractor will start in upon this with a force of men at once — this will enable a large part of the scaffolding to come down — and amongst other things give us a better sight, (& I hope *insight* into the walls —)[.] I staid over at Lawrence's request — to see the effect under the Electric which was turned on last night, and even with the scaffolds filling the hall, we were both gratified with the response of [the] walls to the light — the greys pulling together harmoniously & clearly defined — (of course the arc-light is viciously strong & turns everything black & white, but making allowances for this, I am not afraid to go into court on the result — The red BASE (walls under 1st gallery, we shall tackle like the gold — last — but I do not doubt the wisdom of its use in the end (I refer to the red) We shall need very little

I expect to be back again in a week, or earlier. Lawrence has his hands full, but a clear course on ceiling and walls down to 1st balcony — & am leaving him for New York at one in a good frame of mind —
In haste yrstry
C. F. McK

(59) McKim to Higginson, June 18, 1900, announcing another visit to Boston.[316]

[Letterhead]
June 18th, 1900.

Dear Mr. Higginson:

This is to say that I expect to leave on Wednesday [June 20], probably in the morning, reaching Boston at 3 o'clock, for the purpose of getting the electric that night and also the morning light, on the walls of the Music Hall, the next day.

I want to have a look at the Club House excavation [in Cambridge], and, if possible, catch the 5 o'clock train on Thursday back to New York.

No news is good news, and so long as I hear nothing to the contrary, I am hoping that all is well with the Music Hall interior.

Yours very truly,

C. F. McKim

(60) McKim, Mead & White to Higginson, June 19, 1900, asking authority to proceed with stage lighting.[317]

[Letterhead]
June 19th, 1900.

Dear Sir:

Mr. Caldwell tells us that he has not as yet received any decision from you, in relation to the bracket lights behind the musicians, of which full size details and estimates were sent you some time ago. Will you kindly decide this matter, so that the work may in some form be put in hand. In a recent letter, you acknowledged its receipt, and approved the general character of the design, but gave us no authority to act. The price was, we believe, $750 for the two brackets.

Respectfully,

McKim, Mead & White

(61) McKim to Higginson, from the Music Hall, June 21, 1900, commenting on interior color scheme (excerpt).[318]

Music Hall
11.30 — Thursday

Dear Mr Higginson,
I find Lawrence needs me here, so I shant try to talk Club house with you this m[ornin]g, but send over the photograph of Kings Col. Cambridge Commons Hall —

★ ★ ★

Mr Hooper has just gone — also Mrs Whitman — We are really not yet ready to see visitors — Mrs Whitman was sympathetic —

I have abandoned the use of red in the 2nd and 3rd galleries, for the purpose of being able to secure a stronger accent on the walls of the floor (*under 1st gallery*) —

I have no doubt of the correct use of strong color here, & its assistance to the whole scheme [.]

I have assured Mrs W. that *Red* is the correct note here, *& all right.* (green is beautiful but the right thing in the wrong place.

I shall be here till five — train — returning again as soon as notified by Lawrence probably within a week.
In haste Yrs
C. F. McK.

(62) O. W. Norcross to Higginson, July 13, 1900, reporting on status of construction.[319]

Norcross Brothers,
General Contractors,
Worcester, Mass.
July 13, 1900.

Dear Sir, —
Yours of July 11th at hand. On the day of our last interview I went to New York and did all I could to get a move on the balcony and stairs. The Hecla Iron Works have had a hard time; the work is elaborate and they have been both-

ered all summer by their men. I understand now that they have a full force there. Just as soon as the stage is down we will push the putting in of that floor very fast. They are now taking down the stage. I know of nothing else about the building except a few slate treads which have been delayed somewhere in transit. We expect them every day.

Yours truly,

O. W. Norcross

(63) *George S. Hutchings to Higginson, July 24, 1900, asking instructions on tuning the organ.*[320]

Geo. S. Hutchings & Co.
Church and Chapel
Organ Builders
Boston. New York.
Boston, July 24, 1900.

My dear Mr. Higginson, —

I was at the Music Hall this morning and met Messrs. Cotting, Fox and Ellis, all of whom impressed upon me the necessity of finishing the organ with the utmost despatch.

Now before Mr. [B.J.] Lang left for Europe he sent for one of us to come down and see him. Our superintendent answered the summons. Mr. Lang wished us to wait until his return from Europe before setting the pitch of the organ. Then he wished to get Mr. [Franz] Kneisel with one or two of the Oboe players to go to the hall and start the pitch from this. Now, as I understand it, Mr. Lang will not be here before the 15th of September, then it would take two weeks to tune the organ. Now the question is shall we wait, or shall we proceed with the work as fast as circumstances will permit?

If you care to see me on the subject, drop me a note or telephone me, and I will meet you.

Yours truly,

Geo. S. Hitchings

(64) Ellis to Higginson in Manchester, Massachusetts, August 13, 1900, reporting on construction and decoration.[321]

Lee, Higginson & Company,
44 State Street,
Boston,
August 13, 1900.

Dear Mr. Higginson:

The men are putting two iron panels on the upper balcony today. The rail is all on and the iron work on both balconies will be finished this afternoon with the exception of attaching eight cupids. These figures have not come, but the foreman has been notified that they will be here tomorrow, and he says it will be only a few hours work to put them on.

About one-half the oak rail for the balconies is now in position and the rest will be put on tonight.

The inclined floor is practically all laid, so that the seats can be put in immediately.

The flooring of the aisles is not laid and Mr. French says it will require about four days to lay it, as there is considerable fitting to be done on the wall aisles.

The radiators in the upper balcony are connected and all the painting in the upper balcony has been done.

The staging over the stage is partly down and will be entirely cleared out tomorrow. As soon as this staging is out of the way and the dust is settled, the painters will finish their work in the lower balcony and the gilding of the balcony fronts will be pushed forward.

Davenport's men are at work in the upper balcony and will have to wait for no one.

Mr. Lawrence has selected the plush for covering the balcony rail and is to see how it looks by electric light this evening.

Mr. Mead will be here tomorrow. If you wish to send him any word, I will see that he gets your message.

I enclose four letters.

I hope you will soon be over your lameness.

Yours truly,

C. A. Ellis

(65) Ellis to Higginson, August 15, 1900, reporting further progress (excerpt).[322]

[Letterhead]
August 15, 1900.

Dear Mr. Higginson:
All the staging in Music Hall has been taken down. Several painters are finishing the lower part of the walls of the stage, reached from the floor, and eight men are at work gilding the fronts of the balconies. Mr. Lawrence has asked Mr. Perry to put more men on to this work. The last in the way of painting in the interior of the hall has been finished. Eight cupids are still wanted, otherwise all the iron work in the auditorium is completed. Mr. Freitag telephones that he has been notified that the cupids have been shipped and they should be here tonight or tomorrow morning.

Mr. Davenport has 22 men on his job this morning, and they are at work on the seats both in the upper balcony and on the floor.

The door springs and other trimmings are being put on the balcony doors.

All but two fixtures for the electric lights are in place in the side lobbies of the first floor and lower balcony. The fixtures for the upper balcony lobby and the front floor lobby are yet to come from the factory. A strike delayed the contractor, but the trouble is over and the fixtures are now being made as fast as possible.

A sample shade for the circular windows has been ordered and will be tried soon.

Nobody is being hindered and there are no complaints.

★ ★ ★

Very truly yours,
C. A. Ellis

(66) Ellis to Higginson, August 18, 1900, reporting progress (excerpt).[323]

[Letterhead]
August 18, 1900.

Dear Mr. Higginson:

Mr. Lawrence reports that the painting is practically done in the auditorium and lobbies of Music Hall. The lower portion of the walls of the foyer and one of the side rooms are yet to be done, and will be painted as soon as vacated. The side room is filled with paint pots and the foyer is occupied in part by Davenport's men.

Eleven men are at work gilding the balcony fronts and a larger force will be put on next week.

Mr. Lawrence says that all the painting and gilding will easily be finished by September 1.

The seats are in place on the floor of the hall as far back as the edge of the centre balcony, — i.e., all but ten or a dozen rows on the floor. In the upper balcony the seats are in place except the wall row on the sides. These are being held until the radiators are moved back several inches. Somebody did not allow space enough for the seats here. About a third of the seats are placed in the lower balcony. The seats are being numbered and lettered.

All the iron work is finished and in place except the newell posts in the corridor at the foot of the stairways.

The work on the organ is going along well. Mr. Hutchings tells me that the blowing arrangements and motor are finished and he expects to start the motor this afternoon to blow the dust out. When this has been done, the pipes will go in. The pipes for the front of the organ are being gilded in the side room.

The radiators in the second balcony may make trouble on account of noise and they are apt to "bake" the seats which come snugly against them, but Mr. Cotting considers the radiators necessary.

Our carpenter has finished the platforms for the orchestra, and I have asked Mr. Lawrence to see that they are painted the proper color.

★ ★ ★

Yours truly,
C. A. Ellis

(67) Ellis to Higginson, August 21, 1900, reporting near-completion of construction and decoration.[324]

[Letterhead]
August 21, 1900.

Dear Mr. Higginson:
All the seats in the Music Hall will be in place by six o'clock tonight. A few changes will have to be made in some of the corners, but the work has been done.

More than one-half of the front of the upper balcony has been gilded and, perhaps, a quarter of the lower balcony front. Mr. Lawrence believes that the gilding will be finished next Tuesday. There will then be nothing more for the painters except renewing in spots, where the paint has been scratched, and doing odds and ends.

A performance could be given in the hall tonight, if it were necessary, without the organ.

The platforms for the Handel & Haydn chorus are being built.

★ ★ ★

Yours truly,
C. A. Ellis

(68) Ellis to Higginson, August 24, 1900, suggesting that the building be called "Higginson Hall" (excerpt).[325]

[Letterhead]
August 24, 1900.

Dear Mr. Higginson:

★ ★ ★

The instruments are being tried today in the new lockers. The plan was to number these lockers and let the musicians draw lots for them. This would save somebody the embarrassment of assigning them, and it would not be necessary to label them; but if you wish the names of the musicians marked on the inside or outside, I will have it done.

The fixtures for the coat rooms are going in at the Music Hall, and the little ticket office for the Huntington Ave. corridor is being built.

Work at the hall is going on without any hitches, and the building seems to be very near completion. What it lacks most is a proper title. "New Music Hall" is rather common and would convey the impression to strangers that it was a variety theatre. Mr. Savage continues to use the title "Boston Music Hall" for the old building, and it ~~would~~ will lead to confusion. Can we not call the new building "Higginson Hall"?

I am having envelopes addressed to the stockholders, and they will be ready for whatever notices you wish to send out. If you decide to give the stockholders complimentary tickets, I should think they ought to be notified about the first of September.

I enclose for revision a list of the seats reserved last year for the Symphony rehearsals and concerts.

Yours truly,

C. A. Ellis

[Handwritten postscript:]

It now looks as though there would be a great rush for seats for the inaugural concert and the house will probably be sold out. Herrick has received a great many orders. He says people are bound to go and expect to pay well and they will be disappointed if they don't have to pay a good price for seats — I hope you will decide not to give free tickets to stockholders.

(69) Higginson to McKim, Mead & White, August 28, 1900, reporting his impressions of the new hall.[326]

[Letterhead]

August 28, 1900.

Dear Sirs:

I have yesterday and today seen the Music Hall, which is pretty nearly complete. The front organ pipes are still to be put up and the organ to receive tuning. The painters are finishing and a few little jobs about the floor are to be done, after which the hall and the whole building are to be cleaned. Then, I think, we are done. I wish to say that it all seems to me very handsome. The green has added a good deal to the effect of the gallery and harmonizes the whole house. More than that, the rise from the front to the back, running as it were into the first gallery and so into the second, is very excellent. The stage, (which is somewhat marred by a staging now put up for the Chorus and which is ugly,) is very handsome. I also heard the organ yesterday and, so far as one can judge, the effect of the sound in the hall will be good. I am inclined to think it will be very good.

Two or three small matters remain — objectionable points. In the second gallery the back or second row of seats is too near the front seats. They are thrown out from the proper wall of the hall some six or eight inches by the pilasters and by the radiators. They are so near that people sitting in those seats (even if short-coupled like myself) will touch the hats of the people in front of them. Six inches more of gallery would have saved all this trouble, but it is too late to put those six inches on. The radiators were put in by Mr. Wolff and we cannot take them out, nor shall we touch in any way his arrangements for ventilating and heating. That must have every chance just as he has planned it. Even if the radiators were out, the pilasters would throw the chairs in front of them out of line, as above described. Very likely these chairs will have to be taken out, which will mean a loss of 40 seats. This is a pity. I see no way of changing this matter. If the pilasters were cut off it would deform the hall. Perhaps, you will look at it and see what may be done.

Next, the steps on Massachusetts Avenue, of which you have already been notified, protrude into the street and the city has ordered them off. We are now going to see what can be done to coax the city into a kindly move [sic: mood?], but this is problematical and it would seem as if the change would be merely a delay for a year, — that is, we would have to cut off those steps at the end of a year.

I am sorry for this last trouble, as it will cost a thousand or two dollars and a great deal of dirty work, and might have been avoided. The loss of seats will cost me about $40 a week, — say $1,000 for my season, — which, also, seems a pity.

I wish to thank you for your trouble and for your energy in pushing up the completion of the hall, but I hope this energy will last a little longer until the hall is in concert order.

We are without a name for the hall and you may be able to suggest something. Will you kindly think of it and write me? We should advertize [sic] the tickets very soon and should advertize them from some particular place.
Yours truly,
H. L. Higginson

(70) *Symphony Hall facts: Descriptive article from the* Boston Journal, *reprinted in the* Baltimore American, *October 15, 1900.*[327]

FINE HOME FOR MUSIC
Description of the New Symphony Hall in Boston

Symphony Hall, the new home for the Boston orchestra, in Boston, at Massachusetts and Huntington avenues, is thus described by the Journal, of that city:

Cheerfulness and warmth of color effects were the dominant characteristics of the hall to the Journal reporter who entered the auditorium about eight o'clock last evening.

The walls and ceiling are a very light gray in color, and the general plan of interior decorations being of the style of the Italian renaissance. There are two balconies, the seats in both all commanding a fine view of the stage.

All of the seats in the hall are upholstered in rich, dark green leather. They are about the same pattern as those in the old Music Hall, and are all alike. The seating capacity of the hall is 2,569. Of this number, [1,466] seats are on the floor, 598 in the first balcony, and 505 in the second balcony. The seating capacity of the old Music Hall was 2,307. Some of the best seats in the house are those in the upper balcony, which Major Higginson has decided shall be sold for 25 cents apiece for the Friday afternoon rehearsals. The custom maintained at the old hall is thus continued.

The proscenium arch is, perhaps, the most imposing feature of the hall. It is square and 62 feet by 45 feet in dimensions. A broad band of gold comprises the frame in which is worked a handsome design, consisting of acanthus leaves and fruits. On a wide golden scroll where the keystone of the arch would naturally be is the name of Beethoven.

A fine organ takes up the entire background of the stage. The decoration of this, as well as the walls of the stage, is in light gray, while the pipes are of gold. There are entrances to the stage at the right and left, through which the musicians can enter and retire.

The organ contains 58 stops, 21 combinations, 10 couplers, 3,485 pipes. The console is movable and is attached to the organ by a flexible cable 100 feet in length. The cable contains 372 wires. In the pedal organ there is an open diapason of 32 feet pitch, the longest pipe being large enough for a man to crawl through, turn around and come out again.

Like the proscenium arch, the balcony railings are of gold color and quite showy. The tops of the balcony rails are upholstered in crimson plush.

From the handsomely designed ceiling, done in panels with curved beams, are suspended a number of artistic chandeliers of bronze or brass, which contain hundreds of incandescent lights, of 16 and 32 candle-power, respectively. These chandeliers are placed so near the ceiling that they will not annoy the audience with their glare. The lights on the stage are placed behind the proscenium arch, and are thus out of sight of the people for the most part. Upon the front of the organ are two small clusters of electric lights, too. The lighting arrangements are perfect. There are 2,000 electric lamps in all.

The acoustic properties of the hall have not yet been thoroughly tested. Special attention has been given to the matter, however, and an expert on such matters, Prof. Wallace C. Sabine, of Harvard University, has been employed to make the hall as nearly perfect as possible in this respect.

Last evening Mr. Comee stood upon the stage and talked in an ordinary tone of voice with a gentleman seated in the upper balcony. Both could distinguish what the other said without the least trouble. Several selections were also played upon the organ, and this, too, indicated that the acoustic properties of the hall were excellent.

The general public will have a chance to judge for themselves on the night of Monday, October 15, when the first concert to be held in the hall — the dedicatory concert — will be held. On that night Beethoven's Mass in D will be given by the full Symphony Orchestra, under Mr. Gericke, with a chorus from the Cecelia Society of 200 voices and a quartet composed of Clementine Devere, Gertrude Mayster, Evan Williams and Joseph Beresheim.

Throughout the building is fireproof, and there are 16 exits from each balcony and from the floor, while the corridors are large enough to hold the entire audience comfortably. On the second floor is a large foyer, or promenade, with an arched ceiling and a gem of an echo. This is on the Huntington avenue side, right over the main entrance.

There are four coat-rooms, two on the floor and two in the first balcony, with a capacity of nearly 2,000 boxes. There are also spacious toilet and dressing rooms for ladies and for gentlemen.

A feature of the new hall that will be appreciated is the almost perfect system of heating and ventilation. It is a system said to be in use nowhere else in the world. The cool, fresh air is drawn in from the top of the building, and by means of fans and suction is made to pass through pipes, by which it can be fixed at any temperature, hot or cold, and then is forced into the auditorium from perforations in the ceiling and out again through registers on the floor. In this way it is claimed that the air will be kept constantly cool and fresh.

The rise in the floor of the auditorium begins at the letter K, and extends to the back wall of the hall: rises, also, in both balconies, both in the center and on the sides.

There is a marquise over the Massachusetts avenue entrance, 65 feet in length, which is for the convenience of carriages principally. There will also be ticket offices located at this entrance. The main entrance, however, is on Huntington avenue.

The exterior of the building suggests the architecture of the North Italian Renaissance. It is very plain, but substantial looking. Ground was broken June 12, 1899. The builders were the Norcross Bros.; the architects, McKim, Mead & White, and the heating and ventilating apparatus was put in under the direction of Alfred R. Wolff, heating expert, of New York.

At the recent auction of the seats for the concerts this season a premium of $1,120 was paid for two seats.

(71) Inauguration of Symphony Hall, October 15, 1900: "Report" by H. L. Higginson.[328]

The directors of this building have allowed me the honor and the pleasure of welcoming you to your new Symphony Hall. As no detailed report of the directors' scheme and acts has ever been made to the public, you will perhaps be glad to hear a few words on the subject.

The directors have tried to fulfil the trust imposed on them and to make the hall satisfactory to you. After a long search, they chose this site as the best in Boston, and in 1893 they bought it at about half the price per foot paid for the opposite lot, where the Horticultural Hall is to stand. They pondered long over plans, and finally, laying aside with regret Mr. McKim's beautiful design after the Greek theatre, they adopted the shape of hall which had of late been in vogue because successful. In this decision they have put aside the convictions and wishes of the architect — and they may have erred.

It was no easy matter to achieve the absolute needs of the hall without injury to its beauty and without undue expense. They sought diligently to place a second and smaller room for chamber-music or lectures within the space of the exterior walls, but found that such a plan would only result in a compromise, giving you two poorer halls. Therefore, they have built this hall, of which you will presently hear the quality.

If it is a success, the credit and your thanks are due to four men — Mr. McKim, Mr. Norcross, Professor Sabine, of Harvard University, and last, but not least, Mr. C. E. Cotting, who, with his wide experience, guarded our slender purse. Without his aid the hall might not have been ready tonight; and I rejoice for him that his task is fulfilled. Professor Sabine has studied thoroughly our questions of acoustics, has applied his knowledge to our problem; and I think with success. Professor Cross, of the Institute of Technology, has also given us the benefit of his counsel; and the help of these three gentlemen has been a pure labor of love. You see the handiwork of Mr. Norcross and of his excellent sub-contractors and assistants, but you have not seen their energy and patience in our behalf. As for Mr. McKim, he is here but will not speak for himself, his partners, and his office. Abandoning his pet idea with absolute cheerfulness, he set himself to devise a plan not entirely to his liking, and even in the execution of this plan, he has given up many hopes, wishes, and fancies because the directors had no more money.

Our capital is $500,000, of which $410,700 has been subscribed, and, as this sum was far too small, the directors have borrowed the remaining cost, which is about $350,000, making the total cost rising $750,000. They mortgaged the hall with reluctance, but had no other course, as the money was essential.

The building has been leased by the directors for ten years to me, who am to meet the costs of administration, taxes, and all charges, and to pay to the stockholders the rest of the receipts.

Let me add that the beauty of the hall has been won entirely by Mr. McKim, and I hope that it pleases you. I think it very handsome, and know that it is convenient and entirely safe. With the exception of the wooden floors laid directly on masonry and steel, the hall is built of brick, tile, steel, and plaster.

According to the foreman, Mr. French, it cannot be burned, and thus the fear of fire which has hung over us for twenty years in the old hall is gone forever.

It had long been clear that our home of music in Boston must be moved, for the old Music Hall was faulty in safety, in ventilation, in convenience, in lack of a good organ, and to a certain degree in acoustics. Around the old hall, from the opening night on November 20, 1852, hang the happy memories of fifty years' triumphs — the concerts of the Musical Fund Society, the Handel and Haydn, the Germanians, the Harvard Musical Society, the Apollo, the Cecilia — of Sontag, Albani, Carl Eckert, Bergmann, Thomas, Zerrahn, Thalberg, Rubinstein, Von Bülow, Wieniawski, Ole Bull, Sarasate, Paderewski, Patti, Nilsson, Sembrich, Lehmann, Ternina, and countless artists — of great organ recitals, as well as echoes of noble sermons and church services, of lectures, of great public meetings — nor can any one forget the men who, from public spirit, built the old hall, with one gentleman at their head, whose life and means without stint were devoted to art — Mr. Charles C. Perkins.

The old Music Hall had become a great temple for our city, which had made many generations happy, and which it was sad to leave — but the long-felt need of change, quickened in 1893 by the supposed certainty of a street through the hall, moved you to offer your money freely during a period of financial distress, and thus to give to the city this new home. To me it was of vital moment, for without it the life of the Orchestra would have ceased, and I have never said how deeply your sympathy and generosity touched me.

It is all as it should be. Certain citizens of Boston build a hall, without regard to return in money, and by this act care for the happiness, the convenience, the education of the inhabitants for twenty miles around this spot; and it is fitting in a republic that the citizens and not the government in any form should do such work and bear such burdens. To the more fortunate people of our land belongs the privilege of providing the higher branches of education and of art.

As for the Orchestra, it is always with us, and is always trying to improve itself — thus far with success. It is nearly of age and is always glad to speak for itself. Of its knowledge, its skill, its artistic qualities, its constant devotion to the best work year after year, of its consequent power to play its great repertory, I have no adequate words to speak, nor can I tell you how highly I prize our great string and wind-players, let alone our conductor, who has formed the Orchestra and led it so long, and who has never, even to save his men or me toil and trouble, lowered one jot his lofty standard of performance. I am very proud of him and of them, this band of artists, and I again thank them with all my heart, for they have done our city and our country signal and intelligent service, such as ennobles and educates a nation.

Whether this hall can ever give so much joy to our people as the old Music Hall, no one can tell. Much depends on the public, which has always been loyal and staunch to the Orchestra. I can only promise in return that it will try to do its share.

(72) Sabine to McKim, May 1, 1901, regarding the effect of statuary on Symphony Hall acoustics.[329]

Jefferson Physical Laborary,
Harvard University
Cambridge, Mass.,
May 1, 1901

Dear Mr. McKim: —

My first intimation that there was criticism on the acoustics of Symphony Hall was two weeks ago. How common it is and what form it takes I do not know.

Two things surprise me. First, the conflict between the original opinions which almost everybody expressed and these, to me, new opinions. Second, that the critics are able to locate so definitely the cause, — perhaps, I ought to say, recognize that your statues would make the acoustics less to their taste.

In the acoustics of any hall we have the following several elements to consider, — loudness, clearness, interference, resonance, and reverberation. In a hall of the seating capacity demanded of Symphony Hall all the loudness possible would not be too great, and every configuration of the hall and of the stage was strained to this end, as you know. You remember how the hall was shortened from the idea of an enlarged Gewandhaus, the ceiling lowered, the stage recessed, and the second gallery inserted to maintain the seating capacity to the required amount, — not to enter more intricate considerations. Moreover, I wish to maintain that the volume of sound is not merely great in view of the seating capacity, but that it is more uniformly distributed than in any other hall. It is greater, for example, than in the old hall. Just how much greater on the average than in the old hall I can tell you if you wish. There is, however, no point in the new hall where the sound is as intense as beside the stage in the old hall, but by agreement these seats were removed for the benefit of the rest of the hall.

In the matter of clearness there cannot be two opinions, either in regard to the ideal condition or the satisfactory nearness of its realization. As to the third point, I do not think anybody has yet found a zone of confusion in the Hall. Resonance is a much misused term. It is sometimes applied to reverberation, but should, I think, be kept distinct, to indicate a certain cause of distortion which no one could like, but which there is not time here to explain. The term is, however, popularly used synonymously with reverberation. The latter is the point which I particularly desire to discuss. On all of the other points I cannot believe that there is any difference of opinion.

Reverberation sometimes miscalled resonance is a matter of taste. Recognizing this I sought the opinion of Mr. Gericke, and the Committee in regard to what halls were satisfactory in this respect and accepted this as the best available definition of the desired result. Then I made a special study that this above all things might be quantitative, investigated these halls, was struck by the nice agreement of the opinions expressed, and reproduced this condition in the present hall. On the certainty of my work in this respect I shall not yield.

I have made this analysis in order that I might better discuss the difficulty with which Mrs. Elliot has met. The statues will not in the least affect the reverberation in the hall. This point was specifically investigated. When the Fogg Art Museum was under discussion Mr. Hooper suggested that busts and statues placed around the room might help it. This I tried in another room and satisfied not merely myself but Mr. Hooper as well. Any one can convince himself that plaster statues will not reduce the reverberation in a room by entering the front hall of the Fogg Art Museum, which is almost crowded with them. The only effect which they can have is slightly to *break up the interference* of the sound in the room, an unqualified disideratum [sic], although the effect even in this direction will in Symphony Hall be extremely small. The statues were a part of the original plan not only artistically in your scheme but acoustically.

I shall be extremely sorry if these criticisms in regard to the acoustics of the hall should be allowed to interfere with the completion of your plans, as the point against them is not well taken, even granting that a change of taste justifies a criticism of the hall. I appreciate, however, the wisdom of Mrs. Elliot in avoiding a discussion which is "at an acute stage."

I shall make arrangements to meet you Saturday morning, as you request. Very truly yours,
Wallace C. Sabine

Appendix A

CALCULATION IN ADVANCE
OF CONSTRUCTION

BY WALLACE C. SABINE

THE CONCLUDING CHAPTER OF SABINE'S 1900 PAMPLET, *Architectural Acoustics: Part I — Reverberation*, discussing acoustical considerations in the design and constructions of Boston's New Music Hall (Symphony Hall), is here reproduced in facsimile.

N.B. Sabine's posthumous *Collected Papers* correct the tables on p. 64 (p. 196 of this volume) to show the volume of the Leipzig Gewandhaus as 11,400 cubic meters (407,000 cubic feet) and that of the New Boston Music Hall as 18,300 cubic meters (649,000 cubic feet).

7. — CALCULATION IN ADVANCE OF CONSTRUCTION.

IN the present paper it is the purpose to show the application of the preceding analysis and data, taking as an example the design of the new Boston Music Hall now under construction, Messrs. McKim, Mead & White, architects.

In the introductory paper the general problem of architectural acoustics was shown to be a fairly complicated one, and to involve in its solution considerations of loudness, of interference, of resonance, and of reverberation. All these points received consideration while the Hall was being designed, but it is proposed to discuss here only the case of reverberation. In this respect a music hall is peculiarly interesting. In a theatre for dramatic performances, where the music is of entirely subordinate importance, it is desirable to reduce the reverberation to the lowest possible value in all ways not inimical to loudness; but in a music hall, concert room, or opera house, this is decidedly not the case. To reduce the reverberation in a hall to a minimum, or to make the conditions such that it is very great, may, in certain cases, present practical difficulties to the architect — theoretically it presents none. To adjust, in the original design, the reverberation of a hall to a particular and approved value requires a study of conditions, of materials, and of arrangement, for which it has been the object of the preceding papers to prepare.

It is not at all difficult to show *a priori* that in a hall for orchestral music the reverberation should neither be very great, nor, on the other hand, extremely small. However, in this matter it was not necessary to rely on theoretical considerations. Mr. Gericke, the conductor of the Boston Symphony Orchestra, made the statement that an orchestra, meaning by this a symphony orchestra, is never heard to the best advantage in a theatre, that the sound seems oppressed, and that a certain amount of reverberation is necessary. An examination of all the available plans of the halls cited as more or less satisfactory models, in the preliminary discussion of the plans for the new hall, showed that they were such as to give greater reverberation than the ordinary theatre style of construction. While several plans were thus cursorily examined the real discussion was based on only two buildings — the present Boston Music Hall and the Leipzig Gewandhaus; one was familiar to all and immediately accessible, the other familiar to a number of those in consultation, and its plans in great detail were to be found in " *Das neue Gewandhaus in Leipzig, von Paul Gropius und H. Schmieden.*" It should, perhaps, be immediately added that neither hall served as a model architecturally, but that both were used rather as definitions and starting points on the acoustical side of the discussion. The old Music Hall was not a desirable model in every respect, even acoustically, and the Leipzig Gewandhaus, having a seating capacity about that of Sanders Theatre, 1500, was so small as to be debarred from serving directly, for this if for no other reason.

The history of the new hall is about as follows : A number of years ago, when the subject was first agitated, Mr. McKim prepared plans and a model along classical lines of a most attractive auditorium, and afterwards, at Mr. Higginson's instance, visited Europe for the purpose of consulting with musical and scientific authorities in France and Germany. But the Greek Theatre as a music-hall was an untried experiment, and because untried was regarded as of uncertain merits for the purpose by the conductors consulted by Mr. Higginson and Mr. McKim. It was, therefore, abandoned. Ten years later, when the project was again revived, the conventional rectangular form was adopted, and the intention of the building committee was to follow the general proportions and arrangement of the Leipzig Gewandhaus, so enlarged as to increase its seating capacity about seventy per cent; thus making it a little more than equal to the old hall. At this stage calculation was first applied.

The often-repeated statement that a copy of an auditorium does not necessarily possess the same acoustical qualities is not justified, and invests the subject with an unwarranted mysticism. The fact is that exact copies have rarely been made, and can hardly be expected. The constant changes and improvements in the materials used for interior construction in the line of better fireproofing — wire-lath or the application of the plaster directly to tile walls — have led to the taking of liberties in what were perhaps regarded as non-essentials ; this has resulted, as shown by the preceding tables, in a changed absorbing power of the walls. Our increasing demands in regard to heat and ventilation, the restriction on the dimensions enforced by location, the changes in size imposed by the demands for seating capacity, have prevented, in different degrees, copies from being copies, and models from successfully serving as models. So different have been the results under what was thought to be safe guidance, — but a guidance imperfectly followed, — that the belief has become current that the whole subject is beyond control. Had the new Music Hall been enlarged from the Leipzig Gewandhaus to increase the seating capacity seventy per cent, which, proportions being preserved, would have doubled the volume, and then built, as it is being built, according to the most modern methods of fireproof construction, the result, unfortunately, would have been to confirm the belief. No mistake is more easy to make than that of copying an auditorium, — but in different materials or on a different scale, — in the expectation that the result will be the same. Every departure must be compensated by some other, — a change in material by a change in the size or distribution of the audience, or perhaps by a partly compensating change in the material used in some other part of the hall, — a change in size by a change in the proportions or shape. For moderate departures from the model such compensation can be made, and the model will serve well as a guide to a first approximation. When the departure is great the approved auditorium, unless discriminatingly used, is liable to be a treacherous guide. In this case the departure was necessarily great.

The comparison of halls should be based on the duration of the residual sound after the cessation of a source that has produced over the hall some standard average intensity of sound,— say one million times the minimum audible intensity,

1,000,000 i'. The means for this calculation was furnished in the fifth paper. The values of V and a for the three halls under comparison are as follows: —

DIMENSIONS OF THE THREE HALLS IN METRES.*

	Leipzig Gewandhaus.	Boston Music Hall, Old.	Boston Music Hall, New.
Length.	(38)	39.2	(39.5)
Breadth.	19	23.5	22 8
Height.	15.5	20.0	17.9
Volume.	(11,200)	18,400	(16,200)

The length given for the Leipzig Gewandhaus, 38 metres, is measured from the organ front to the architecturally principal wall in the rear. On the floor and by boxes in the balconies the seats extend 3 metres farther back, making the whole length of the hall, exclusive of the organ niche, 41 metres. This increases the volume of the hall about 200 cubic metres, making the total volume 11,400 cubic metres.

The height given for the new Boston Music Hall, 17.9, is the average height from the sloping floor. The length is measured on the floor of the main part of the hall; above the second gallery it extends back 2.74 metres, giving an additional volume of 580 cubic metres. The stage, instead of being out in the room, is in a contracted recess having a depth of 7.9

*DIMENSIONS OF THE THREE HALLS IN FEET.

	Leipzig Gewandhaus.	Boston Music Hall, Old.	Boston Music Hall, New.
Length.	(124)	129	(130)
Breadth.	62	77	75
Height.	52	66	59
Volume.	(400,000)	656,000	(575,000)

The length given for the Leipzig Gewandhaus, 124 feet, is measured from the organ front to the architecturally principal wall in the rear. On the floor and by boxes in the balconies the seats extend 10 feet farther back, making the total length of the hall, exclusive of the organ niche, 134 feet. This increases the volume 7,000 cubic feet, making the total volume 407,000 cubic feet.

The height given for the new hall, 59 feet, is the average height from the sloping floor. The length is measured on the floor of the main part of the hall; above the second gallery it extends back 9 feet, giving an additional volume of 20,000 cubic feet. The stage, instead of being out in the room, is in a contracted recess, having a depth of 26 feet, a breadth, front and back, of 60 feet and 45 feet, respectively, and a height, front and back, of 44 feet and 35 feet, respectively, with a volume of 54,000 cubic feet. The total volume of the new Music-Hall is, therefore, 649,000 cubic feet.

metres, a breadth, front and back, of 18.3 and 13.6, respectively, and a height, front and back, of 13.4 and 10.6, respectively, with a volume of 1,500 cubic metres. The height

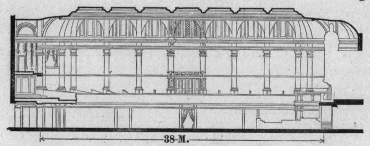

Fig. 20. The Leipzig Gewandhaus.

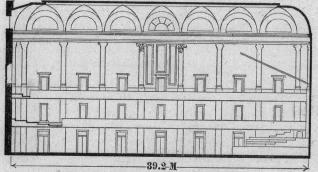

Fig. 21. The Old Boston Music Hall.

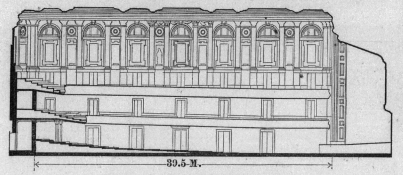

Fig. 22. The New Boston Music Hall.

of the stage-recess is determined by the absolute requirements of the large organ to be built by Mr. Geo. S. Hutchings. This organ will extend across the whole breadth of the stage.

The total volume of the new Boston Music Hall is, therefore, 18.300 cubic metres.

In the following table of materials in the three halls no distinction is made between plaster on wire-lath and plaster on wood-lath, the experiments recorded in the preceding paper having shown no certain difference in absorbing power. The areas of wall-surface are expressed in square metres. The number of persons in the audience is reckoned from the number of seats, no account being taken of standing room.

ABSORBING MATERIAL.

	Leipzig Gewandhaus.	Boston Music Hall, Old.	Boston Music Hall, New.
Plaster on lath.	2,206	3,030	1,040
Plaster on tile.	0	0	1,830
Glass.	17	55	22
Wood.	235	771	625
Drapery.	80	4	0
Audience:			
on floor.	990	1,251	1,466
in 1st balcony.	494	680	606
in 2d balcony.	33	460	507
Total audience.	1,517	2,391	2,579
Orchestra.	80	80	80

The drapery in the Leipzig Gewandhaus will be rated as shelia, and in the old Music Hall as cretonne, to which it approximates in each case. It is an almost needless refinement to rate differently the orchestra and the audience merely because the members of the orchestra sit more or less clear of each other, but for the sake of a certain formal completeness it will be done. For the above materials the coefficients, taken from the preceding paper, are as follows : —

COEFFICIENTS OF ABSORPTION.

Plaster on lath.................................. .033
Plaster on tile.................................. .025
Glass... .027
Wood.. .061
Drapery { shelia................................ .23
{ cretonne............................. .15
Audience per person............................. .44
Orchestra per man............................... .48

In the following table is entered the total absorbing power contributed by each of these elements. As this is the first example of such calculation all the elements will be shown, although it will then be immediately evident that some are of wholly negligible magnitude.

ABSORBING POWER.

	Leipzig Gewandhaus.	Boston Music Hall, Old.	Boston Music Hall, New.
Plaster on lath.	73	100	34
Plaster on tile.	0	0	46
Glass.	0.4	1.5	0.6
Wood.	14	47	38
Drapery.	18	0.6	0
Audience.	667	1,052	1,135
Orchestra.	38	38	38
Total = a.	810	1,239	1,292

V and a being determined for each of the three halls, the duration, T, of the residual sound after standard initial intensity can be calculated.

The results, in seconds, are as follows: —

    Leipzig Gewandhaus...................... 2.30
    Old Boston Music Hall.................... 2.44
    New Boston Music Hall................... 2.31

In other words, the new hall, although having a seating-capacity for over a thousand more than the Gewandhaus and nearly two hundred more than the old hall, will have a reverberation between the two, and nearer that of the Gewandhaus than that of the old hall.

It is interesting to contrast this with the result that would have been obtained had the plan been followed of reproducing on an enlarged scale the Gewandhaus. Assuming perfect reproduction of all proportions with like materials, the volume would have been 25,300 cubic metres, and the absorbing power 1,370, resulting in the value, $T = 3.02$. This would have differed from the chosen result by an amount that would have been very noticeable.

The new Boston Music Hall is, therefore, not a copy of the Gewandhaus, but the desired results have been attained in a very different way.

A few general considerations, not directly connected with reverberation, may be of interest. The three halls are of nearly the same length on the floor; but in the old hall and in the Gewandhaus the platform for the orchestra is out in the hall, and the galleries extend along both sides of it; while in the new hall the orchestra is not out in the main body of the room, and for this reason is slightly farther from the rear of the hall; but this is more than compensated for in respect to loudness by the orchestra being in a somewhat contracted stage recess, from the side walls of which the reflection is better because they are nearer and not occupied by an audience. Also it may be noted that the new hall is not so high as the old and is not so broad.

Thus is opened up the question of loudness, and this has been solved to a first approximation for the case of sustained tones. But as the series of papers now concluded is devoted to the question of reverberation, this new problem must be reserved for a subsequent discussion.

Appendix B

COLLATERAL
OBSERVATIONS

BY LEO L. BERANEK

O N SUNDAY, OCTOBER 30, 1898, WALLACE C. SABINE, ASSISTANT professor at Harvard University, wrote to the president of Harvard, Charles W. Eliot, that he was willing to act as acoustical advisor to Henry Lee Higginson in regard to the projected "New Music Hall." His acceptance of an invitation followed his discovery of an equation for predicting the reverberation time of a hall from a knowledge of its cubic volume, the number of people in the audience and the acoustical properties of the walls and ceiling. Possessing these, "he flatly declared that the application of the scientific principles resulting from his experiments would guarantee successful results."[330]

Early in the saga, Sabine appears largely to have been acoustical consultant to Henry Lee Higginson and the directors of the New Music Hall. None of the available records indicate that Charles F. McKim, lead architect, had any direct correspondence or contact with Sabine until the latter's visit to McKim's office on February 25, 1899. Nor is there evidence in the various documents reproduced in this volume that Sabine actually applied his calculations as a guide to the architectural design of Symphony Hall. We must turn to Sabine's published papers and Orcutt's biography of Sabine to infer the probable sequence of events.[331]

Higginson's earliest detailed letter to McKim, November 27, 1892, said: "The hall should hold about 2200 to 2500 people . . . have an ample stage . . . have a good space for an organ."[332] After a six-year interim, Higginson communicated another basic instruction to McKim: "We shall . . . turn to the general plan of our [present] Music Hall and of the halls in Vienna and Leipsic, the latter being the best of all, and Mr. [C. E.] Cotting will ask for a plan on those lines."[333] Several days later,

President Eliot wrote to Sabine on October 31, 1898: "I have written to Major Higginson telling him of the kind of help I think he could get from you towards the construction of a satisfactory Music Hall for Boston."[334]

Wallace Sabine published an account of his consultation on the new hall in a paper dated June 16, 1900: "the intention of the building committee was to follow the general proportions and arrangement of the Leipzig Gewandhaus, so enlarged as to increase its seating capacity about seventy per cent; thus making it a little more than equal to the old [Boston Music] hall. At this stage *calculation was first applied*."[335] One must presume that this was the first request by Higginson and the building committee for Sabine's active services using his newly-found theory.

The Gewandhaus seated 1560 and the proposal of the committee was to enlarge the seating capacity by a factor of 1.7 to achieve a capacity of about 2600. This would require an increase in all linear dimensions by a factor of 1.3, and an increase in cubic volume of 2.2, more than double that of the Gewandhaus. Figure B-1 shows a comparison between the actual Gewandhaus and a version expanded 1.3 times. The width would increase from 62 feet to 81 feet, and the height from 48 feet to 62 feet. Note that there are two small balconies at the rear of the Gewandhaus and one that extends over the stage on each side wall.

Sabine's calculations showed that the reverberation time at middle tones in the expanded hall (occupied) would be 1.31 times that in the actual Leipzig Hall. An increase by a factor of 1.31 would have meant a reverberation time of almost 2.5 seconds compared to today's measured value of 1.9 seconds (occupied) for Boston Symphony Hall (which Sabine later calculated to be the same as that of the Gewandhaus). Sabine called this "an amount that would have been very noticeable."[336] By today's standards, a new hall with a reverberation time of 2.5 seconds would be an acoustical disaster. Sabine would also have remarked that, from his equation, a hall whose cubic volume was 2.2 times that of the Leipzig hall would need to have its cubic volume reduced by a factor of 1.3 (if no changes were made in the 2500+ seating area) to achieve the desired reverberation time. It is not known how the building committee used this information, but it may have been helpful to the committee in the December 2, 1898, conference where McKim presented several sketches of which one was provisionally accepted.[337]

McKim submitted his first serious plan for the new hall to the directors in December 1898. That plan must be inferred from the Documents in this volume, from Sabine's *Collected Papers*, and from the Orcutt biography of Sabine. Fortunately, certain critical dimensions are spelled out in a letter between Higginson and McKim.[338] Besides the required reduction in cubic volume, McKim made two other changes from the simple expansion shown in Figure B-1. First, Higginson had informed McKim earlier that the 77-foot breadth of the old Music Hall was too wide, so in his December 1898 plan, McKim probably showed a width of 75 feet (the present

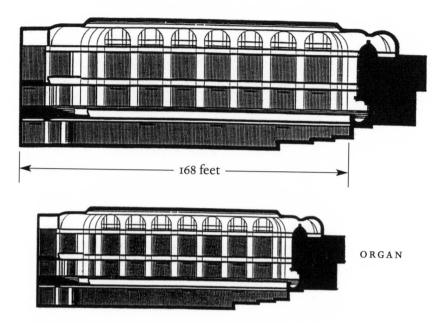

FIGURE B-1. *The lower drawing shows the [Neues] Leipzig Gewandhaus as it was before destruction in World War II. The upper drawing shows the result of expanding all of its dimensions by a factor of 1.3, as suggested by the building committee to achieve an increase in seating capacity from 1560 to 2600. In both renditions, there are one balcony along the sidewalls and two balconies at the rear.*

width of Boston Symphony Hall). Second, McKim planned to make the row-to-row spacing of the seating in the new hall 36 inches (compared to the 30 inches in the Gewandhaus). To achieve space for at least 2500 seats, he had to enlarge the two rear balconies greatly, and to introduce two rows of four boxes each on the side walls. A plan that fits these criteria is presented in Figure B-2, which thus shows what McKim's December 1898 plan may have looked like.

The old Boston Music Hall, which this hall was to replace, also had a calculated reverberation time nearly equal to that of the Leipzig Gewandhaus, and it was generally well liked by the Boston community and most of the local music critics. Its seating capacity was 2,391, including two shallow balconies on each of the side walls that extended over the stage, and two small balconies at the rear (see Figure B-3a).

Sabine had access to McKim's December drawings about the first of January 1899; after study he passed his analysis on to Higginson and the building committee. On January 26, Higginson wrote McKim with Sabine's recommendations, apparently the first time that McKim was told of Sabine's participation. His review included: The hall (Figure B-2) was altogether too long and he was very much afraid of a tunnel effect. The upper tier of boxes was too high to be useful. To shorten the hall, and not lose seats, a second balcony should be included along each of the side walls.

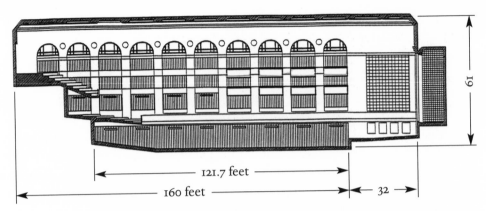

FIGURE B-2. *The probable design of Boston Symphony Hall by McKim as of early December 1898. The front four bays contain two layers of boxes above a single balcony. The back six bays are decoration. This longitudinal section is based on descriptions and dimensions in the text and the referenced books. It was prepared through the courtesy of Mr. John Prokos of Graham Gund Architects, Cambridge, Massachusetts.*

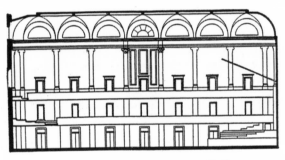

a. Old Boston Music Hall

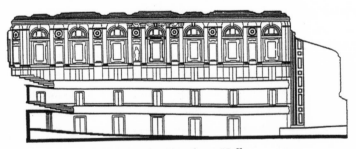

b. Boston Symphony Hall

FIGURE B-3. *Comparison of (a) the old Boston Music Hall with (b) the Boston Symphony Hall as built. Note that both halls have two balconies on the side and rear walls (from Col-lected Papers on Acoustics, Wallace Clement Sabine [Cambridge: Harvard University Press, 1922; reprint, Los Altos, California: Peninsula Publishing, 1992]).*

The stage should be narrower and a separate stage house built with a lower sloping ceiling. The space under the stage should be hollow and neither balcony seating, nor boxes or draperies, should be in the enclosure. To shorten the hall further, Higginson suggested that the row-to-row spacing be narrower by five inches, equaling that in the old hall.

McKim must have been unhappy with those recommendations, because they dictated a new hall that would look very much like the old Music Hall, differing only in that the stage was moved forward into its own enclosure (see comparison in Figure B-3). He had lost an opportunity to create an unique architectural monument such as he had envisioned when he presented the neo-Greek Theatre a half-decade before. He must have communicated this frustration to Higginson, because it was arranged for Sabine to go to New York on February 25, 1899, to present his case. After the visit, Sabine wrote to Higginson expressing McKim's acquiescence in the changes, saying, "Mr. McKim feels that he has evolved a beautiful and artistic plan *in spite of*, or rather, as he puts it, with the aid of the second gallery, and apparently takes pleasure and interest in the architectural problem *because of the difficulties and restrictions to be overcome.*"[339]

Sabine later wrote, "the real discussion was based on only two buildings — the present Boston Music Hall and the Leipzig Gewandhaus . . . both were used rather as definitions and starting points on the acoustical side of the discussion."[340]

"Then came the announcement," writes Orcutt, "that McKim, Mead & White, architects of the new Symphony Hall, in Boston, had placed the responsibility for the acoustics unreservedly in Sabine's hands, and were preparing their plans . . . in conformity to . . . [his] ideas."[341] This statement was probably made soon after Sabine's visit of February 25. As would be true for most architects today, McKim, Mead & White probably chose to make such an announcement because they wanted to make it clear that the responsibility for the acoustics was not theirs, and that the less-than-original architectural design was the result of acoustical demands.

In the news releases issued upon completion of Symphony Hall, an attempt was made to present it as a copy of the Leipzig Gewandhaus. It is easy to see from Figure B-3 that with two side balconies and nearly the same ceiling height, Boston Symphony Hall is more like the old Boston Music Hall, except for a stage house added at the front, than like the Leipzig Gewandhaus, shown in the lower drawing of Figure B-1. This is particularly apparent if one terminates the length of the Gewandhaus at the organ front, as is done in the drawing of Symphony Hall.

Appendix C

WHO WAS WHO

ADAMS, HENRY (1838–1918), Boston-bred American historian.

AGASSIZ, LOUIS (1807–1873), Swiss-born naturalist and Harvard professor, father of Higginson's wife, Ida Agassiz Higginson.

APTHORP, WILLIAM FOSTER (1848–1913), Bostonian musicologist, *Boston Transcript* music critic and BSO program annotator.

BACON, FRED P., Boston music commentator.

BIGELOW, WILLIAM STURGIS (1856–1926), Orientalist and art connoisseur, a director of New Boston Music Hall.

BOARDMAN, T. DENNIE, Boston realtor, collected subscriptions for new Music Hall.

BRADFORD, EDWARD H. (1848–1926), orthopedic surgeon, faculty member (later dean, 1912–18) of Harvard Medical School.

BULFINCH, CHARLES (1763–1844), Boston-based architect, designer of Massachusetts State House and other area buildings.

CAPRONI, PIETRO P., Italian-born maker and dealer in plaster statuary, located at Washington and Newcomb Streets in Roxbury.

COMEE, FREDERIC ROBBINS (1854–1909), BSO assistant manager, ca. 1886–1909.

COTTING, CHARLES EDWARD (c. 1856–1920), Boston trust and real estate agent, treasurer and clerk of New Boston Music Hall corporation; father of Charles E. Cotting, Jr., later president and treasurer of Lee, Higginson Corp.

CRAWFORD, THOMAS (1813–1857), American sculptor.

CROSS, CHARLES R. (1848–1921), Massachusetts Institute of Technology graduate, 1870; headed MIT physics department, 1876; founded MIT electrical engineering department, 1882.

DE GERSDORFF, GEORGE B. (ca. 1866–1964), junior architect in McKim firm, oversaw construction of Harvard Stadium.

DEXTER, F. GORDON, previous owner of Symphony Hall land; described as a "socially prominent clubman."

ELIOT, CHARLES WILLIAM (1834–1926), Harvard president, 1869–1909.

ELLIOT, MARY LEE (Mrs. John Wheelock Elliot), cousin of H.L. Higginson; procured Symphony Hall statues in 1901–02.

ELLIS, CHARLES ADAMS (1855–1937), BSO manager, 1885–1918.

ELSON, LOUIS C. (1848–1920), Boston musicologist, lecturer, and *Boston Advertiser* music critic.

EPSTEIN, JULIUS (1832–1926), Viennese pianist, professor and Higginson friend.

FOX, THOMAS A., Boston architect, assisted in Symphony Hall construction.

FRENCH, DANIEL CHESTER (1850–1931), American sculptor.

GARDNER, ISABELLA STEWART (Mrs. John Lowell Gardner or "Mrs. Jack") (1834–1919), Boston hostess and art collector.

GARDNER, JOHN LOWELL (1837–1898), Boston banker.

GERICKE, WILHELM (1845–1925), Austrian-born BSO conductor, 1884–89 and 1898–1906.

GOODRICH, J. WALLACE (1871–1952), organist and New England Conservatory faculty member, later director.

GREGERSON, JAMES R., Boston architect, one of the designers of Boston Music Hall.

HALE, PHILIP (1854–1934), *Boston Journal* music editor and BSO program annotator, succeeding William Foster Apthorp; *Boston Herald* music critic, 1903–1934.

HERRICK, Boston concert and theatrical agency.

HIGGINSON, HENRY LEE (1834–1919), Boston financier and philanthropist, founder of BSO, president of New Boston Music Hall, benefactor of Harvard University and other institutions.

HOOPER, EDWARD W. (1839–1901), treasurer of Harvard College, 1876–98; a director of New Boston Music Hall and trustee of the Museum of Fine Arts.

HOWARD, JOHN GALEN (1864–1931), American architect, assisted McKim in Paris; later headed School of Architecture at University of California, Berkeley.

HOWE, M.A. DEWOLFE (1864–1960), Boston biographer and historian.

HUNTINGTON, ARTHUR, Boston philanthropist, benefactor of MIT; gave name to Huntington Avenue.

HUTCHINGS, GEORGE S., Boston–New York organ builder.

KNEISEL, FRANZ (1865–1926), BSO concertmaster, 1885–1903.

KOUSSEVITZKY, SERGE (1874–1951), Russian-born BSO conductor, 1924–46, and music director, 1947–49.

KREHBIEL, H.E. (1854–1923), American musicologist and *New York Tribune* music critic.

LA FARGE, JOHN (1835–1910), American artist.

LALOUX, VICTOR (1850–1937), Paris Beaux-Arts professor, trained numerous Americans.

LAMOUREUX, CHARLES (1835–1910), French conductor.

LANG, BENJAMIN JOHNSON (B.J.) (1837–1909), leading Boston organist and choral conductor.

LANGERFELDT, THEODORE OTTO (1841–1906), German-born landscape and architectural painter, in Boston from 1868.

LOW, SETH (1850–1916), Columbia University president, 1889–1901; mayor of New York City, 1901–03.

MACMONNIES, FREDERICK WILLIAM (1863–1937), American sculptor.

MATTHEWS, NATHAN (1854–1927), Boston lawyer and Democratic politician; elected mayor, 1890; reelected 1891, 1892, 1893.

MCKIM, CHARLES FOLLEN (1847–1909), American architect, established firm of McKim, Mead & White; founder and first president of American Academy in Rome.

MEAD, WILLIAM RUTHERFORD (1846–1928), American architect, partner in McKim, Mead & White.

MUDGETT, LOUIS H. (1860–1924), manager of Boston Music Hall, 1891–1900; of Symphony Hall, 1900–22; of Boston Opera House, 1922–24.

NIKISCH, ARTHUR (1855–1922), Hungarian-born BSO conductor, 1889–93.

NORCROSS, ORLANDO W. (1839–1920), head of Norcross Brothers, Builders, of Worcester, Mass.

PAUR, EMIL (1855–1932), Austrian-born BSO conductor, 1893–98.

PERKINS, CHARLES C. (1823–1886), Boston art historian, critic, and etcher; gave Beethoven statue to Boston Music Hall.

PERKINS, CHARLES E., railroad builder and operator and Higginson friend.

RICHARDSON, HENRY HOBSON (H.H.) (1838–1886), architect of Trinity Church, Boston, and other area buildings.

RICHTER, HANS (1843–1906), German-born conductor, led Vienna Court Opera and Philharmonic in 1890s.

SABINE, WALLACE CLEMENT (1868–1919), Harvard physicist and acoustical scientist; aeronautical adviser in World War I.

SAVAGE, HENRY W., Boston realtor, in charge of Boston Music Hall reconstruction.

SEARS, HENRY F., benefactor of Harvard Medical School, a director of the New Boston Music Hall and member of the "Committee of Three" with Higginson and Hooper.

SHAW, ROBERT GOULD (1837–63), colonel of 54th Massachusetts Regiment in Civil War; killed leading his troops at Fort Wagner, SC.

STRUBE, GUSTAVE (1867–1953), BSO violinist, 1891–1913; later professor and director of Peabody Conservatory, Baltimore.

THOMAS, THEODORE (1835–1905), German-born American conductor and educator.

WHITE, STANFORD (1853–1906), American architect; partner in McKim, Mead & White.

WHITMAN, SARAH (Mrs. Henry S.), Boston hostess.

WISTER, OWEN (1860–1938), American writer, delivered ode at Symphony Hall dedication.

WOLFF, ALFRED R., New York heating specialist, installed Symphony Hall equipment.

WOLTERS, G.E., represented McKim firm on Boston projects.

ZACH, MAX (1864–1921), BSO first viola, 1886–1907; frequent Pops conductor, 1896–1907.

NOTES

1. See "A Note on Sources," pp. 108–09 of this volume.

2. Walter Muir Whitehill, *Boston: A Topographical History*, 2nd ed., enlarged (Cambridge: Belknap Press of Harvard University Press, 1976), p. 236.

3. Whitehill, *Boston: A Topographical History*, pp. 185 and 241–46; and Douglass Shand-Tucci, *Built in Boston: City and Suburb 1800–1950*, 2nd ed. (Amherst: University of Massachusetts Press, 1988), p. 106.

4. Document 2 (in this volume): Henry Lee Higginson to Charles F. McKim, October 27, 1892.

5. Town Topics (New York), May 30, 1901 (Scrapbook, vol. 18, p. 60). (Citations to Scrapbooks in Boston Symphony Orchestra archives are explained in Note on Sources, pp. 108–09.)

6. Document 1: James R. Gregerson to Henry Lee Higginson, March 11, 1887.

7. M. A. DeWolfe Howe, *A Partial (and not impartial) Semi-Centennial History of the Tavern Club, 1884–1934* (Cambridge, MA: The Riverside Press, printed for the Tavern Club, 1934), pp. 98–9.

8. *Bacon's Dictionary of Boston*, with an historical introduction by George E. Ellis (Boston and New York: Houghton, Mifflin, 1886), p. 256.

9. *Boston Herald*, November 22, 1852, quoted in *Boston Sunday Herald*, March 13, 1898 (Scrapbook, vol. 11, p. 92).

10. Fred P. Bacon, music critic and publicist, in *Boston Transcript*, March 15, 1898 (Scrapbook, vol. 11, p. 92). A more balanced summation is found in the *New York Musical Courier*, November 7, 1900 (Scrapbook, vol. 16, pp. 38–39). Not to be overlooked in any account of the Music Hall's varied uses was its employment by Henry James for the climactic episode of his 1886 novel *The Bostonians*.

11. *Bacon's Dictionary of Boston*, p. 257. The Boston Music Hall was nominally operated by a corporation in which Higginson was believed to hold three-fourths of the shares. *Boston Daily Globe*, March 22, 1893 (Scrapbook, vol. 5, p. 126).

12. *Boston Transcript*, probably February 8, 1892 (Scrapbook, vol. 5, p. 102).

13. Letter to the editor of the *Boston Transcript*, ca. February 19, 1898 (Baker XII-5-93). (Baker Library citations explained in Note on Sources.)

14. Suffolk County Deeds Book 2092, p. 193.

15. Ibid., p. 194.

16. Ibid., p. 200.

17. The so-called New Gewandhaus (Neues Gewandhaus) was completed in 1884 to replace the original Gewandhaus or Drapers' Hall, a medieval building whose concert hall was much celebrated in the later eighteenth and earlier nineteenth centuries. The New Gewandhaus of 1884, irretrievably damaged by Allied bombing in World War II, was replaced in 1981 by a second New Gewandhaus (Neues Gewandhaus) of ultramodern design, and the 1884 building was retrospectively designated the New Concert House (Neues Konzerthaus). See Rudolf Skoda (the architect of the 1981 building), *Das Gewandhaus Leipzig: Geschichte und Gegenwart* (Berlin: Wilhelm Ernst und Sohn, 1986); and Leo Beranek, *Concert and Opera Halls: How They Sound* (Woodbury, N.Y.: Acoustical Society of America, 1996), pp. 253–8.

18. Skoda, *Das Gewandhaus Leipzig*, pp. 22–3. The winners of the competition were Martin Gropius (uncle of Walter Gropius of Bauhaus fame) and Heino Schmieden, who carried out the design after Martin Gropius' death in 1880.

19. Charles Moore, *The Life and Times of Charles Follen McKim* (Boston and New York: Houghton Mifflin Co., 1929), p. 101.

20. Document 2: Higginson to McKim, October 27, 1892. The circumstances surrounding Higginson's invitation remain obscure. Charles Moore stated that Higginson impulsively caused his note of October 27 to be delivered "as McKim was taking the train for New York" on the 28th. Moore, *Life and Times*, p. 101. McKim confirmed in his reply of the 29th (Document 3) that he had received it "last night . . . at the moment of leaving" and had telegraphed Higginson from the train. Although McKim's typewritten letter lacks the usual printed letterhead, it reads as though written from his New York office after consultation with his colleagues.

21. Document 3: McKim to Higginson, October 29, 1892.

22. Document 4: McKim to Higginson, November 10, 1892.

23. Document 5: McKim to Higginson, November 22, 1892.

24. Document 6: Higginson to McKim, November 27, 1892.

25. Boston's population grew from 136,788 in 1850 to 560,892 in 1900, the year Symphony Hall opened. Much of this increase, however, was the result of immigration and the absorption of adjacent municipalities such as Roxbury, Dorchester, Charlestown, and Brighton.

26. Document 6: Higginson to McKim, November 27, 1892.

27. Skoda, *Das Gewandhaus Leipzig*, pp. 16, 51, and 84. The quotation is from Lucius Annaeus Seneca, *Epistolae morales ad Lucilium*, Letter 23; the original text reads, *"Mihi crede, verum gaudium res severa est"* (Believe me, true joy is a serious matter). This motto was conspicuously displayed, in slightly different forms, both inside the original Gewandhaus and on the facade of the "New" Gewandhaus of 1884.

28. Document 23: McKim to Higginson, October 28, 1898.

29. Moore, *The Life and Times of Charles Follen McKim*, p. 102. Some slightly different details emerge from the correspondence reproduced in Document 7: McKim to Higginson, March 3, 1893; Document 8: William R. Mead to Higginson, April 28, 1893; and Document 9: McKim to Higginson, May 3, 1893.

30. Document 8: Mead to Higginson, April 28, 1893.

31. Document 9: McKim to Higginson, May 3, 1893.

32. *Boston Transcript*, March 20, 1893; further details in *Boston Daily Globe*, March 22, 1893, and other papers (Scrapbook, vol. 5, pp. 125–26).

33. Massachusetts Acts and Resolves, 1893, Chapter 481.

34. These particular requirements applied specifically to the portion of the strip "from Court square to a point at or near the junction of Shawmut avenue and Tremont street." A glimpse of traffic conditions along Tremont Street at this period is given by Childe Hassam's painting of 1885–86, *Boston Common at Twilight*, in Boston's Museum of Fine Arts.

35. *Boston Herald*, June 16, 1893 (Scrapbook, vol. 5, p. 169).

36. Document 10a: Statement by "several prominent gentlemen," June 14, 1893.

37. Document 10b: Communication from the Committee for a New Music Hall, June 17, 1893.

38. M.A. DeWolfe Howe, *Later Years of the Saturday Club, 1870–1920* (Boston: Houghton Mifflin, 1927), p. 260; other details from Harvard University Archives, Biographical File (HUG 130); Otto Friedrich, *Clover* (New York: Simon and Schuster, 1979); and Eugenia Kaledin, *The Education of Mrs. Henry Adams* (Philadelphia: Temple University Press, 1981).

39. Document 10c: Letter of H.L. Higginson to the editors of Boston newspapers, June 20, 1893.

40. Although this sum exceeded the target amount, it was later revised downward to about $402,000, from 406 subscribers. *Boston Transcript*, November 22, 1893 (Scrapbook, vol. 6, p. 36); ibid., January 11, 1899 (Scrapbook., vol. 13, p. 84).

41. *Boston Post*, June 27, 1893 (Scrapbook annex).

42. *Boston Herald*, December 2, 1898 (Scrapbook, vol. 13, p. 64). Leading supporters of the plan were listed in a public appeal dated June 21, 1893, printed in M.A. DeWolfe Howe, *The Boston Symphony Orchestra, 1881–1931* (Boston and New York: Houghton Mifflin Co., 1931), pp. 95–6.

43. Higginson to C.E. Cotting, April 2, 1919 (Baker XII-22-Cotting 1919).

44. Thomas Russell Sullivan, *Passages from the Journal. . . 1891–1903* (Boston and New York: Houghton Mifflin Co., 1917), p. 101.

45. Henry Adams, *The Education of Henry Adams* (New York: Modern Library, 1931; copyright Massachusetts Historical Society, 1918), pp. 41, 337, 338.

46. Bliss Perry, *Life and Letters of Henry Lee Higginson* (Boston: Atlantic Monthly Press, 1921), pp. 338–39.

47. Adams, *The Education of Henry Adams*, p. 339.

48. Document 11: Circular letter to subscribers from the Committee for a New Music Hall, October 30, 1893.

49. The official records of the New Boston Music Hall have not been located, but the essentials of its organization and activity have been gleaned from contemporary press reports and other documentation cited.

50. *New England Historical and Genealogical Register*, vol. 75 (1921), p. lxxii.

51. *Boston Journal*, January 7, 1894 (Scrapbook, vol. 6, p. 67); Suffolk County Deeds Book 2174, p. 437.

52. Document 12: McKim to Higginson, July 5, 1893.

53. Document 13: Hooper to McKim, September 1, 1893.

54. Document 14: McKim to Hooper, September 2, 1893. The cost to the New Boston Music Hall did, however, ultimately reach $3,517.39, exclusive of storage and other incidentals. Cotting to Higginson, February 14, 1898 (Baker XII-5-93).

55. Document 15: McKim to Hooper, December 21, 1893.

56. The leading modern authority on the work of the McKim firm prints illustrations purporting to show a perspective and second-floor plan of the proposed Greek theatre, and states that "[t]he facade somewhat resembled that of the Paris Opera but . . . without its Baroque plasticity." Leland M. Roth, *McKim, Mead and White* (New York: Harper and Row, 1983), p. 225. Elsewhere, Roth states that his description was based on "sketch drawings preserved in the archives." Leland Roth, *The Urban Architecture of McKim, Mead and White, 1870–1910* (Ann Arbor: University Microfilms, 1973), p. 471. Contemporary press reports make it clear, however, that the model displayed in Boston provided no indication of the architect's views concerning the exterior. The *Boston Daily Globe* of January 9, 1894, reported: "No attempt is made to outline the exterior, as that can easily be adapted to the interior." The *Boston Evening Transcript* of January 8, 1894, stated that although the model was limited to the interior, the architectural treatment of the exterior would echo that of the interior, and "[t]he outlines of the façade apparently will all be curved." The *Boston Journal*, in contrast, reported on January 9, 1894, that the exterior would probably be "cubical," with a tower at each corner. Scrapbook, vol. 6, pp. 68, 69, and 71.

57. *Boston Herald*, January 9, 1894 (Scrapbook, vol. 6, p. 70); other press comment, Scrapbook, vol. 6, pp. 68–70, and Document 16: Description of the model, on view January 8, 1894.

58. French to McKim, October 18 and December 20, 1893 (New-York Historical Society). (New-York Historical Society citations are explained in Note on Sources.)

59. French later concluded that it would be difficult to find a sufficient number of appropriate sculptures with musical associations.

60. Document 16: Description of the model, on view January 8, 1894.

61. Scrapbook, vol. 6, p. 69.

62. See, for example, Moore, *The Life and Times of Charles Follen McKim*, p. 102.

63. Ednah D. Cheney to Hooper, January 16, 1894, in BSO Archives, Henry Lee Higginson Papers, MC31 series 220, Box 2.

64. Document 15: McKim to Hooper, December 21, 1893.

65. *Boston Herald*, December 2, 1898 (Scrapbook, vol. 13, 1898–99, p. 64); *Boston Transcript*, January 11, 1899 (Scrapbook, vol. 13, p. 84). It has been stated by both Moore and Roth that the directors' misgivings were reinforced by criticism from Professor Wallace C. Sabine, who later served as acoustical consultant on the building of Symphony Hall in 1899–1900. Moore, *The Life and Times of Charles Follen McKim*, p. 103; Roth, *The Urban Architecture of McKim, Mead and White*, p. 472. Such an intervention on Sabine's part in 1893–94 seems quite improbable, however, since he can have had little acquaintance with any of the directors, and his own involvement in acoustical research did not begin until after this period. Roth himself notes that, "only after construction [of Symphony Hall] was well advanced did Sabine have an opportunity to study McKim's Greek plan, for he had been absent from Boston during the early controversy; he then realized that the acoustics of McKim's Greek plan would have been satisfactory." For these statements, Roth cites a let-

ter of August 12, 1899, from McKim to E.A. Darling in the Charles Moore Papers, Manuscript Division, Library of Congress.

66. Hooper to McKim, February 14, 1894 (New-York Historical Society; two sentences transposed).

67. *Boston Post*, April 6, 1894 (Scrapbook, vol. 6, p. 106).

68. Document 17: Higginson to McKim, April 23, 1894.

69. Document 18: McKim to Higginson, April 26, 1894.

70. Document 19: McKim to Hooper, July 9, 1894.

71. *New York Evening Post*, October 16, 1900 (Scrapbook, vol. 16, p. 21); Francesco Passanti, "The Design of Columbia in the 1890s," *Journal of the Society of Architectural Historians*, vol. 36 (May 1977), pp. 68–84, esp. pp. 73–5, 78.

72. Document 19: McKim to Hooper, July 9, 1894.

73. Cotting to Higginson, February 14, 1898, and April 28, 1899 (Baker XII-5-93 and XII-6-32).

74. Adams, *The Education of Henry Adams*, p. 346.

75. *Boston Transcript*, November 12, 1894 (Scrapbook, vol. 7, p. 50).

76. Document 20: Report to stockholders of the New Boston Music Hall, November 17, 1894.

77. *Boston Transcript*, February 20, 1895 (Scrapbook, vol. 7, pp. 98–99).

78. Walter Muir Whitehill, *Boston Public Library: A Centennial History* (Cambridge: Harvard University Press, 1956), pp. 167 and 192. The exact figure for construction costs was eventually calculated at $2,558,559.

79. Moore, *The Life and Times of Charles Follen McKim*, pp. 97–8 and 104–5.

80. *Gradus ad Parnassum*, a treatise on counterpoint, was published in 1725 by the Viennese composer Johann Joseph Fux, Kapellmeister at St. Stephen's Cathedral and the Imperial Hapsburg Court. In 1817 the composer Muzio Clementi used the same title for his famous book of exercises for the pianoforte.

81. *Boston Journal*, March 11 and 12, 1898 (Scrapbook, vol. 11, p. 9). The stockholders of the (old) Boston Music Hall Association approved the sale on March 22, 1898; *Boston Journal*, March 23 (Scrapbook, vol. 11, p. 91).

82. *Boston Sunday Globe*, January 26, 1902 (Scrapbook, vol. 17, p. 64).

83. Baker XV-1.

84. Document 21: Hooper to Higginson, October 22, 1898.

85. Document 22: Higginson to McKim, October 27, 1898. The archaic spelling of "Leipsic" for Leipzig is retained only in quoted material.

86. Document 23: McKim to Higginson, October 28, 1898.

87. Document 24: Higginson to McKim, October 31; see also Document 25: McKim to Higginson, November 5, 1898.

88. Document 26: McKim to Higginson, November 23, 1898.

89. Document 27: Report of the *Boston Herald*, December 2, 1898.

90. A cryptic note from Higginson to McKim, dated December 2, 1898, and now in the archives of the New-York Historical Society, creates some mystery: "We abandon the little hall — so we all think. Of course we would rather have it, but the lot gives you and us a fine chance, & we must use it." It is unclear whether Higginson is here talking about the lounging hall referred to in the *Herald* or about a small hall for chamber music, an idea to which he would revert a few weeks later.

91. Edwin H. Hall, "Wallace Clement Sabine," *Dictionary of American Biography*, vol. 8, part 2, pp. 277–78.

92. Wallace C. Sabine, *Collected Papers on Acoustics* (Cambridge: Harvard University Press, 1922; reprinted Los Altos, Calif.: Peninsula Publishing, 1993).

93. William Dana Orcutt, *Wallace Clement Sabine: A Study in Achievement* (Norwood, Mass.: Plimpton Press, 1933), pp. 130–49.

94. Eliot to Higginson, June 22, 1893 (Baker XII-4-11).

95. Orcutt, *Wallace Clement Sabine*, pp. 133–5.

96. Orcutt, *Wallace Clement Sabine*, pp. 133–4.

97. Harvard University Archives, C.W. Eliot Correspondence (UAI 5.150, Box 120, folder 329).

98. Leo L. Beranek, "Boston Symphony Hall: An Acoustician's Tour," *Journal of the Audio Engineering Society*, vol. 86, no. 11, November 1988, pp. 919–30, at p. 920. Reverberation, classified by Sabine as one of the four key factors in architectural acoustics — the other three being loudness, interference, and resonance — is a measure of the length of time a given sound persists after its source has fallen silent. Too much reverberation produces a confused and jangling sound; too little reverberation may result in a dry and labored effect.

99. Orcutt, *Wallace Clement Sabine*, p. 131; similarly pp. 130 and 137 (Orcutt's emphasis).

100. Scrapbook, vol. 16, p. 20; also in Orcutt, *Wallace Clement Sabine*, p. 145.

101. Orcutt, *Wallace Clement Sabine*, pp. 135–6.

102. Quoted in Orcutt, *Wallace Clement Sabine*, p. 138.

103. Document 28: Charles A. Ellis to Charles E. Cotting, Clerk of the New Boston Music Hall, from Washington, D.C., January 6, 1899.

104. Wallace C. Sabine, "Architectural Acoustics: Reverberation," *The American Architect and Building News*, vol. 68, April–June 1900; reprinted in Wallace C. Sabine, *Reprints from the American Architect on Architectural Acoustics — Part I: Reverberation* (Cambridge, Mass.: no publisher's name, 1900); and in Sabine's *Collected Papers*. Sabine's discussion of "the new Boston music hall" appeared in the periodical version, vol. 68, no. 1277 (June 16, 1900), pp. 83–4, and in the 1900 reprint at pp. 61–68, and is reproduced in Appendix A, below.

105. Beranek, "Boston Symphony Hall: An Acoustician's Tour," p. 921.

106. Dr. Beranek's current views are set forth in detail in Appendix B, below.

107. Appendix A. Beranek rebuts the prevalent notion, based on Sabine's calculations, that Symphony Hall has a reverberation time of 2.3 seconds at 500 Hz. when fully occupied. Reverberation time measured under those conditions in 1996–97, Beranek states, was only 1.9 seconds. The difference, in Beranek's view, is due to variances in the amount of sound absorption by the audience, which was calculated by Sabine based on measurements made in a Harvard lecture hall where 20-year-old students occupied wooden benches, whereas contemporary Symphony Hall audiences tend to be larger individuals occupying wider, upholstered seats with armrests, thus absorbing more sound and reducing the reverberation time.

108. Appendix A.

109. Orcutt, *Wallace Clement Sabine*, p. 138.

110. Appendix A.

111. Document 72: Sabine to McKim, May 1, 1901.

112. Document 29: Higginson to McKim, January 26, 1899.

113. Sabine to Eliot, June 8 and November 3, 1897, in Harvard University Archives, C.W. Eliot Correspondence (UAI 5.150, Box 120, Folder 329).

114. Appendix B, below.

115. Document 31: McKim to Higginson, February 27, 1899.

116. Document 30: Sabine to Higginson, February 26, 1899.

117. Document 32: Higginson to McKim, March [5 ?], 1899.

118. Orcutt, *Wallace Clement Sabine*, p. 137.

119. *Boston Herald*, February 15, 1899 (Scrapbook, vol. 13, p. 102).

120. *Boston Transcript, Boston Daily Globe, Boston Evening Record*, February 15, 1899; *Boston Post*, February 16, 1899 (Scrapbook, vol. 13, pp. 101–3).

121. Scrapbook, vol. 16, p. 4.

122. Appendix A.

123. Document 36: Higginson to McKim, March 24, 1899.

124. Sabine to Eliot, August 2, 1900, in Harvard University Archives, C.W. Eliot Correspondence (UAI 5.150, Box 120, folder 329).

125. Document 49 (Sabine to Higginson, March 8, 1900) and Document 51 (Sabine to Ellis, March 22, 1900) show that Sabine accompanied the orchestra on its final trip of the 1899–1900 season on March 19–24, 1900, at a time when Symphony Hall was already half built.

126. Wallace C. Sabine, "Architectural Acoustics," *Proceedings of the American Academy of Arts and Sciences*, vol. 42, no. 2 (June 1906), p. 58 (in Sabine, *Collected Papers*, pp. 71–72).

127. Document 29: Higginson to McKim, January 26, 1899. Dr. Beranek notes that, "Sabine also played an important part in designing the ventilation system. Nobody had designed a quiet ventilation system before; in fact most halls were not ventilated except by opening windows. By 1897 there were electric motors, and large fans were just coming into existence. Sabine recommended that about one fifth of the ceiling should be perforated, allowing fresh air to drop down. The exhaust air goes out through the grilles that you see on the lower side walls. The air simply falls through the hall, making no noise." Beranek, "Boston Symphony Hall: An Acoustician's Tour," p. 922.

128. Orcutt, *Wallace Clement Sabine*, p. 142.

129. Appendix A. "The stage," Sabine adds, "instead of being out in the room, is in a contracted recess, having a depth of 26 feet, a breadth, front and back, of 60 feet and 45 feet, respectively, and a height, front and back, of 44 feet and 35 feet, respectively, with a volume of 54,000 cubic feet."

130. Orcutt, *Wallace Clement Sabine*, pp. 142–43.

131. Howe, *The Boston Symphony Orchestra*, pp. 243–4.

132. Beranek, "Boston Symphony Hall: An Acoustician's Tour," p. 923.

133. Document 33: McKim to Higginson, March 10, 1899.

134. See especially Document 34, descriptive article in the *Boston Transcript*, March 13, 1899. A further selection of architectural plans and drawings from the BSO archives will be found on pp. 144–149 of this volume.

135. The last phrase was used by Paul Goldenberger in Boston Symphony Orchestra Program Book, April 11–13, 1990, p. 13.

136. Appendix A. "The length," Sabine explains, "is measured on the floor of the main part of the hall; above the second gallery it extends back [an additional 9 feet]. . . . The height . . .

is the average height from the sloping floor." Beranek offers 1996 measurements of 128, 75, and 61 feet respectively; Beranek, *Concert and Opera Halls*, p. 82.

137. Document 34: descriptive article in *Boston Transcript*, March 13, 1899.

138. *Boston Herald*, March 14, 1899 (Scrapbook, vol. 13, p. 117).

139. Document 6: Higginson to McKim, November 27, 1892.

140. Document 35: McKim to Higginson, March 17, 1899; see also Document 37: George B. de Gersdorff to Higginson, March 31, 1899.

141. Barton and Rackemann, Counsellors at Law, to McKim, Mead & White, March 15 and May 3, 1899 (New-York Historical Society).

142. Cotting to McKim, Mead & White, June 28, 1899 (New-York Historical Society).

143. New-York Historical Society.

144. Robert Campbell, "The Acoustical Magic of Symphony Hall," *Boston Globe Magazine*, October 18, 1981, pp. 36–42, at p. 36.

145. *Boston Transcript*, December 5, 1898 (Scrapbook, vol. 13, p. 69).

146. Clippings in Scrapbook, vol. 13, pp. 46, 64, 69. Minor discrepancies in the figures cited are presumably the result of rounding and recalculations over time.

147. Document 22: Higginson to McKim, October 27, 1898.

148. *Boston Transcript*, January 11, and *Boston Journal*, January 12, 1899 (Scrapbook, vol. 13, pp. 84–85). The purchase by Higginson, Sears, and Bigelow, on December 29, 1898, of additional land adjacent to the Music Hall lot, with a frontage of 96.77 feet on Huntington Avenue, a depth of 125 feet, and an area of 12,096 square feet, was recorded in Suffolk County Deeds Book 2576, p. 601. A five-foot-wide strip of this land, running inward from Huntington Avenue and flanking Symphony Hall on the southwest, was transferred by the purchasers to the New Boston Music Hall on March 20, 1901; Suffolk County Deeds Book 2748, pp. 565, 567.

149. Press reports, February 15, 1899 (Scrapbook, vol. 13, pp. 101–103). On the Bacon campaign, see further Scrapbook, vol. 11, p. 92; vol. 13, pp. 69 and 99.

150. *Boston Herald*, March 28, 1899 (Scrapbook, vol. 13, p. 128).

151. *Boston Transcript*, probably May 1, 1899 (Scrapbook, vol. 13, p. 137). A reminiscence of one of the directors, William Sturgis Bigelow, reflects the spirit in which the members of Higginson's inner circle rallied round when needed. Writing in 1923 to Judge Frederick P. Cabot, then President of the BSO Board of Trustees, Bigelow recalled: "You know — or perhaps you do not happen to have heard — that, strange to say, when the hall was being built, the money seemed likely to run short at one time, and some of us put in a little to help. I don't remember who there was or how much they put in, but doubtless it is all a matter of record. I put in fifteen thousand dollars." Bigelow to Cabot, January 15, 1923, in BSO Archives, F.P. Cabot correspondence, TRUS Series 51x, Box 1.

152. Document 38: Open letter of Major Higginson to the people of Boston, June 5, 1899.

153. Document 71: Inauguration of Symphony Hall, October 15, 1900, "Report" by H.L. Higginson.

154. *Boston Evening Transcript*, June 12, 1899.

155. Suffolk County Deeds Book 2613, p. 610. A second mortgage in the amount of $36,000 was arranged with the same institution on February 9, 1902; Suffolk County Deeds Book 2808, p. 437. With an aggregate indebtedness of $361,000, the two mortgages were carried for-

ward through the years and assumed by the BSO when it took over the Symphony Hall property from the New Boston Music Hall on March 27, 1934. The 1902 mortgage, with a principal of $36,000, was retired by the BSO on December 9, 1936. The 1899 mortgage, with a principal amount of $325,000, remained in effect, with partial payments and extensions, until its final liquidation during the financial year ending August 31, 1955.

156. Lease and accompanying documents in BSO Archives, Board of Trustees, Office of the Treasurer, Financial Records, TRUS Series 52. Renewed May 27, 1910, for a second ten-year period, the lease was transferred by Higginson to the Boston Symphony Orchestra, Inc. with effect from August 1, 1918. The BSO, in turn, acquired title to Symphony Hall by purchase from the New Boston Music Hall in 1934.

157. Document 38: Open letter of Major Higginson to the people of Boston, June 5, 1899.

158. Higginson to John A. Sullivan, Boston Corporation Counsel, April 28, 1914 (Baker XII-15-1914 Music); Higginson to Henry Wilder Foote, July 22, 1915 (Baker XII-17-1915 Music). The earlier letter puts the annual drain at $13,000–19,000; the 1915 letter puts the drain at a more plausible $13,000–14,000.

159. Document 38: Open letter to the people of Boston.

160. Richard Herndon, *Boston of Today* (Boston: Post Publishing Company, 1898), pp. 325–26; *Boston Directory*, 1897, pp. 1172, 2117; obituary notice in *Boston Transcript*, February 27, 1920.

161. Higginson to Eliot, July 13, 1899, in Harvard University Archives, C.W. Eliot Papers, UAI 5.150, Box 111, Folder 152.

162. *Boston Evening Transcript*, June 13, 1899. The *Transcript*'s reference to "tow-horse" carts presumably results from a typographical error.

163. Document 36: Higginson to McKim, March 24, 1899.

164. O.W. Norcross to McKim, Mead & White, enclosing report of B.F. Smith & Bro. dated April 24, 1899 (New-York Historical Society).

165. Cotting and others to McKim, Mead & White, June 20 and 23, 1899 (New-York Historical Society).

166. Enclosure in letter of Thomas A. Fox to McKim, Mead & White, June 23, 1899 (New-York Historical Society; punctuation edited for clarity.)

167. *Boston Transcript*, October 20, 1899 (Scrapbook, vol. 14, p. 27).

168. In spite of differences in size, shape, and purpose, the two buildings display a certain stylistic kinship in their use of a mellowed red brick with limestone facings. A recorded McKim touch at Symphony Hall was the use of so-called "Harvard brick," specially treated by overburning in an attempt to match the old brickwork of Harvard Hall and other early Harvard buildings. Alfred Hoyt Granger, *Charles Follen McKim: A Study of His Life and Work* (Boston, 1913; reprinted New York: Benjamin Blom, Inc., 1972), p. 36.

169. Document 39: McKim to Higginson, November 3, 1899; Document 40: George S. Hutchings & Company to McKim, Mead & White, November 7, 1899; Document 41: McKim to Higginson, November 8, 1899.

170. Orcutt, *Wallace Clement Sabine*, p. 143.

171. Ibid.

172. Document 42: Sabine to McKim, November 12, 1899.

173. Orcutt, *Wallace Clement Sabine*, p. 144.

174. *Boston Globe*, October 13, 1900 (Scrapbook, vol. 16, p. 16).

175. Document 43: McKim to Higginson, November 15, 1899.

176. Typescript, "Suggestions for the large front panel. W.S.B. & E.H.B. Boston, Nov. 23, 1899" (New-York Historical Society). In a subsequent letter to McKim (Document 45, December 19, 1899), Hooper suggested that the date 1900 (MDCCCC) be presented in an ornate Roman numeral style then in use at Harvard.

177. Document 44: McKim to Higginson, December 1, 1899.

178. Document 45: Hooper to McKim, December 19, 1899.

179. Van Wyck Brooks, *New England: Indian Summer 1865–1915* (New York: E.P. Dutton, 1940), p. 104n.

180. Document 46: McKim to Higginson, December 29, 1899.

181. *Boston Sunday Journal*, March 18, and *Boston Post*, March 19, 1900 (Scrapbook, vol. 14, p. 85). The *Herald* had already published on March 1 a drawing of the half-completed hall (Scrapbook, vol. 14, p. 77), enlivened by pedestrian and vehicular traffic and showing electric streetcar lines on both Massachusetts and Huntington Avenues.

182. *Boston Transcript*, January 4, 1900 (Scrapbook, vol. 14, p. 58).

183. Scrapbook, vol. 14, p. 77; further reports, apparently from the same source, ibid., pp. 77 and 85.

184. Document 50: Thomas A. Fox to Higginson, March 20, 1900; Document 52: McKim to Higginson, March 26, 1900.

185. Document 47: Higginson to McKim, Mead & White, January 18, 1900.

186. Document 48: de Gersdorff to Higginson, January 19, 1900.

187. Document 54: McKim to Higginson, April 20, 1900. See also Document 53: McKim to Higginson, April 14, 1900; Document 56: McKim, Mead & White to Higginson, April 28, 1900.

188. Document 55: McKim to Higginson, April 24, 1900.

189. According to the *New York Evening Post* of October 16, 1900 (Scrapbook, vol. 16, p. 21), official stationery had also been printed with the name of the "New Music Hall," which had then to be hand-corrected on outgoing correspondence.

190. *Boston Post*, October 21, 1899 and March 23 and 24, 1900 (Scrapbook, vol. 14, pp. 26 and 88).

191. *Boston Daily Advertiser*, April 30, 1900 (Scrapbook, vol. 14, p. 103).

192. Ibid.

193. *Boston Post*, April 29, 1900 (Scrapbook, vol. 14, p. 104).

194. *Boston Transcript*, May 3, 1900 (Scrapbook, vol. 14, p. 106).

195. The post-1900 history of the former Boston Music Hall is reviewed by Shand-Tucci, *Built in Boston*, p. 214.

196. Scrapbook, vol. 15, pp. 113–17.

197. All Boston papers, May 6, 1900 (Scrapbook, vol. 15, pp. 119–20).

198. Document 57: McKim, Mead & White to Higginson, May 18, 1900.

199. Document 58: McKim to Higginson, from Boston, June 15, 1900; Document 61: McKim to Higginson, from the Music Hall, June 21, 1900.

200. Document 59: McKim to Higginson, June 18, 1900; Document 60: McKim, Mead & White to Higginson, June 19, 1900; Document 61, McKim to Higginson, June 21, 1900; Document 62: O.W. Norcross to Higginson, July 13, 1900; Document 63: George S. Hutchings to Higginson, July 24, 1900.

201. Quoted phrase from Baker XII-15-1914 Music, April 7, 1914.

202. Document 64: Ellis to Higginson, August 13, 1900; Document 65: Ellis to Higginson, August 15, 1900.

203. Document 66: Ellis to Higginson, August 18, 1900; Document 67: Ellis to Higginson, August 21, 1900.

204. Document 68: Ellis to Higginson, August 24, 1900.

205. Document 69: Higginson to McKim, Mead & White, August 28, 1900.

206. Ibid.

207. *Boston Daily Globe*, September 28, 1900; *Boston Post*, September 29, 1900; and *Boston Herald*, October 21, 1900 (Scrapbook, vol. 16, pp. 2, 3, and 18). For the 2000–2001 season, the same seats were priced at $1,618 each for twenty-three Saturday evening concerts.

208. *Boston Transcript*, September 24, 1900 (Scrapbook, vol. 16, p. 4).

209. *Boston Evening Record*, September 26, 1900 (Scrapbook, vol. 16, p. 2).

210. *Boston Sunday Herald*, October 14, 1900 (Scrapbook, vol. 16, p. 17).

211. *New York Daily Tribune*, October 16, 1900 (Scrapbook, vol. 16, p. 20). For a detailed description of the hall on the eve of the formal opening, see Document 70: Symphony Hall Facts: Descriptive article from the *Boston Journal*, October 15, 1900.

212. *Musical Courier*, October 24, 1900 (Scrapbook, vol. 16, p. 27). The reader may note a similarity in the tone of this anonymous comment to that of earlier quoted remarks by Fred P. Bacon.

213. Document 72: Sabine to McKim, May 1, 1901.

214. *Boston Journal*, September 25, 1900 (Scrapbook, vol. 16, p. 4).

215. *Boston Transcript*, February 16, 1901 (Scrapbook, vol. 16, p. 79).

216. Document 72: Sabine to McKim, May 1, 1901.

217. Quotation supplied by Leo L. Beranek.

218. *Boston Herald*, October 9, 1902 (BPL Scrapbook, vol. 22, pp. 22–24). (BPL Scrapbook citations explained in Note on Sources.)

219. *Boston Herald*, October 9, 1902 (BPL Scrapbook, vol. 22, pp. 22–24); *Boston Transcript*, October 9, 1902 (BSO Scrapbook, vol. 19, p. 13); BSO Program Book, April 17–18, 1903, p. 1233.

220. French to McKim, March 7, 1902 (New-York Historical Society).

221. For further discussion see H. Earle Johnson, *Symphony Hall* (Boston: Little, Brown, 1950), pp. 12–13; Beranek, "Boston Symphony Hall: An Acoustician's Tour," p. 922; and especially Caroline E. Hessberg, "The Symphony Statues: Casts of Character," *BSO: The Boston Symphony's Monthly Newsletter*, November–December 1980, pp. 1 and 4; and Caroline Smedvig, "The Symphony Statues: Casts of Character," BSO Program Book, Season 1990–91, Week 14 (January 24–26, 1991), pp. 12–17.

222. Document 68: Ellis to Higginson, August 24, 1900.

223. Scrapbook, vol. 16, pp. 7 and 20.

224. Philip Hale in *Boston Journal*, October 16, 1900; *Boston Herald*, October 17, 1900 (Scrapbook, vol. 16, p. 18).

225. *Boston Sunday Herald*, October 14, 1900 (Scrapbook, vol. 16, p. 16).

226. *New York Daily Tribune*, October 16, 1900 (Scrapbook, vol. 16, p. 20).

227. *New York Evening Post*, October 16, 1900, quoted in Orcutt, *Wallace Clement Sabine*, p. 147.

228. *Boston Transcript*, October 16, 1900 (Scrapbook, vol. 16, p. 18).

229. *Boston Transcript*, October 22, 1900 (Scrapbook, vol. 16, p. 25).

230. *Boston Transcript*, December 31, 1902 (BPL Scrapbook, vol. 22, p. 120).

231. Leo L. Beranek and John W. Kopec, "Wallace C. Sabine, Acoustical Consultant," *Journal of the Acoustical Society of America*, vol. 69 (1), January 1981, p. 3.

232. "Boston Symphony Hall: An Acoustician's Tour," p. 923.

233. Beranek, *Concert and Opera Halls: How They Sound*, p. 58.

234. Document 72: Sabine to McKim, May 1, 1901.

235. Beranek speculates that Sabine's complete silence on a matter of such personal importance may reflect embarrassment on having realized that "the measured reverberation times [in Symphony Hall] were at least 20% shorter than his predictions." (Beranek's explanation of this discrepancy appears in note 107 above). Beranek, "The Notebooks of Wallace C. Sabine," *Journal of the Acoustical Society of America*, vol. 61, no. 3 (March 1977), pp. 629–39, at pp. 636–37.

236. Orcutt, *Wallace Clement Sabine*, p. 147.

237. Ibid.

238. *New York Tribune*, October 16, 1900 (Scrapbook, vol. 16, p. 20).

239. Quoted by Darwin Payne, *Owen Wister* (Dallas: Southern Methodist University Press, 1985), pp. 187–88. A partial text of Wister's poem is printed in Howe, *The Boston Symphony Orchestra*, pp. 111–12.

240. *Boston Herald*, October 16, 1900 (Scrapbook, vol. 16, p. 7).

241. Document 71: "Report" by H.L. Higginson at the Inauguration of Symphony Hall, October 15, 1900.

242. Rounded figures as of January 1, 1906, from annual financial statements of the New Boston Music Hall (Baker XIV-6-3).

243. Whitehill, *Boston Public Library*, p. 192. Higginson boasted in his report that the land acquired for Symphony Hall in 1893 had cost only "about half the price per foot paid for the opposite lot, where the Horticultural Hall is to stand." The official history of the Massachusetts Horticultural Society reports that its richly ornamented headquarters, dated 1900 but completed in 1901 or later, cost $290,997 for the building and $515,997 for the building and land. Albert Emerson Benson, *History of the Massachusetts Horticultural Society* (Norwood, Mass.: Plimpton Press, for the Massachusetts Horticultural Society, 1929), p. 367. The construction of Horticultural Hall, formally authorized May 26, 1900, was still incomplete at the time of its dedication on November 9, 1901 (ibid., pp. 349–51, 368, 376).

244. Campbell, "The Acoustical Magic of Symphony Hall," p. 42.

245. Baker XII-2-53.

246. Handwritten original in New-York Historical Society, McKim, Mead & White Collection, Box M-10 Misc. Folder: Boston Music Hall. (All subsequent citations to the New-York Historical Society are to this folder.) Despite the evidence of the letterhead, Higginson's letter appears from its content and from McKim's reply (Document 3) to have been written from Boston during one of McKim's frequent visits to that city.

247. New-York Historical Society.

248. Unless otherwise noted, other communications from McKim and associates bear office letterheads as shown in Documents 4 and 19.

249. Baker XII-3-91.

250. Baker XII-3-91.

251. In answer to McKim's telegraphic request of November 14, 1892 (Baker XII-3-91), Higginson on November 16, 1892 telegraphed as follows (text from New-York Historical Society): "The lot is nearly rectangular two hundred twenty five feet ten inches on [West Chester] park two hundred twenty five feet rear line — one hundred and fifty feet on [Huntington] avenue and one hundred and fifty two feet one inch on side street. Set back on Huntington avenue fifteen feet."

252. Interpreted by Higginson as a suggestion "that we may perhaps be able to use some of these 34,000 ft for other purposes" (Document 6).

253. Typewritten transcript of penciled note, from New-York Historical Society. Emphasis indicated by underlinings on Higginson's penciled draft.

254. Baker XII-3-118.

255. John Galen Howard, McKim's assistant in Paris, had cabled, "Sketches forwarded today" in reference to sketches he had prepared in connection with the Music Hall project (Baker XII-3-118).

256. Baker XII-4-11.

257. Baker XII-3-118.

258. Published in several newspapers; text from *Boston Post*, June 15, 1893 (Scrapbook, vol. 5, p. 166).

259. The text as printed in ibid. says "definitively."

260. Text from *Boston Transcript*, June 19, 1893 (Scrapbook, vol. 5, p. 170).

261. Text from *Boston Herald*, June 21, 1893 (Scrapbook, vol. 5, p. 171). The identical letter appeared in several other newspapers and is reprinted (but incorrectly dated July 20, 1893) in Howe, *The Boston Symphony Orchestra*, pp. 96–7.

262. Text from *Boston Transcript*, November 22, 1893 (Scrapbook, vol. 6, p. 49); date from committee circular of April 17, 1899 in *Boston Transcript*, May 1, 1899 (Scrapbook, vol. 13, p. 137).

263. Baker XII-3-118; text edited for clarity.

264. New-York Historical Society (handwritten).

265. BSO Archives, Henry Lee Higginson Papers, MC 31 Series 220, Box 2.

266. Reference to an inquiry dated August 15, 1893, from the New York office of the *Boston Transcript* about a report that the McKim firm had been "definitely given the planning of the new Music Hall in Boston" — to which the firm had replied that such a report was "wholly unauthorized" (Baker XII-3-118).

267. Baker XII-3-118.

268. Scrapbook, vol. 6, p. 71.

269. New-York Historical Society (handwritten).

270. Baker XII-4-64.

271. BSO Archives, Henry Lee Higginson Papers, MC 31 Series 220, Box 2.

272. *Boston Transcript*, November 17, 1894 (Scrapbook, vol. 7, p. 51).

273. Baker XII-5-93 (handwritten).

274. New-York Historical Society. The letter was addressed to McKim at his firm's new offices.

275. Baker XII-5-93.

276. New-York Historical Society.

277. Baker XII-5-93.

278. Baker XII-5-93.

279. Western Union telegram, November 17, 1898 (Baker XII-5-93): "Norcross is here today estimating upon alternate plans based on your scheme which we hope to be able to submit next week."

280. Scrapbook, vol. 13, p. 64.

281. New-York Historical Society (typewritten copy). Mr. Ellis was apparently on tour with the Damrosch Opera Company, of which he was one of the organizers.

282. New-York Historical Society.

283. Baker XII-6-32 (handwritten).

284. Baker XII-6-18.

285. New-York Historical Society (handwritten).

286. Baker XII-6-18.

287. Scrapbook, vol. 13, p. 120; other press comment ibid., pp. 115–18.

288. Baker XII-6-18.

289. New-York Historical Society.

290. Baker XI-6-18 (handwritten).

291. *Boston Evening Transcript*, June 5, 1899.

292. Baker XII-6-18.

293. Baker XII-6-18; apparently a typewritten copy made in the McKim office.

294. Baker XII-6-18. This letter was written before McKim received the Hutchings letter of November 7, 1899 (Document 40). Having read that letter, McKim wrote again to Higginson on November 13, 1899 (Baker XII-6-18) to emphasize that he had seen Hutchings only once and had given him no authority to take any action without the approval of "the Committee."

295. New-York Historical Society (handwritten). Professor Sabine wrote Mr. Higginson on November 13, 1899 (Baker XII-6-32) to acquaint him with the substance of this letter.

296. Baker XII-6-18.

297. Baker XII-6-18.

298. Hooper to McKim, November 29, 1899 (New-York Historical Society).

299. New-York Historical Society (handwritten).

300. Baker XII-6-18.

301. New-York Historical Society.

302. Baker XII-6-57 (handwritten).

303. Boston architect serving as McKim's on-site representative.

304. Baker XII-6-67 (handwritten).

305. Baker XII-6-67 (handwritten).

306. Baker XII-6-32 (typewritten).

307. Baker XII-6-57.

308. Should probably read PAULUS V. Many minor anomalies in McKim's letters appear to be the result of imperfect communication with a stenographer.

309. Baker XII-6-57.

310. Baker XII-6-57.

311. Baker XII-6-57.

312. Baker XII-6-57.

313. Baker XII-6-57.

314. Baker XII-6-57.

315. Baker XII-6-57 (handwritten on Norcross Brothers stationery).

316. Baker XII-6-57.

317. Baker XII-6-57.

318. Baker XII-6-57 (handwritten on notebook or memorandum paper).

319. Baker XII-6-57.

320. Baker XII-6-67.

321. Baker XII-6-47.

322. Baker XII-6-47.

323. Baker XII-6-47.

324. Baker XII-6-47.

325. Baker XII-6-47.

326. New-York Historical Society.

327. Scrapbook, vol. 16, p. 6.

328. Text from Howe, *The Boston Symphony Orchestra, 1881–1931*, pp. 112–115.

329. New-York Historical Society.

330. Orcutt, *Wallace Clement Sabine*, p. 131.

331. Sabine, *Collected Papers on Acoustics*.

332. Document 6: Higginson to McKim, November 27, 1892.

333. Document 22: Higginson to McKim, October 27, 1898.

334. Orcutt, *Wallace Clement Sabine*, p. 135.

335. Wallace C. Sabine, ""Architectural Acoustics: Part I — Reverberation: Calculation in advance of construction," *American Architect*, vol. 58, no. 1277, June 16, 1900 (emphasis added); also in Sabine, *Collected Papers*, p. 62; and in Appendix A, above.

336. Wallace C. Sabine, *Collected Papers on Acoustics*, p. 67.

337. Document 27: Report of the *Boston Herald*, December 2, 1898.

338. Document 29: Higginson to McKim, January 26, 1899.

339. Document 30: Sabine to Higginson, Cambridge, Massachusetts, February 26, 1899 (emphasis added).

340. Sabine, *Collected Papers on Acoustics*, p. 61.

341. Orcutt, *Wallace Clement Sabine*, p. 130.

INDEX

ABOUT THE AUTHOR

RICHARD POATE STEBBINS first entered Symphony Hall to attend Young People's Concerts in the 1920s, and mounted its stage in the 1930s to sing with the Harvard-Radcliffe chorus under the direction of Serge Koussevitzky. After graduating from Harvard in 1933 with highest honors in English, he earned his A.M. and Ph.D. in history. As a world affairs specialist, he served with the U.S. Office of Strategic Services, the Department of State, and the Council on Foreign Relations, and was the recipient in 1945 of a Guggenheim Fellowship. The author, co-author, or editor of some forty books on international, musical, and biographical topics, Dr. Stebbins returned to Symphony Hall in the 1990s as a volunteer assistant in the BSO Archives.